T4-ABL-604

Small Business in a Regulated Economy

Recent Titles from Quorum Books

The Modern Economics of Housing: A Guide to Theory and Policy for Finance and Real Estate Professionals
Randall Johnston Pozdena

Productivity and Quality through Science and Technology
Y. K. Shetty and Vernon M. Buehler, editors

Interactive Corporate Compliance: An Alternative to Regulatory Compulsion
Jay A. Sigler and Joseph Murphy

Voluntary Corporate Liquidations
Ronald J. Kudla

Business-Government Relations and Interdependence: A Managerial and Analytic Perspective
John M. Stevens, Steven L. Wartick, and John W. Bagby

Career Growth and Human Resource Strategies: The Role of the Human Resource Professional in Employee Development
Manuel London and Edward M. Mone, editors

Guide to International Real Estate Investment
M. A. Hines

Occupational Job Evaluation: A Research-Based Approach to Job Classification
Wilfredo R. Manese

The Professionals' Guide to Fund Raising, Corporate Giving, and Philanthropy: People Give to People
Lynda Lee Adams-Chau

Financial Forecasting and Planning: A Guide for Accounting, Marketing, and Planning Managers
Sharon Hatten Garrison, Wallace N. Davidson, Jr., and Michael A. Garrison

Professional Accounting Practice Management
Joseph T. Kastantin

The New Oil Crisis and Fuel Economy Technologies: Preparing the Light Transportation Industry for the 1990s
Deborah Lynn Bleviss

Small Business in a Regulated Economy
ISSUES AND POLICY IMPLICATIONS

EDITED BY
Richard J. Judd, William T. Greenwood, and Fred W. Becker

PREPARED UNDER THE AUSPICES OF THE
POLICY STUDIES ORGANIZATION

Quorum Books
NEW YORK • WESTPORT, CONNECTICUT • LONDON

Library of Congress Cataloging-in-Publication Data

Small business in a regulated economy: issues and policy implications
 / edited by Richard J. Judd, William T. Greenwood, and Fred W.
 Becker.
   p.   cm.
   Bibliography: p.
   Includes index.
   ISBN 0-89930-343-9 (lib. bdg. : alk. paper)
   1. Small business—Government policy—United States. 2. Small
business—Law and legislation—United States. 3. Small business—
Government policy. 4. Small business—Law and legislation.
I. Judd, Richard J., 1941-   . II. Greenwood, William T.
III. Becker, Fred W.
HD2346.U5S627   1988
338.6'42'0973—dc19   87-32611

British Library Cataloguing in Publication Data is available.

Copyright © 1988 by the Policy Studies Organization

All rights reserved. No portion of this book may be
reproduced, by any process or technique, without the
express written consent of the publisher.

Library of Congress Catalog Card Number: 87-32611
ISBN: 0-89930-343-9

First published in 1988 by Quorum Books

Greenwood Press, Inc.
88 Post Road West, Westport, Connecticut 06881

Printed in the United States of America

The paper used in this book complies with the
Permanent Paper Standard issued by the National
Information Standards Organization (Z39.48-1984).

10 9 8 7 6 5 4 3 2 1

Contents

Figures and Tables ix

Preface xiii

Introduction: Emerging Relationships between
Public Policies and Small Business 1
Richard J. Judd and William T. Greenwood

I. SMALL BUSINESS IMPACTS ON PUBLIC POLICY ISSUES

1. A Multi-Sector Approach to Small Business Policy Development 17
   Bruce A. Kirchhoff

2. Flexible Specialization Technologies, Innovation, and Small Business 41
   Zoltan J. Acs

II. PUBLIC POLICY IMPACTS ON SMALL BUSINESS

3. The Costs of Complying with Government Requirements: Are Small Firms Disproportionately Impacted? 53
   Paul Sommers and Roland J. Cole

4. Employment Disincentives and Small Business: A Pilot Study 67
   Herbert R. Northrup and Evelyn M. Erb

5. The Impact of Tax Reform on Small Business　79
Thomas S. McCaleb

6. Stages of Development and Stages of the Exporting Process in a Small Business Context　95
George S. Vozikis and Timothy S. Mescon

7. Economic Development Programs of State and Local Governments and the Site Selection Decisions of Smaller Firms　111
William L. Waugh, Jr., and Deborah McCorkle Waugh

8. Small Business Challenging Contemporary Public Policy: A Coalition for Action　127
Donald F. Kuratko

III. PUBLIC POLICY IMPLICATIONS FOR SMALL BUSINESS

9. Firm Size and Productivity Growth in Manufacturing Industries　141
Steven A. Lustgarten

10. Encouraging Small Business Startups: An Alternative to Smokestack Chasing?　155
Benjamin W. Mokry

11. Linking Small, Advanced Technology Firms and Universities　169
Victor Levine and David N. Allen

12. Divergent Perspectives on Social Responsibility: Big Business versus Small　181
Philip M. Van Auken and R. Duane Ireland

13. A Geographic Structure for Black Small Business Research　187
David B. Longbrake and Woodrow W. Nichols, Jr.

SUMMARY: IMPLICATIONS FOR SMALL BUSINESS AND PUBLIC POLICY

14. A Model for Contemporary Small Business Policy Issues　205
Robert E. Berney and Ed Owens

15. Regulation, Small Business, and Economic
    Development: A Historical Perspective on Regulation
    of Business   221
    Richard J. Judd and Barbra K. Sanders

    Selected Bibliography   231

    Index   233

    About the Editors and Contributors   239

Figures and Tables

FIGURES

1.1	Categorization Matrix for Small Firms	24
3.1	Analysis of Variance (ANOVA) of Size on Cost Measures	56
8.1	Percentage Distribution of Employment and Establishments by Employment—Size Class	129
11.1	The Role of the University in the Activities of Advanced Technology Firms	171
13.1	U.S. Census Geography: Regions and Divisions	190
13.2	Black Business Geography: Regions and Divisions	197
14.1	The Net Impact of Government Policy on Firms of Varying Size	213
14.2	Maximum and Minimum Reasonable Compliance Costs	214
14.3	Annual Costs of Compliance by Business Size	215

TABLES

1.1	Effect of ERTA Tax Provisions on the Five Small Business Sectors	35
3.1	Areas of Requirements Affecting Sample Firms	58
3.2	Ranking of Impacts by Level of Government	59
3.3	Costs of Compliance: Estimated Regression Coefficients	61
3.4	Estimated Compliance Costs for Five- and 100-Employee Firms	63
4.1	Index Values Correlated by Industry	69

6.1	Frequencies of Surveyed Firms by Stage of Development	101
6.2	Frequencies of Surveyed Firms by Stages of Export Development	102
6.3	Results of Chi-square Analyses for Differences of Overall Functional Problems of Small Exporters in Stages I, II, and III of Overall Development	103
6.4	Results of Chi-square Analyses for Differences of Exporting Functional Problems of Small Exporting Firms in Stages I, II, and III of Overall Development	104
6.5	Results of Chi-square Analyses for Differences of Overall Functional Problems of Small Exporting Firms in Stages I, II, and III of Exporting Development	105
6.6	Results of Chi-square Analyses for Differences of Exporting Functional Problems of Small Exporting Firms in Stages I, II, and III of Exporting Development	107
7.1	Site Selection Criteria: Mean and Rank by Firm Size	120
7.2	Importance of Transfers of Scientific Knowledge from Universities by Firm Size	121
7.3	Preference for Locations near Universities by Firm Size	121
7.4	Factors Affecting Importance of University-Related Sites, Mean and Rank by Firm Size	122
7.5	Use of Professional Site Selection Consultants or Firms in Decision Making by Firm Size	122
7.6	Involvement of Personnel Being Moved to New Site in Site Selection Decision by Firm Size	123
9.1	Average Annual Percentage Rates of Growth of Factor Inputs and Industry Output for Manufacturing Industries Classified by Industry Average Firm Size	144
9.2	Average Factor Shares Classified by Industry Average Firm Size	146
9.3	Average Annual Percentage Rates of Productivity Growth for Manufacturing Industries Classified by Industry Average Firm Size	149
9.4	Regression Equations Relating Average Firm Size and Productivity Growth Using Continuous Variables for Firm Size	152
10.1	Operating Definition of Policy Entrepreneurship	158
10.2	Effect of Location on Mean Birthrates: First Location Compared to Second	161
10.3	Effect of Location on Change Scores	163
11.1	Importance of the University in Nine Roles	173
11.2	Firm Characteristics and University Importance—Stepwise Multiple Regression	175
13.1	Black Regions and Divisions: Selected Variables	192

13.2	Black State-Level Spatial Dimensions: Component Loadings	194
13.3	Black Business Participation Rates	198
14.1	Percentage of New Jobs Created by Businesses of Varying Size	210
14.2	Comparison of Brookings and Birch Data on Employment Growth	211
14.3	Employment Growth in Single-Establishment Firms, by Size Class	211
14.4	Percentage Share of GNP by Firm Size: 1958, 1963, 1972, and 1977	217
14.5	Share of Total Value Added in Manufacturing by the Top 200 Companies	218

Preface

This book explores issues related to the operation of small business in a regulatory economy. This subject has not been examined comprehensively, and only now are its boundaries being defined. By identifying the implications of government policies that inhibit or encourage the growth and development of small business, this book seeks to add to the public's understanding of this important policy area.

The introductory chapter by Richard J. Judd and William Greenwood reflects the primary orientation of the book: identifying the public policy issues affecting small business in the late 1980s. Some of these issues have arisen because of recent changes in the structure of the U.S. economy, and others because of the challenges small business must confront in a regulated economy. Moreover, the consequences of government actions to aid small businesses have become a current topic of debate. The Judd and Greenwood chapter also provides a guide to the respective issues addressed by the authors in this book. Some of the reforms which these authors have suggested may be considered to be controversial. Judd and Greenwood also provide a guide to these recommended policy reforms.

A close inspection of the references cited in some of the chapters in this book will reveal the changing emphases in the nature of the debate regarding small business in a regulated economy. The editors wish to emphasize that references to the earlier literature appear by design rather than by happenstance. We feel fortunate that several of the contributors to this book have provided a sense of continuity between discussions of current issues and the formative literature. In doing so, they have substantially aided the attempt to define the policy area of small business operating in a regulated—and sometimes paternalistic—economy.

Finally, the editors wish to express their appreciation to three people who helped make this book a reality. The first is Stuart Nagel of the University of Illinois who originally suggested the need for this book and encouraged its development. The second is Michael Ayers, Vice President for Academic Affairs at Sangamon State University, who had the vision to support the commitment of the necessary financial and human resources required for this effort. The third is Barbra Sanders, the production manager and one of the contributors to this book, whose unselfish devotion to this project was—perhaps—only exceeded by the energy she expended on its fruition.

Introduction: Emerging Relationships between Public Policies and Small Business

RICHARD J. JUDD and
WILLIAM T. GREENWOOD

Public policy issues and small business are influencing each other so extensively that this relationship has become a national issue for all Americans. Because the small business sector has often served as a forerunner of change for the American economy, in this chapter we will focus on the emerging relationships between public policies and small business.

SMALL BUSINESS IMPACTS ON PUBLIC POLICY ISSUES

In 1986 there were over 15 million small business firms in the United States, approximately 40 percent of which were identified as part-time, nonfarm, nonemployer businesses. Small business firms have tended to concentrate in the retail and service sectors, and this trend is expected to continue through the end of the 1980s.

Small business is not itself a primary public policy issue, but it has aroused attention because of growing evidence that small business successfully addresses a policy issue of national priority—economic growth.

Small Business and Economic Growth

According to Bruce A. Kirchhoff in Chapter 1, public policy development must make economic growth its central issue. Economic growth is achieved by only a small percentage of small businesses. Moreover, it is difficult to identify such firms inasmuch as the small business sector is a heterogeneous mixture that tends to defy efforts to identify predictors of business success in generating economic growth. Furthermore, there is no adequate theory base that links public policies such as monetary policy, tax regulations, or national banking regulations with economic performance, firms' structural or technological features, or entrepreneurial behavior attributes. As a result, policymakers do not have a common conception of what constitutes small business.

Because small business does not have as much influence as large business and is seemingly diffuse with individual special interests, policymakers tend to focus on issues and interests of the large corporation. Kirchhoff discusses the role of small business through a review of economic theory with perspectives on economic growth to describe the current small business environment within which policy is formulated. From this context he develops a classification scheme for describing various types of small business efforts. He applies this scheme to recent tax legislation to demonstrate the scheme's effectiveness in clarifying the policy effects for small business and entrepreneurship.

The importance of small business can be gauged by examining industry sales and how these sales are distributed among small and large firms. For all industries, 41.7 percent of sales in 1982 were made by firms with fewer than 500 employees. Variation among industrial categories suggests that some sectors can be accurately categorized as dominated by small business, that is, agriculture, construction, wholesale, retail, and the service sectors.[1] In contrast, industries such as transportation, energy, and extractive enterprises are generally dominated by large firms.

Creation of New Jobs

Between 1978 and 1980, 64 percent of the increase in employment was attributable to expansion of existing small firms, whereas the remaining 36 percent resulted from new venture creation. Between 1980 and 1982, overall employment grew in small firms but declined in large firms in virtually every industry. During this period net employment increased by 984,000 jobs. This increase is derived from the following statistics: about 19.6 million jobs created through birth and/or expansion of existing firms, less 18.6 million jobs lost through business contractions or dissolutions. Fifty-nine percent (59.2) of total employment changes occurred through the creation of jobs in small firms versus 46.5 percent of employment change through the creation of jobs in large firms. These percentages represent jobs created in both newly established firms and existing firms that underwent expansion. The remaining 40.8 percent of small firms and 53.5 percent of large firms lost employees when they either contracted in size or were dissolved during that period.[2]

During the 1980–82 period, an increase in the number of small firms with fewer than 100 employees accounted for 43 percent of the net increase in jobs created.

Technology and Innovation

The small business sector of the U.S. economy coexists with large business. The larger business mass production sector was considered to be dominant until the early 1970s. As a result of the economic crisis of the 1970s, American business and public policymakers could not preserve the position of mass production in the economy while maintaining price stability. In Chapter 2, Zoltan J. Acs examines the emergence of flexible technologies through a case study of mini-mills in the steel industry. He argues that the emergence of new flexible specialization technologies provides opportunity for smaller firms to effectively compete with large firms. The newer technologies require much less capital with shorter payback periods, are less dedicated to single-purpose processing, and can be used to produce a wider range of products than "older" forms of technology. Indeed, newer, flexible technologies which can be used by small business can compete with older, mass production technologies in terms of both price and quality, and, in some instances, can outperform the older technologies.

Until recently, the mass production sector of the steel industry dominated that industry. Today, the nonintegrated sector of the steel industry is made up of small, efficient, and expanding firms—the mini-mills. These small firms rely on a different technology than their integrated, mass production counterparts—flexible specialization technologies—and their technology minimizes the advantages that formerly accrued to large-scale integrated operations. Acs reports that the expansion of mini-mills has not been a result of poor domestic performance by large-scale, integrated mass production mills because markets in which mini-mills have a substantial share also tend to have a lower than average import share. Moreover, the trend of imports in mini-mill product lines has contrasted sharply with the overall trend toward an increased import share.

According to Acs, the distinctive feature of flexible specialization technologies is a return to technology as the focal point of competition. Innovation is the primary ingredient as the focus of innovation shifts from refinement of existing products to the production of new products. Through a cross-sectional and international comparison, Acs illustrates how mini-mills can display distinct advantages in production output. He suggests that vertical integration, an asset during the mass production era, becomes a liability in an era of flexible production; that use of flexible technologies tends to minimize operating costs; and that flexible specialization technologies create the need for craft workers—people willing and able to perform several tasks within a plant and to foster paternal relationships within a workforce.

PUBLIC POLICY IMPACT ON SMALL BUSINESS

Public policy can impact small business in a variety of ways. In theory, government regulation is meant to correct flaws in the competitive nature of a marketplace, but in practice, government intervention into a marketplace may have unintended, dysfunctional consequences. For example, government incentives to enhance business may, in fact, be disincentives. Likewise, federal tax policy can affect a business's financial and market decisions whether the business is large or small. Moreover, international trade is a virtually untapped market potential for small business. This market opportunity may have great impact on the small business sector if uncertainties can become understood and methods of selecting appropriate approaches for entry into export processes are determined. State and local governments, universities, professional associations, and the banking community can become partners in revitalizing the role of small business in the economy through neutral regulation and management assistance, and in providing sufficient opportunity for capital formation and debt availability.

The Impact of Government Regulation

In theory, government regulation is society's way of handling flaws in our competitive economic system. Governmental intervention becomes necessary as a result of five areas of market failure: natural monopoly, natural resource regulation, destructive competition, external diseconomies or externalities, and inadequate or complex information.[3]

In practice, government regulation is not perceived so altruistically. In a survey of small business owners in New Orleans, "too much red tape in dealing with federal government" was identified as the third most critical problem confronting small businesses—just behind "inability to get working capital loans," and "taxes are too high."[4] In 1980 small businesses filled out 850 million pages of federally mandated forms, costing millions of dollars in employee man-hours.[5] Thus, few small firms are beyond the reach of government regulations. An unmeasurable effect of government regulation is what it does to the basic entrepreneurial nature of the private enterprise system. Yet, one can theorize that, to the extent that management's attention is diverted from traditional product development, production, and marketing concerns to meeting governmentally updated social requirements, a significant bureaucratization of business activity results.[6]

The general view of government regulation is one of increasing requirements and monitoring effects of business. On the other hand, governmental movement toward deregulation has occurred. This movement may be a catalyst for revitalizing small business activity. For example, deregulation in the airline industry has provided opportunities for heretofore obscure air carriers and has renewed interest in the use of railroads for freight transportation.[7]

The costs of complying with government regulations and their effects on small and larger firms are discussed in the Paul Sommers and Roland J. Cole study in Chapter 3. Their research covered firms in Washington, Georgia, and Massachusetts; they designated as "small" firms those with fewer than fifty employees and as "larger" those with fifty or more employees. They found that larger firms were more likely to engage in frequent challenges to the government requirements, and that small firms were much less likely to use lawyers or consultants. With compliance costs so high per dollar of sales, some small firms chose partial or noncompliance. In addition, compliance costs per employee were reported to be higher for small firms than for larger firms.

Sommers and Cole conclude that (1) a very broad-scale government effort will be required to make regulatory compliance costs neutral with respect to firm size; (2) the compliance burden varies significantly among industries and, therefore, these differences should be taken into account in performing cost-benefit analyses; and (3) the paperwork cost is significant and, therefore, should be considered in formulating policy initiatives.

Government Incentives or Disincentives

Although the government offers a variety of incentives to business, most incentives are of greater benefit to large firms and, in fact, too often serve as disincentives for small business. The Small Business Administration commissioned the Wharton School to study these disincentives, and the results are presented by Herbert R. Northrup and Evelyn M. Erb in Chapter 4.

Of the numerous governmental regulatory acts and commissions studied, the following were found to have the most adverse impact on small business: the National Labor Relations Act (NLRA-Taft Hartley), the Equal Employment Opportunity Commission (EEOC) or the Office of Federal Contract Compliance Programs (OFCCP), and the Occupational Safety and Health Administration (OSHA). The companies found that employment legislation was generally adverse to small business and, in particular, in the employee-selection process. The legal costs, especially of proving their innocence, constituted the main complaints.

Moreover, the small businesspeople are greatly burdened by government-required increases in employment costs for which they must make out-of-pocket payments. Although businesspersons recognize that some employment legislation is beneficial, most believe it should be held to the minimum.

Taxation Impacts

Taxation is always a major question relating to business policy. Because greater reliance is placed on personal and family resources as sources of capital, taxation has a greater impact on the small firm than on the larger firm. In addition, income taxes become more burdensome in times of inflation. When a fixed-rate tax structure exists, a business may be forced into a higher bracket, even though there may be no change in the *real* economic position of the business. Tax shelters and high tax rates provide incentives to invest in low-productivity rather than high-productivity areas. High tax rates also distort the incentives to save and increase work effort.

The economic implications of recent developments in federal tax policy for small business are presented by Thomas S. McCaleb in Chapter 5. He found that, although the absolute level of taxes on all businesses has been reduced, no signficant conclusion can be made as regards its effects on small versus large business, since both experienced beneficial and adverse effects. At the 1980 White House Conference on Small Business, eleven of sixty participants were found to be concerned with taxation. They felt that tax relief was the most important means of capital formation for small business.

McCaleb reports that the impact of tax legislation on small and large business cannot be definitively measured. Therefore, it now remains an open question.

World Trade Impacts

The international marketplace holds the greatest untapped market potential for small business, but small business owners or managers lack the information for informed decision making and the channels for distribution and sales.

In Chapter 6 George S. Vozikis and Timothy S. Mescon provide a much more detailed evaluation of the problems and opportunities presented by world trade exporting. Finding the small businessperson overwhelmed by the risks and unknowns of exporting, they investigated the specific functional problems in general management, marketing, production operations, and finance for small business firms at different stages of growth (start-up, early growth, and later growth stages) and at different stages of exporting (Stage I, Inactive; Stage II, Explorer; and Stage III, Experienced Exporter). They tested four hypotheses concerning overall functional problems, exporting functional problems, and problems at different stages of exporting development. Based on their findings, they developed a checklist to aid the small businessperson in identifying and selecting the most appropriate stage of the business life cycle and exporting process to the situation of the firm. The checklist identifies the most likely problems encountered, their solutions, and tips for survival.

Vozikis and Mescon also cite the policy implications of the need for legislation and present guidelines to ensure quality versus quantity of small business exports. These guidelines should result in more permanent positive results on the United States' trade balance. The suggested guidelines include differentiation within legislative provisions for the different stages of firm development and recommendations for the Small Business Administration as it provides export assistance for the firm's specific stages of development and for stages of export development. The result will be custom "export" financial and management consulting resources.

State and Local Government Impacts

Although most assistance to small business is directed at the federal level, it should also be examined at the state and local levels. Industrial development commissions have been active at the state and local levels for decades, and it may now be appropriate for more detailed emphases on small business recruitment and growth.

Site selection problems and state and local programs are evaluated by William L. Waugh and Deborah McCorkle Waugh in Chapter 7. They explain why small businesses should be attractive to states and communities, one of the reasons being the often unrecognized "political clout" of this group. They focus particularly on the site selection incentives used to attract large and small businesses. In a survey of 200 firms with large research and development budgets, they found that smaller firms did *not* have special preferences or needs relative to site selections. However, medium-sized firms were more emphatic about their preferences. Waugh and Waugh found only "lukewarm" confirmation of the consultants' conclusions as to the factors most important to the decisions. The availability of labor was found to be the most important factor; taxes and regulatory practices were also important concerns.

Financial Services and Venture Capital Impacts

In most instances public policy issues have greater impact on small business than on other businesses in the economy. For example, overall, small firms owe 20 to 30 percent of their total liabilities to banks. About one-third of the banks' total outstanding commercial and industrial loans go to small businesses. Yet, short-term loans to big business constituted almost all of the increase in bank lending during 1980 to 1982. Short-term loans to small firms increased 20 to 30 percent, compared to approximately 400 percent for large firms.[8]

Venture capital generally comes from three sources: independent private funds, small business investment corporations (SBICs), and corporate sources.[9] Between 1977 and 1982, independent sources of capital have become more important while SBIC and corporate sources have declined in relative importance. Therefore, the impact is far greater on small business than on others.

Coalitions for Contemporary Public Policies

Government concerns about small business have grown dramatically in recent years. In Chapter 8, Donald F. Kuratko states that government has now become a new partner with business, as we now enter a full decade of small business realization and revitalization. He identifies as the five main problems faced by small business—inflation and cash flow, taxes, sources of capital, innovations, and government regulation—all of which revolve around the impacts of government public policy. Government regulation, the largest of the five problems, is cited as a new trend in current policy formation; of special note among these regulations are the Regulatory Flexibility Accounting Tax Incentives, social policies, and a reinvigorated Small Business Administration (SBA). To meet these needs, Kuratko recommends a "Coalition for Action" composed of the SBA, Chambers of Commerce, unions, professional societies, universities, associations, and state commerce departments. Kuratko contends that only through coalition can the diverse aspects of the nation's small businesses be considered.

PUBLIC POLICY IMPLICATIONS FOR SMALL BUSINESS

Financial Services Implications

In many instances public policy issues affect small business far more than other businesses in the economy. As stated above, overall, small firms owe 20 to 30 percent of their total liabilities to banks, whereas about one-third of the banks' total commercial and industrial loans are made to small businesses. In view of this relationship, almost all of the increase in bank lending during the 1980–1982 period was in short-term loans to big business. Small firms tend to receive proportionately less of the increase in loan money available than do large firms. If, as suggested, small firms represent the greatest potential for economic growth, and if growth for small firms is financed primarily through debt, then the small business sector is not receiving its "share" of the increase in funds available for financing economic growth.

Economic Growth Impacts and Issues

External factors such as economic recession, overall employment trends, federal posture in regulation and deregulation, as well as general demand conditions of a business cycle influence new business formations. According to the U.S. Department of Labor, in industries where overall employment has had an upward trend, employment in the subset of industries dominated by small business rose more than the subset of industries dominated by large business.[10]

Steven A. Lustgarten in Chapter 9 provides additional insight on this topic by comparing productivity growth in industries with different average firm sizes in order to assess the contribution of small firms to technical progress. His study shows that, over most of the range of firm sizes, the influence of size on productivity growth is not statistically significant. Yet, the largest firms have experienced significantly greater growth in productivity than all other industries. Lustgarten's analysis suggests that, whereas productivity growth is not inhibited by very small firm size, it is promoted by very large firm size.

Benjamin W. Mokry addresses yet another facet of the economic growth issue in Chapter 10. Because it is politically fashionable for local, county, and state governments to encourage economic development initiatives, the tendency has been to focus on small, new, high tech firms. The argument is that young firms with fewer than twenty employees tend to create most of the net new jobs in the country and are most likely to need and benefit from government help. This economic development posture is considered "entrepreneurial" because it requires local governments to serve business in innovative ways, such as encouraging development of venture capital pools, organizing small business incubators and information clearinghouses, cutting red tape, and becoming advocates of small business. Thus, offering "policies" that help small business would encourage more people to think of a particular state, county, or town as a good place to do business because of the positive business climate.

Mokry studies two counties with markedly different policies toward business, measuring business birthrates in six selected manufacturing and service industries. The results suggest that entrepreneurial government policies do not appear to have a significant impact on new business start-up decisions.

Government Assistance to Small Business

Another area in which government can influence economic development is through assistance to the small business community from colleges and universities. Strong interest has been shown in the linkage between small advanced technology firms and universities in collaborative partnerships in research and training. Victor Levine and David N. Allen test a descriptive model by which small, advanced technology firms can evaluate the relative importance of nine university "roles." Their survey findings suggest that the universities are considered important because they produce graduates and provide access to university libraries, information systems, and cultural amenities. However, the importance of the university-business linkage differs systematically with the firm's characteristics. Although there is clear indication that the advanced technological business community is interested in access to universities, obstacles to collaboration also exist. Levine and Allen urge that the interactions between university and advanced technology firms be examined carefully before large-scale programs are implemented.

Social Responsibility

Perhaps the greatest and most pervasive imbalance of power between workers and managers is found in small businesses located in small towns with low labor mobility. This imbalance is sufficiently serious to justify characterizing this condition as an unrecognized public policy issue. In Chapter 12, Philip M. Van Auken and R. Duane Ireland conclude that social responsibility is different for small business. Instead of attempting to assume the social activist functions found widely for large firms, they recommend that small business avoid social irresponsibility. Because the wide variety of social activities would be uneconomic and impracticable for the small firm, small businesses should identify and avoid socially irresponsible activities such as violating laws and governmental regulations, taking advantage of the consumer, damaging the environment, and discriminating against minorities. Therefore, the avoidance of social irresponsibility becomes the primary measurement of social responsibility for small business.

Minority Business Development

In Chapter 13, David B. Longbrake and Woodrow W. Nichols examine minority business enterprises (MBEs) as a subset of the larger category of independently owned small businesses. Longbrake and Nichols provide insight into how the geographic structure of regions and divisions might provide a useful reference framework for research efforts involving the formation, growth, and failure of black enterprises. They have found that, overall, with the exception of the southeast, there is a marked regional trend in black business participation rates from east to west. In fact, there is very little differentiation in business participation rates by blacks between three of the four census regions.

Longbrake and Nichols propose a six-region structure as the most appropriate format for viewing or conducting research on black businesses when a spatial dimension is important to the research effort. Because many economic analyses include geographic variables, such a regional perspective, based on descriptive and distributional business characteristics, can be very important in studies attempting to understand the formation and function of black-owned businesses.

SUMMARY: IMPLICATIONS FOR SMALL BUSINESS AND PUBLIC POLICY

To date, public policy and small business issues have been fragmented in the literature. The variety and extent of these issues are summarized in the first three parts of this book: Small Business Impacts on Public Policy Issues; Public Policy Impacts on Small Business; and Public Policy Implications for Small Business. A view of these issues and their implications in aggregated form suggests far more impact for both small business and public policymaking than the sum of its parts.

Robert E. Berney and Ed Owens cite the necessity of public policy support for small business as a means of insuring approximation of pure competition and delineate the externalities contributed by small business. With small business's relative lack of power position and lack of public policy support, the achievement of economic goals will be diminished.

In their appeal for "neutral" tax policies, Berney and Owens identify a major overall goal of small business and public policy. Rather than general assistance or restrictions on either large or small business, the goal should be to neutralize both in providing competition and economic benefits. Although public policy actions may appear as a result to subsidize small business, they, in fact, may be neutralizing the small versus large areas of competitive action in order to maximize small business externalities and optimize the economy.

In the concluding chapter, Richard J. Judd and Barbra K. Sanders provide an historical perspective on regulation of business. They suggest that government regulation of business is rooted largely in the nineteenth century, when government perceived its role as that of helping to create environmental stability wherein fledgling developing industries could undertake long-term investment and production plans on a calculable basis. Thus, governmental policy has been not only useful, but also essential to the oligopolization of basic energy, extraction, and manufacturing industries. With these policies, the United States became the mass producer of tangible goods for the world.

As the American economy slowed down in the 1970s and 1980s, and significant competition was felt from abroad, government policymakers became reluctant to identify a central public policy dilemma: if American industry wants to produce domestically on the same terms that it has done historically, then it must be willing to accept prevailing world wage rates for semi- and unskilled labor. If it does accept these rates, the United States should prepare for a significant decline in its standard of living. In contrast, if the nation chooses to relinquish its dominant position as a major mass production supplier of goods in the world economy, then it may need to abandon the mass production model as the centerpiece of its national economic output and, along with it, signal the decline of its largest industrial corporations.

At the core of this public policy issue is economic development. It is becoming more evident that small business is successfully addressing this policy issue. The vertically integrated, large-scale, mass production organization is gradually being replaced by smaller scale, horizontally integrated, "flexible" specialization firms. This development has been spawned by technological advances, particularly in microelectronics, telecommunications, and biotechnology.

From a governmental policy perspective, unfortunately we do not have sufficient theoretical understanding to forge linkages between the newer growth firms and growth industries with economic public policies such as tax regulation, banking regulation, industry deregulation, or monetary policy.

As economic development becomes more important nationally, state and local government officials are being faced with declining productivity, plant closings, and rising unemployment. Many states are taking the cue from the federal level and are making regulatory reform central to their own economic development plans concerning factors such as capital availability, technology transfer, job training programs, entrepreneurship studies, and other features designed to improve the climate for small business development.

The small firm creates most of the jobs that have to be replaced when large firms constrict their size, close down, or relocate. However, the issue of how to create an economic climate that sparks new ventures is not well understood. Public policies concerning the regulation of business are in the forefront of America's interest. There is little question that we are experiencing a revolution in economic development policymaking. The two thematic lines appear to be: (1) attempting to "get out of the way" of business development, and (2) creating programs and policies that encourage business formation and job creation in order to contribute to economic vitality and growth.

NOTES

1. *The state of small business: A report of the President*, March 1983, Washington, D.C.: U.S. Government Printing Office.

2. Ibid. 25-27.

3. George Steiner and John Miner, 1980, *Business, government and society: A managerial perspective*, 3rd ed., New York: Random House, 148-49.

4. Jane Juhn, Daniel Cromartie, and Kenneth Lacho, 1982, Information search behavior of small businessmen, in *Southwestern small business institute association proceedings*, Southwest Federation of Administrative Disciplines annual meeting, Dallas, Texas, March, 48.

5. People and so forth, *Arizona Magazine*, October 28, 1980:1. See also Timothy Mescon et al., 1982, The regulation of small business—let our people go, in *Southwestern small business institute association proceedings*, Southwest Federation of Administrative Disciplines annual meeting, Dallas, Texas, March, 14.

6. Murray Weidenbaum, 1977, The forgotten consumer: Hidden costs of government regulation, National Federation of Independent Business, Public Policy Discussion Series pamphlet.

7. Mescon et al., 15.

8. *The state of small business: A report of the President*, 1983, 100.

9. *Venture capital journal*, 1982, Capital Publishing Corporation, October, 22:7.

10. William T. Greenwood and Richard J. Judd, 1984, The emerging relationships of public policy issues and small business, in *Small business/entrepreneurship proceedings*, Chicago, Midwest Business Administration Association, April, 34-35.

I

SMALL BUSINESS IMPACTS ON PUBLIC POLICY ISSUES

1 A Multi-Sector Approach to Small Business Policy Development

BRUCE A. KIRCHHOFF

Small business in and of itself is not a primary public policy issue in U.S. society today. Public attention has begun to focus on small business because of emerging evidence that small business successfully addresses a primary policy issue—economic growth. Economic growth is of concern to our society as a whole because our growing population needs more jobs to earn incomes necessary for life fullfillment.

Policy development must make economic growth its central issue. Achieving this objective is a challenge inasmuch as most economic growth is produced by a small percentage of all small businesses, less than 15 percent by several estimates. Identifying this 15 percent is very difficult because the small business sector is a heterogeneous mix that defies researchers' efforts to systematically identify attributes that predict success. Furthermore, we do not have a theory base that predicts linkages between major policy variables (e.g., monetary policy, national banking, tax regulations) and entrepreneurial behavior.

Small businesses have long had a role in influencing public policy formation. Their influence is evident in the development of antitrust legislation, fair pricing laws such as the Robinson/Patman Act, and even changing government procurement policy during World War II. The last-named effort eventually led to the formation of the U.S. Small Business Administration. Over time, the terms *entrepreneurship* and *small business* have become synonymous, that is, it is widely assumed that entrepreneurs form and operate small businesses.

Sustained entrepreneurial behavior is the key relating small business and economic growth. Entrepreneurship is the act of forming and developing an independent business. By this definition all small business formations are entrepreneurial. However, some small businesses cease to grow after an initial formation/growth period; in other words, the initial entrepreneurial behavior diminishes. Other small businesses continue to be entrepreneurial and grow, thereby creating many new jobs. This second group is the 15 percent that make a disproportionately large contribution to new job formation. Policymakers seldom perceive this difference between entrepreneurship and sustained entrepreneurship, and this difference rarely surfaces in discussions of small business policy.

Not surprisingly, currently small businesses are attempting to influence public policy formation from widely differing directions, presenting a variety of issues with conflicting views on most. Policymakers have lost sight of any "mainstream" policy interests of small business; the "small business economic sector" has lost its identity; and with it, small business has become a blurred subject. Policymakers are now inclined to perceive small businesses as a hodgepodge of individual special interests, all striving for a bigger piece of the pie. While some squabble over price protection, others ask for reduced taxes on capital rollover. Because no small business has as much influence as that of a single megabusiness, policymakers find it easier to attend to large corporate interests.

Still, the small business sector and entrepreneurship are clearly identified as engines of economic growth. Research shows that small businesses create the majority of jobs and innovations. How, then, does it happen that an economic sector simultaneously loses its identity and influence while gaining increasing importance in economic affairs? Apparently, some major change in the identity of the small business sector is required.

The following discussion examines what small business means and what role small business plays in economic growth. It begins by examining the meaning of the original designation "small business" and then reviews an established economic theory that effectively describes the current small business environment within which policy is being formulated. From this theoretical base, a classification scheme is developed. This classification scheme is applied to recent tax legislation to demonstrate its effectiveness in clarifying policy effects for small businesses and entrepreneurship.

THE MEANING OF SMALL

Use of "small size" as a business designation differentiates one set of businesses from others. Members of such a differentiated set supposedly share unique problems compared to nonmembers. In the case of business firms, small businesses (members) are expected to have a unique set of problems attendant to their "smallness" that differentiates them from large firms (nonmembers). This unique set of problems can be addressed by policy prescriptions that serve the needs of most or all members of one sector. Definitions of needs have varied in the twentieth century. The "traditional view" deriving from classical economics dominated from the turn of the century through World War II. After the war, a new economic view of small business needs emerged as economic thought began to focus on large corporations as the central actors in economic activity. This view, the "New Industrial State," has only recently been challenged by researchers who have identified the "economic engine" aspect of the small business sector.

The Traditional View

Even though classical economic theory largely ignores size as a causal variable, conventional wisdom has long held that the small size designation is appropriate. The traditional belief is that small businesses preserve the fundamental capitalist virtue of "competition"; small businesses serve as the classical economists' exemplification of "perfect competition" as modeled in capitalist theory.

Historically, the policy influence of small business has been based on this view. Small business owners perceive themselves as models of capitalistic competitors and extol the virtues of operating in "free markets." Markets dominated by large oligopolistic or monopolistic businesses are seen as less efficient in serving consumer needs and distributing wealth. Such large businesses are "nonvirtuous" in a capitalistic sense because they deviate from perfect competition.

In the past, small businesses sought and received government protection from the powers of monopolistic (and therefore evil) large businesses. This image of small business as idealizing free markets and competition made small business a politically powerful voice with the ability to shape American economic policy, for example, federal antitrust legislation, state fair pricing laws, and laws against chain store competition.

The New Industrial State

After the Second World War, perceptions of large businesses began to change as more economists focused on the efficiencies of scale brought to industry by large businesses. John Kenneth Galbraith's *New Industrial State* (1972) epitomizes this view. He describes the virtues of a large business-dominated economy, and he discounts the classical perfect competition model as unrealistic and at best irrelevant to modern capitalism. The economy, Galbraith claims, was run by the "technostructure" extant in large business, large government, and large labor organizations which serve society's interests and their own equally well. Thus, as the evil image of large business faded, the virtuous image of small business as the "keeper of perfect competition" also disappeared. As their virtue fades, economists increasingly portray small businesses as anachronisms, inefficient and economically unprofitable. Economists routinely use stories of "mom and pop" stores succumbing to the distribution and marketing efficiency (and power) of large retailers to demonstrate the effects and benefits of the large business's use of economies of scale.

The economies of scale assumption is that larger businesses are more profitable because their size allows them to produce and distribute at lower cost. Thus, small businesses are less profitable and, therefore, less efficient users of resources. Economists conclude that, as less efficient users of resources, small businesses exist primarily for reasons outside of economic theory, for example, personal, social, or political reasons. Furthermore, political protection of the economically inefficient is undesirable; therefore, small businesses should have little or no influence on government policy.

In this way, Galbraith's theory base served to gradually erode the influence of small business on public policy. Even before Galbraith documented the emergence of corporate economic dominance, William H. Whyte (1956) noted that society increasingly admired the *organization man*, that individual who is employed by and provides service to a large corporation. Meanwhile, the entrepreneur became the measure of one who fails to achieve the organization person's status. Therefore, small business operators were those who were unable or unwilling to become a part of the influential large corporations, that is, misfits.

The Economic Engine

But now another view of small business is emerging, a view that is based on the role of small business in economic growth. This view is convincing in its economic logic and has revitalized small business as a significant economic sector. The economic growth view of small business discards the conventional wisdom that small businesses are the keepers of capitalistic competitive virtue. It also attacks the notion that small businesses are archaic, economically inefficient misfits. By so doing, it has cast traditional and Galbraithian policy prescriptions into turmoil and further confused the logic base for policy formation.

To a great extent, the economic growth view is a result of recent research activity based on new research methods. As such, it carries the persuasion of empiricism and, therefore, dominates current research thinking. However, since it casts conventional views into turmoil, it is appropriate to review not only the new view itself but also the errors of classical economics, and to provide a new conceptual scheme to guide policymakers in formulating policy for this important economic sector.

THE NEW VIEW OF SMALL BUSINESS

Both the traditional and New Industrial State views of small business had their roots in economic theory, and so, too, does the new view. Unfortunately, few small business advocates have searched for and identified the theoretical base. It is not new—it has merely been dormant for forty years.

Forty years ago, Joseph A. Schumpeter (1976) criticized classical and neoclassical economics for its distorted view of capitalism. He noted that, contrary to classical economic theory, perfect competition is neither an accurate descriptive, nor useful, explanatory model of working capitalism. Capitalist markets are dominated by monopolists and oligopolists who strive to increase profits by reducing competition. In so doing, they create profit opportunities for entrepreneurs who develop innovations and use these to form new firms that enter existing markets and destroy the monopolists' economic structures. These entrepreneurs start as small businesses and grow to become monopolists/oligopolists who then create new opportunities for other entrepreneurs. This is Schumpeter's "creative destruction" model (Schumpeter 1976).

In other words, Schumpeter does not perceive the small business sector's role as that of "keeper of competition." In his view, true capitalist competition originates with entrepreneurs who start new innovative small firms that attack and destroy existing economic structures, structures established specifically to defend the monopolists' position. The small business sector is the *birthplace* and *cradle* of competition, not its keeper. Capitalism's strength lies not in the static condition of an economic sector (e.g., perfect competition or monopoly), but instead in the dynamics of entrepreneurs creatively destroying the existing economic structure. The small business sector is the origin of these dynamics.

Schumpeter's theory of creative destruction was largely ignored for forty years. During the last ten years, however, empirical evidence supporting his theory has emerged from several sources. Research reported by the National Science Foundation has demonstrated that Schumpeter was correct about innovation; small businesses are 2.5 times more innovative and twenty-four times more cost efficient in their innovations than large businesses (National Science Board 1977:116-18). In addition, research at the Massachusetts Institute of Technology (MIT) demonstrates that Schumpeter was right about small businesses generating economic growth. David L. Birch (1979) found that small businesses create 86 percent of all new jobs, a far larger number than do large businesses, thereby confirming Schumpeter's theory of entrepreneurship as the "engine of growth."

According to Schumpeter, the traditional view of small businesses as keepers of American capitalistic values is an unimportant static concept. Economists' views that small businesses are archaic and inefficient are also static and meaningless. His emphasis shifts from these static views of sector structure to the dynamic views of creative destruction of economic structure. And creative destruction originates within the small business sector of our economy.

IN SEARCH OF DEFINITION

Because of this significant transition in theoretical base, policy formulators face a dilemma in defining small business: What does the designation "small business" mean? Is it a sector populated by free market capitalists, the "keepers of capitalist competitive virtue"? Is it economically inefficient "mom and pop" stores—social misfits—falling victim to economies of scale resident in large businesses? Or is it the cradle of creative destruction that dynamically destroys economic structures in order to create growth? Without a defined theory base, policies will lack direction and fall short of their designed intention.

This is the current dilemma of policy formulators. Smallness by itself does not identify any set of unique problems common to all small businesses. Instead, smallness identifies a hodgepodge of businesses ranging from family-owned neighborhood stores to venture-capital-owned, innovative computer manufacturing firms. Identification of problems common to such widely differing business entities clearly is difficult. Policymakers have the choice either of becoming mired in a plethora of minutiae by prescribing policies for each retail store, service station, or computer manufacturing firm almost individually, or of seeking a new, more useful segmentation of the small business sector that identifies common problems amenable to policy prescriptions.

A BASIS FOR CLASSIFYING SMALL FIRMS

As noted earlier, small business itself has never been a primary public policy issue; small business was and is a public policy issue because of its role in economic activity. Thus, a useful small business classification scheme needs to build on Schumpeter's concept of creative destruction since Schumpeter provides a theory that addresses economic growth in a way that is consistent with recent research findings. The two components of Schumpeter's theory of economic growth are entrepreneurial innovation and use of innovation to destroy economic structures.

The firm's rate of innovation is clearly a central aspect. Small firms that initiate and sustain entrepreneurial innovation and create many innovations have more effect on destroying economic structure and creating economic growth than those that create only one or a few innovations. The more innovations, the more the firm's potential for creatively destroying the existing, established economic structure(s). But a firm's innovation rate does not necessarily dictate its economic growth. It is possible to have growth even when innovation rates are low; a single innovation can be sufficient to destroy an existing market structure and cause growth of the new innovative firm. On the other hand, it is possible to have high rates of innovation when growth is low. Established economic structures can be so rigid that new innovative firms are unable to destroy them with one or even many innovations.

If a firm is to contribute to economic growth, it must successfully exploit its innovation(s) by entering and destroying the existing economic structure. Given the monopolists' desire to maintain the existing structure, the entrepreneur may or may not find a successful exploitation mechanism. So, although innovation is a necessary condition for creative destruction, it is not sufficient.

Real economic growth, therefore, occurs as a combination of two events: enterpreneurial innovation combined with penetration and destruction of existing economic structure. When an innovative entrepreneurial firm successfully destroys an economic structure, the firm experiences high growth, thereby contributing to economic growth. A surrogate for creative destruction is success of the new firm itself, that is, the firm's growth rate. Any new firm with a high rate of growth must successfully destroy the existing economic structure.

CATEGORIES OF SMALL BUSINESSES

When we combine creative destruction and innovation rates into a two-dimensional categorization matrix, four distinctly different categories of small businesses emerge: *economic core, ambitious, constrained growth, and glamorous* (Figure 1.1).

Economic Core Firms

By far the greatest number of small businesses belong to this category, defined as low-structure destruction and low-innovation, economic core firms. Entrepreneurs who start such firms are not usually attempting to

Figure 1.1
Categorization Matrix for Small Firms

Internal Constrained Growth	Resource Constrained Growth	Glamorous
Economic Core		Ambitious

FIRM'S INNOVATION RATE: HIGH / LOW

FIRM'S CREATIVE DESTRUCTION RATE: LOW / HIGH

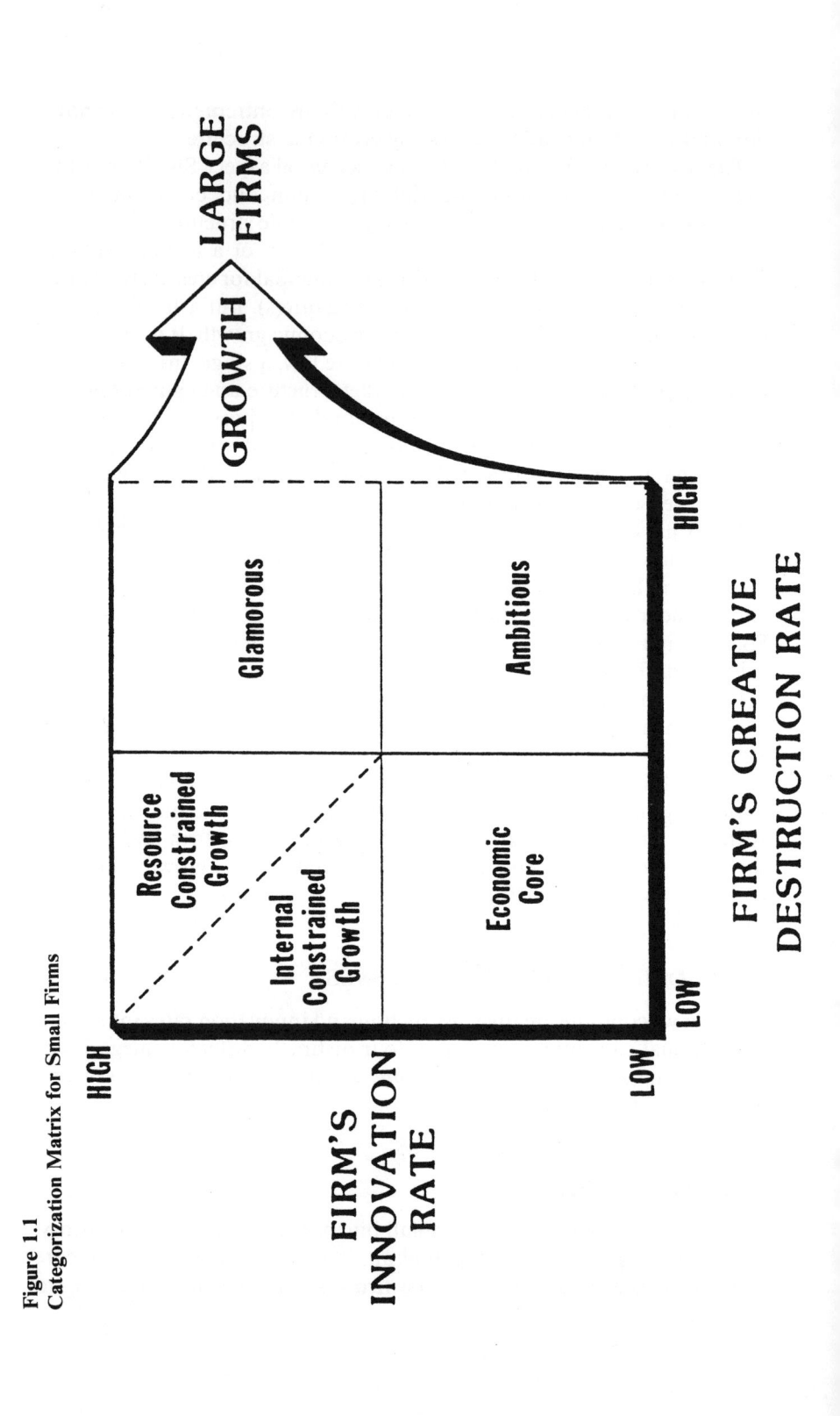

GROWTH → LARGE FIRMS

destroy large segments of economic structure. They simply wish to "upset" a small portion of economic structure, such as a local market or specialized part of a national market, in an effort to carve out a market that will establish and maintain their firms. These firms tend to be relatively stable, low-growth, technologically mature firms in which innovation plays a minimal role. Many of them are retail and service firms, such as neighborhood auto repair shops, retail boutiques, and restaurants. Even the locally owned franchises of national fast food chains can be cited as examples.

Once established, such firms become the economic core structure of our economy. But as Schumpeter so accurately stated, these firms are not "free market" competitors in the classical economic sense. These entrepreneurs recognize the economic suicide of undifferentiated, cutthroat competition just as do larger firms. Although not desiring the heady title of oligopolist or monopolist, these entrepreneurs try hard to establish defensible economic structures through mechanisms of product differentiation, advertising, location, and so on. Such defenses take many forms; among their tools, small firms use trade associations, local business groups, and cooperative purchasing as ways to establish barriers to the entry of new firms. As these firms build their own economic structures, they become vulnerable to entrepreneurial innovation that destroys existing economic structure. In the past, such small firms have been "creatively destroyed" through economies of scale wielded by large firms.

This does not mean that economic core entrepreneurship is unimportant; on the contrary, such entrepreneurship makes significant and important contributions to the economy. The products and services of small firms are those we use daily. These firms employ millions of workers, and their ranks are expanding; franchising has expanded the extent of local ownership of major retail and service organizations. In most geographical areas, economic core entrepreneurs have become the backbone of the local housing construction industry. Many of us found our first job working full- or part-time within such firms. In rural America, nearly the entire wholesale and retail distribution network that supports our immense agricultural production system rests on economic core small firms.

Economic core small firms are important in yet another way. Although few entrepreneurs enter this type of firm with innovations of obvious major importance, or with the intention of having regional or national effect on economic structure, a small but important part of such firms evolves into firms with high creative destruction. For example, Southland Corporation began its existence as a locally owned ice-making firm in Dallas. One of its managers had an appreciation for convenient retail service, and today, its chain of retail Seven/Eleven Stores places it seventh in size among retail firms within the Fortune "Service 500" for 1984 (*Fortune* 1985:190). Its impact on retail marketing has been felt in every major population center of the United States where it has spawned a host of competitors; in 1980, it became the largest nonrefining gasoline retailer in the country. Its founders had no notion that it would revolutionize retailing nationwide and become the giant it is today (Brown and Thiel 1981:375-96).

Economic core firms, then, make two contributions to our economy. First, formation and growth to their initial size creates economic growth. If such firms remain small, that is, decline in entrepreneurial behavior, this initial growth is their principal direct contribution to sustained economic growth. Second, economic core firms also harbor potential for significant growth by expanding their innovation(s) to a national scale. From this cradle of the economic core spring *ambitious firms.*

Ambitious Firms

This group of firms is often confused with the highly innovative, high-growth firms that are the popular topics of press reports. But these firms are not highly innovative. They are high growth, but their growth is derived from one, or a few, highly successful innovations. These are "ambitious entrepreneurs" who recognize the benefits of high growth and pursue it as their highest priority objective. Their sustained entrepreneurial behavior is expressed in their pursuit of growth. Innovation, although basic to their beginnings, takes a lower priority in their objectives since they seek to exploit growth opportunities of economic structure destruction with their existing innovations.

Godfather's Pizza is typical of ambitious firms. Beginning as an economic core firm in 1973 (a neighborhood bar with an adjacent restaurant), it identified an innovative product, price, decor, and advertising scheme that suited the consumer's tastes. Within ten years, this combination of innovations had rocketed Godfather's into the highest growth rate among food franchise operators in the United States. Godfather's creatively destroyed the existing economic structure of the pizza restaurant business in order to increase the total market and its overall market share. As Godfather's expanded the market, it also eroded the market positions of other established franchises; Pizza Inn and Shakey's were significantly reduced nationwide. Eventually, Godfather's growth tapered off as geographical coverage expansion was completed and additional growth had to come from increased market share within existing markets.

Throughout its growth, Godfather's Pizza did not develop new innovations that were on the scale of the original; instead, it used its original innovation to gain national and international market share. Now it has become an integral part of the new economic structure. Its focus is shifting to protecting its position in this new economic structure. For example, it recently introduced a "pan pizza" to compete with Pizza Hut's product. This is a traditional defensive marketing act rather than an innovation of the entrepreneurial form.

Examples of ambitious entrepreneurs among franchise food firms abound, although not all begin with the intention of being an economic core firm. Wendy's was established with the expressed intention of becoming an ambitious firm. Wendy's founder, an experienced fast food owner/manager, had an innovative approach to the hamburger restaurant business and a plan for a high-growth, ambitious firm. Wendy's most copied innovation is the "drive-through" window now found in nearly all fast food hamburger restaurants (Pilgreen 1979:326-39). After ten years of high growth and significant destruction of market structure, Wendy's growth slowed in 1980. Wendy's is now part of the existing economic structure, struggling to maintain its position by expanding its product line to include competitive product offerings such as salad bars and chicken sandwiches.

All of these entrepreneurs brought their innovative influence on the economic structure already dominated by large firms. Godfather's drove the existing fast food pizza restaurateurs to become more competitive or fail. Wendy's demonstrated that the consumer desired hot fresh food served through a drive-in window, a consumer interest ignored by the leading fast food hamburger chains at the time. In each of these examples, the desire of the entrepreneur to achieve growth through exploitation of an initial innovation led to increased competition and greater consumer variety, that is, to new economic structures. In both examples, however, growth eventually declined as the innovation achieved geographical coverage and creative destruction became an incremental process. Simultaneous with declining growth, the entrepreneurial firm became a big firm.

The strategy of exploiting one or a few innovations to achieve high growth has worked again and again, with benefits of increased national employment, greater product and service variety for consumers, and better quality and/or lower prices in the true Schumpeterian tradition. Yet, the strategy incorporates its own seeds of eventual slowing as the source of growth—creative destruction of the existing economic structure—eventually declines. The new firm becomes part of the existing economic structure. The only mechanism available for continuous high growth is continuous entrepreneurial innovation.

Interestingly, venture capital firms have long recognized the value of ambitious firms in achieving high growth and high profits. Research funded by the National Science Foundation has revealed that prior to 1979, venture capital investment placed between 48 and 63 percent of the investments with the least innovative firms while investing only 19 to 34 percent in the most innovative firms. A reversal of this pattern appears in the 1979-82 period, but lack of more current analysis leaves us without any knowledge of whether this pattern is a long- or short-term phenomenon (Timmons, Fast, and Bygrave, 1983:316-34). Venture capitalists readily admit that not all of their investments succeed and that between 50 and 60 percent of their investment portfolios fail to achieve the desired growth levels. Apparently, some, and perhaps most, ambitious firms slide back into the economic core.

Constrained Growth Firms

Entrepreneurial innovation, by definition, should lead to creative destruction of the existing economic structure. When a highly innovative firm fails to successfully destroy the economic structure, something must be constraining its ability to attack it. Constrained growth firms are those highly innovative firms that have not achieved extensive creative destruction, that is, they have a low growth rate. Contrary to popular images, not all highly innovative firms are growth firms; this is true even thought "high tech" and "new ventrue" publicity purports to describe all highly innovative firms. Constrained growth firms should be high-growth firms, but something constrains the entrepreneurs' efforts to carry out creative destruction. These constraints fall into two classes: (1) internal constraints and (2) external constraints.

Internally Constrained Firms. Internal constraints are constraints on the firm's activity which are imposed by the entrepreneur. Such entrepreneurs are unwilling or unable to grow for reasons within their own control.They accept lower levels of market penetration, market change, or economic structure change as necessary conditions to achieve their other objectives. In other words, some of their objectives differ from Schumpeter's theoretical entrepreneurial objectives. These other objectives may be maintenance of individual or family control, avoidance of high rates of internal change (and the strife and trauma associated with such change), fear of failure, or simply satisfaction with maintaining a secure and adequate personal income flow.

Maintenance of control is the most common constraint. The entrepreneurs recognize that achieving high growth rates requires large sums of capital, sums that exceed the firms' internal cash-generating and -borrowing capability. Thus, they need either to constrain the growth of the firm or to seek outside sources of equity capital. They choose to avoid funding equity needs from outside sources because they fear loss of control with dilution of internal ownership. Slower growth results.

Another common reason is income targeting. The entrepreneur(s) seeks to achieve a level of income that satisfies personal or family needs. Once this level of income is achieved, the need to commercialize inventions and expand applications declines and growth slows. Income maintenance dominates decision making, and risk of failure makes innovating and growing appear as a threat rather than an opportunity. Owner income-constrained firms are susceptible to "buy out" as a solution to their growth constraint. To the extent that the innovativeness is transferred to the new owner and the new owner is growth oriented, the firm will realize its growth potential. Otherwise, the firm's growth and innovativeness will decline and the firm will become part of the economic core.

Creative destruction of economic structure by constrained growth firms lags far behind their potential. If the innovation(s) are attractive enough, competitors eventually copy them, enter the market, and carry out the creative destruction. Inventors who start firms based on a patented invention are often surprised to discover that competitive entry is not prohibited by patents and that in the end, unless they aggressively destroy economic structure, a competitor will willfully violate their patent simply because the profits from destroying economic structure are sufficient to justify patent infringement penalties. For example, the battery-power conserving circuit in today's "pocket pager" was invented and patented by Reach Electronics Corporation. The patented circuit extended the life of the battery from thirty days to over one year and made the pocket pager a truly reliable device. Motorola copied the circuit and eventually lost a multimillion dollar patent infringement suit to Reach Electronics. But Reach constrained its growth and moved slowly into the market while Motorola moved quickly. By the time Reach won its patent suit, Motorola had 95 percent of the U.S. pager market.

There are other ways by which competitors fill the gap created by self-constrained entrepreneurs. Licensing of patents or buying out the firms are common mechanisms used by larger firms. But until ownership of internally constrained growth firms changes, growth rates remain low. Such firms meet their owners' needs but fall short of fulfilling their potential for sustained economic growth. Many constrained growth firms have the potential to challenge the major firms that have established economic structure. Instead, the firm offers its products in a much narrower market; customers, or potential customers, may never know that the innovation exists. If the major firms choose to license or otherwise obtain dominance over the innovation, they will market these products less aggressively since their primary objective is to protect the existing economic structure, or at least to allow only a gradual change in it. The greatest sustained economic growth impact occurs when a new firm aggressively destroys the existing economic structure.

Externally Constrained Firms. Some entrepreneurs are unable to obtain the resources they need to exploit their innovations. These tend to be new, early developing, innovative firms. This is because the cost of innovation is so high that firms either overcome their constraints or fail within a few years. Their products/services have not yet demonstrated market worthiness, and/or management has not yet proven itself capable of performing. Thus, suppliers restrict or withhold credit, banks limit their lending, and venture capitalists hesitate to invest, asking instead for evidence of ability to succeed.

Suppliers of special resources, parts, or subassemblies hesitate to supply small quantities because of high startup costs and credit risk. At the same time, distributors are reluctant to stock the firm's product or even actively sell it until the market is defined and/or the firm shows itself to be a survivor. If such a firm successfully survives and demonstrates market potential for its product/service, resource constraints will disappear. In the meantime, the firm struggles for survival and remains resource starved with an economic growth potential unfulfilled.

If an externally constrained firm is bought out by a large firm before its potential is realized, its potential will probably never be realized because its threat to the existing economic structures of the large firm will deter the new owner from exploiting the innovations except in an orderly way that does not destroy the existing markets. Thus, externally constrained firms represent a category of small firms that are of particular interest to Schumpeterian thinkers. Such firms have considerable potential for "creative destruction" but are teetering on the brink of failure. The extent to which they remain independent and successfully overcome their constraints will determine whether they do or do not contribute to economic growth.

Overview. Constrained growth entrepreneurs are in fact small firms whose potential contribution to economic growth has not been realized. As highly innovative entities, they possess the capability to become high-growth firms.

Highly innovative, constrained growth firms deserve special attention since their potential is so great. Capital, especially start-up capital to turn inventions into innovations, is the most frequent growth-constraining resource for such firms. Venture capitalists see many such firms but turn most away because they lack defined markets and management expertise. Some evidence exists to confirm this belief. Research funded by the National Science Foundation suggests that venture capitalists rarely invest in externally constrained firms. An analysis of average dollar investment by venture capital firms and number of investments in highly technologically innovative firms during the "early" and "seed" stages of firm development reveals a significantly lower investment rate than at later stages of firm development (Timmons, Fast, and Bygrave 1983). Venture capital firms seem to prefer less risky investments. On the other hand, research for the Small Business Administration suggests that informal investors appear to be the predominant investors in externally constrained firms. However, such "investing angels" usually invest only an average of $25,000 (Wetzel and Seymour 1981). Furthermore, such firms are among the riskiest of investment ventures and are, therefore, at considerable disadvantage when they attempt to borrow through banking institutions. Kirchhoff (1985:735-46) has demonstrated that the financial markets will simply refuse to lend to such firms rather than lending at interest rates adjusted for risk. Thus, although ambitious firms usually encounter capital problems associated with their growth, constrained growth firms face capital problems before growth is or can be realized.

Externally constrained growth firms must overcome the barrier which Schumpeter (1976) believed would eventually destroy capitalism, that is, obtaining the resources necessary to innovate. Schumpeter believed that large corporations would usurp the capable innovators, drawing them out of the general population and enmeshing them in the bureaucracy. He further believed that large corporate research and development laboratories possessed significant economies of scale that made entrepreneurial innovation less likely. But forty years after he expressed his concern over the "crumbling walls" of capitalism (Schumpeter 1976:132), increasing evidence exists to demonstrate that innovation is alive and well in the small business sector (National Science Board 1977). In a recent study, Gellman Research Associates, Inc. (1982) found further evidence of the proclivity of small businesses for innovation and also reaffirmed its efficiency in innovating. Creative destruction goes on.

It is difficult to know whether constrained growth or economic core firms serve as the primary "cradle" of those firms that go on to creative destruction and economic growth. Ambitious firms arise out of economic core but are not nearly as newsworthy as the highly innovative firms that arise out of the constrained growth category. By and large, the success stories of "high tech" firms dominate press reports, even though the portfolios of venture capital firms are full of the less newsworthy ambitious firms.

Glamorous Firms

Of all the firm categories, glamorous firms demonstrate the effects of sustained high growth. These firms have high rates of innovation and achieve high growth rates successfully because they have exploited their innovations. Growth continues as long as the firm develops innovations and uses them to destroy the existing economic structure.

These firms are called glamorous firms because they receive the most publicity for their contribution to economic growth. Such firms start small but rarely remain small very long. For example, Apple Computer Company achieved Fortune 500 status in 1982, only eight years after its founding. Once such a firm passes the period of constrained growth, it is catapulted into the large firm sector. The founders become locally (or nationally) renowned, and the press extols the virtues of successful entrepreneurship. Only the founders understand the agony of the start up and the initial struggle to survive.

Such entrepreneurs prioritize innovation over growth. They believe that growth is the outcome of innovation and therefore pursue innovation. Alternatively, they may simply prefer innovation as a way of life. As such, the firm's growth can be sustained as long as it creates innovations that destroy the exciting economic structure. Many of today's large firms began as glamorous small firms. For example, Control Data Corporation was started by several scientists who wanted to innovate outside the constraints of their previous employer. Their commitment to innovation carried them into a long series of new computers and applications, and they grew into a large corporation. Wang Laboratories and Digital Equipment Company have similar stories.

But even highly innovative firms eventually experience declining rates of innovation and subsequently declining growth. Once the entrepreneurial spirit of innovation wanes, large bureaucracies have difficulty refreshing it. Instead, large firms begin to focus on lower risk strategies, concentrating on defending existing economic structures and thereby becoming the target of entrepreneurs. This conclusion is supported by Gellman's (1982) research findings that small firms produce 2.5 times as many innovations per employee as do large firms.

In terms of number of firms, glamorous firms probably represent the smallest component of the small firm sector. Glamorous and ambitious firms together constitute no more than 12 to 15 percent of the total number of small firms as evidenced by research findings (Report of the President 1983:67), and venture capital data suggest that ambitious firms dominate within this group (Timmons, Fast, and Bygrave 1983:316-34).

As small firms, glamorous and ambitious firms face many of the problems common to small firms, for example, lack of access to markets, lack of influence with suppliers, and poor information about resource availability. But, more importantly, since they have chosen to creatively destroy economic structures dominated by large firms, they also face problems associated with distribution systems that primarily serve established large suppliers, advertising and marketing organizations that function mainly to serve large accounts, trade associations that are dominated by large members, and so on. In other words, these firms may need to create a whole new support system as they pursue their own growth. Apple Computer created an entirely new retail distribution system for computers in order to reach its market. The growth of these retailers (e.g., Computerland) is a success story in itself. Godfather's Pizza used a small, local advertising firm to develop its successful "godfather" image. This advertising firm grew to become a larger regional firm based on the growth of Godfather's. Obviously, growth of a single firm has a significant multiplier effect on all the firms around it.

POLICY IMPLICATIONS OF THE NEW CATEGORIZATION

Glamorous, ambitious, economic core, and constrained growth firms have a vital role to play in sustained economic growth. Each segment of the small business sector contributes in a different way, and each segment has different policy needs. Entrepreneurship is an essential element in each segment, yet the entrepreneurs' interests and needs vary from segment to segment.

To demonstrate this point, let us examine the Economic Recovery Tax Act (ERTA) of 1981 to determine how it separately affects each segment. This act is particularly relevant because many lobbying groups for small firms, including the one with the largest membership, supported the act in nearly all of its components, and many of its provisions have been and are under attack because of the size of the federal deficit and the "apparent" inequities between business and personal tax rates.[1]

In March 1982 President Reagan described the benefits of ERTA to the small business sector within his message to Congress in his report entitled: "The State of Small Business: A Report of the President" (1982). His list of direct benefits included the following:

1. Reductions in marginal personal income tax rates.
2. Lower business tax rates on incomes less than $100,000.
3. Simplification of LIFO (last-in first-out) inventory accounting.
4. Increased allowance for accumulated earnings.
5. More liberal treatment of stock option plans.
6. Liberalization of Subchapter S provisions.
7 Expanded expensing of depreciable assets.
8 Larger allowance for investment tax credit on used property.
9. Expanded funding allowances on Keogh plans and IRAs.
10. Liberalized estate and gift tax laws.

The President states that these provisions benefit "small businesses." The implication is that all small businesses benefit, except for the provision on estate and gift taxes which he specifically limits to "family owned and closely held" small businesses (Report of the President 1982:13). When analyzed relative to the five small business segments, however, the benefits of these tax provisions are evidently directed largely to economic core businesses.

Financial Condition of Segment Firms

Analysis of these provisions requires that assumptions be made about the financial condition of the firms in each segment. This analysis will follow the financial model of small firms described in the widely used conceptual scheme published in *Venture and Equity Capital for Small Busi-*

ness (1977), often referred to as the "Casey Report" because William J. Casey served as chairman of the task force. The report notes six phases in the life cycle of a new enterprise: "(0) R&D, (1) Start Up, (2) Early Growth, (3) Accelerating Growth, (4) Sustaining Growth, (5) Maturity." During the first three phases (zero through 2), small firms make no profits and have negative cash flows (Casey Report 1977:5).

Although the Casey report erroneously assumes that all new enterprises are typically growth oriented (ambitious or glamorous) and that mature firms will have annual sales in excess of $40 million, the conceptual scheme is useful for describing the categories of our classification matrix. Economic core and internally constrained firms are in sustaining growth or maturity phases (i.e., low growth); ambitious firms are in the early growth or accelerating growth phases; externally constrained growth firms are in R&D, startup, or early growth phases; and glamorous firms are in accelerating growth and sustaining growth phases.

Table 1.1 provides a summary of ERTA's provisions and lists which category each affects. The Casey Report phases are presented in the first row of this table since the life cycle phase determines both profitability and cash flow. For example, the Casey report (1977:7) notes that tax rates have no effect on firms in the first three phases because they have no reportable income. Thus, none of the tax reduction provisions has any effect on externally constrained small firms since all these firms are within the first three phases. As shown in Table 1.1, only two of ERTA's provisions have any effect on externally constrained firms. The first, more liberal stock options, allows such firms to provide equity to vital employees as compensation and incentive for high risks. The second, liberalization of Subchapter S rules, may encourage investors to provide capital in exchange for using the corporation's losses to reduce their personal income taxes.

In the same way, glamorous and ambitious firms, the categories that contribute most to economic growth, are assisted by only two of the ten ERTA provisions. Even though these firms are profitable, the lower tax rate provisions are of only minor value to them since their profitability is so high. A reduction of the corporate tax rate from 48 to 46 percent adds little significant value to a firm reporting before-tax earnings of 20 to 30 percent. Actually, glamorous and ambitious firms could pay higher rates without upsetting their financial strength, whereas mature large firms with much lower earnings would experience considerable stress from higher tax rates.

Eight of ERTA's ten provisions benefit economic core and internally constrained firms. The two provisions that are exceptions are the more liberal treatment of stock option plans and liberalized Subchapter S rules. Stock options are useful only if the firm's stock is publicly traded and has a rising market price, or if it is a candidate for a buy-out bid from a large

Table 1.1
Effect of ERTA Tax Provisions on the Five Small Business Sectors

Casey Life Cycle Phases	Economic Core Sust Growth Maturity	Ambitious Early Growth Accel Growth	Internal Constrained Sust Growth Maturity	External Constrained R&D Start-Up Early Growth	Glamorous Accel Growth Sust Growth
ERTA TAX PROVISIONS					
Lower Personal Tax Rates	yes	minor	yes	no	minor
Lower Bus Tax on $100,000	yes	minor	yes	no	minor
Simplify LIFO Accounting	some	minor	some	no	minor
Increase Allow - Accum Earn	yes	no	yes	no	no
Liberalized Stock Options	no	yes	no	yes	yes
Liberalized Subchapter S	no	maybe	no	maybe	maybe
Expensing Assets	yes	no	yes	no	no
Used Asset Inv Tax Credit	yes	no	yes	no	no
Expand Keogh and IRA	yes	minor	yes	no	minor
Liberalize Estate & Gift Tax	yes	no	yes	no	no

firm. The old Subchapter S rules allowed up to thirty-five shareholders, far more than the number which the typical closely held firm has.

That ERTA actually focuses nearly all of its small firm benefits on economic core firms is not suprising. This is consistent with the long-held policy view of small firms as the 'keepers of capitalistic virtue." But this view fails to stimulate those categories of the small business sector that create economic growth. Most economic growth comes from those categories that are relatively unaffected by tax policy, at least by ERTA's tax policy provisions. It is clear that the President's view, like those of most policymakers, falls short of understanding the complex role small firms play in creative destruction and economic growth.

CONCLUSION

It has been over forty years since Schumpeter described his theory of capitalism as a process of changing economic structures driven by entrepreneurial creative destruction. Although he feared that entrepreneurial behavior would eventually be crushed by large business organizations, the last forty years have shown that small business is still alive and remains the source of growth in the U.S. economic system.

Yet, unless policymakers recognize the importance of Schumpeter's creative destruction to sustained economic growth, it is probable that they will develop policies that undermine the process. The classification scheme proposed here uses the two components of Schumpeter's theory, innovation and extent of creative destruction, to divide the small business sector into five categories; each category contains firms with identifiably different policy needs. Although statistics do not yet exist to measure firms along these two dimensions, it is possible to conceptualize the policy needs of businesses so that policy analysis can be conducted for each category separately.

Perhaps the most important feature of the categorization is that it clarifies differences rather than similarities that characterize entrepreneurs. For example, not all entrepreneurs create sustained economic growth; economic core entrepreneurs initially create growth and then cease to grow further. Collectively, however, economic core firms create sustained economic growth through the continuous process of entrepreneurship, that is, new entrepreneurs enter business daily, thereby creating new jobs and increasing the total economic activity. A small but important percentage of these entrepreneurs leap out of the economic core by becoming ambitious firms.

Policies designed to facilitate sustained economic growth need to specifically address one or more of the five categories of the small business sector. Policies that focus on economic core firms, for example, should be designed to promote formation of new economic core firms. The more such firms that are formed, the more economic growth occurs; and the more economic core firms that exist, the greater the potential for ambitious small firms to develop.

Policies that maintain or protect the existing economic structure, even in the small business sector, reduce the opportunity for new entrepreneurial entry and slow the rate of growth. Policies directed toward revitalizing economic growth in our industrial sector need to be assessed relative to this caveat. The results of such an evaluation will be in sharp contrast with recent proposals for "industrial policy." The various proposals for industrial policy have focused on revitalizing industries dominated by large firms. Policies directed toward sustaining large firms are, at best, short-run prescriptions that will ease the transition from the current economic structure to the next structure that is being designed by a host of entrepreneurs now toiling within small firms. At worst, it is likely that large firm policy prescriptions will increase the ability of large firms to defend the existing economic structure, thereby slowing the process of creative destruction and strangling our economic growth rate. A tripartite board of big labor, big business, and big government, as specifically recommended in Robert Reich's *The Next American Frontier* (1983), will certainly create additional barriers to creative destruction. Large institutional cooperation is exactly what Schumpeter described as one of the impending causes of the collapse of capitalism in the economy.

Federal policymakers should act now to revise the federal data collection and reporting methods to focus on dynamics. Business growth rates and innovation rates should become routinely measured. In this way, policymakers can begin to track trends that will note when our economy experiences declines or increases in sustained economic growth. Only then can we clearly define the effect of policies on creative destruction. The need for such data was formally recognized in an interagency study completed in 1980 (*Statistical Reporter* 1981). A first effort by the Bureau of the Census has created the *Longitudinal Establishment Data File* from the Census of Manufactures data files (Monahan 1983), and the U.S. Small Business Administration has created a ten-year longitudinal data file from Dun and Bradstreet data (Armington and Odle 1983). These are steps in the right direction but much more is required.

In the meantime, more emphasis on the role of small firms in sustained economic growth is necessary among policymakers, along with use of the classification matrix to clarify how small business creates economic growth. The policy focus should shift from overly simplistic classifications based on firm size to classification based on innovation and creative destruction.

NOTE

1. In 1984 the National Federation of Independent Business was actively defending the asset depreciation provisions of ERTA-1981. See "It's do-or-die time for tax lobbyists," *Business Week*, June 25.

REFERENCES

Armington, Catherine, and Marjorie Odle. 1983. *U.S. establishment longitudinal microdata: The weighted integrated USEEM 1976-1982 sample.* Washington, D.C.: Brookings Institution.

Birch, David L. 1979. *The job generation process.* Cambridge, Mass.: MIT Program on Neighborhood and Regional Change.

Brown, J. W., and John Thiel. 1981. The Southland Corporation. In *Strategy and policy,* ed. Arthur A. Thompson, Jr., and A. J. Strickland, III. Plano, Tex.: Business Publications.

Galbraith, John Kenneth. 1972. *The new industrial state.* New York: Mentor Books.

Gellman Research Associates. 1982. *The relationship between industrial concentration, firm size, and technological innovation.* Jenkintown, Pa.: Gellman Research Associates.

It's do-or-die time for tax lobbyists. 1984. *Business Week* (June 25):30.

Kirchhoff, Bruce A. 1985. Analyzing the cost of debt for small firms. *Policy Studies Journal* 13 (June):735-746.

Monahan, James L. 1983. *Procedures for using the longitudinal establishment data file.* Washington, D.C.: U.S. Department of Commerce, Bureau of the Census.

National Science Board. 1977. Science indicators 1976. *Report of the National Science Board.* Washington, D.C.: U.S. Government Printing Office.

Pilgreen, Pep. 1979. Wendy's International, Inc.: Old fashioned hamburgers. In *Organizational policy and strategic management: Text and cases.* ed. James A. Higgins. Hinsdale, Ill.: Dryden Press.

The President's Reorganization Project for the Federal Statistical System. 1981. Improving the federal statistical system: Issues and options. *Statistical Reporter* 81-5 (February):133-221.

Reich, Robert. 1983. *The next American frontier.* New York: Time Books.

Schumpeter, Joseph A. 1976. *Capitalism, socialism and democracy.* New York: Harper and Row.

The service 500. 1985. *Fortune* (June 10):190.

The state of small business: A report of the President. 1983. Washington, D.C.: U.S. Government Printing Office.

Timmons, Jeffry A., Norman D. Fast, and William D. Bygrave. 1983. The flow of venture capital to highly innovative technological ventures. In *Frontiers of entrepreneurship research-1983,* ed. John A. Hornaday, Jeffry A. Timmons, and Karl H. Vesper. Wellesley, Mass.: Babson College.

U.S. Small Business Administration. 1977. *Report of the SBA task force on venture and equity capital for small business.* Washington, D.C.: U.S. Small Business Administration.

Wetzel, W. E., Jr., and C. R. Seymour. 1981. Informal risk capital in New England. *Report to the Small Business Administration.* Durham, N.H.: University of New Hampshire.

Whyte, William H. 1956. *The organization man.* New York: Simon and Schuster.

2 Flexible Specialization Technologies, Innovation, and Small Business

ZOLTAN J. ACS

What impact has small business innovation had on the U.S. economy? Before such a broad question can be answered, a much more fundamental question should be addressed: Why has there been a growing interest in small business in the United States over the past fifteen years? Although interest has been shown recently in the growth of small business, particularly in terms of innovation and job creation, the contribution of small business and its relationship to other major components of our economy has not been demonstrated.

This chapter discusses the current political economy from a perspective that focuses on technological development and innovation; uses the steel industry as a case study, not of big business decline, but of small business innovation and technological change; and examines small business innovation with regard to public policy.

STATE OF THE ECONOMY

The postwar model of economic development illustrates the large corporation, with mass production technologies, embedded in an environment of stable prices. The large corporation, through vertical and horizontal integration, had been able to fix input and output prices; collective bargaining ensured that wages were fixed; and public policy stabilized the price level, interest and exchange rate (Chandler 1977). This stable environment was necessary to house mass production technologies characteristic of big business in this era. The dedicated machinery that this technology needed was expensive and had to be amortized over a long period of time. This "fixprice" environment—stable wages, prices, and exchange rates—made the existence of mass production technologies possible in an otherwise unstable world (Acs 1980).

The small business sector of the economy existed side by side with the mass production sector. However, it existed at the forbearance of the large firm, and it existed in an environment that was characterized as technologically less sophisticated. The small business sector used more general-purpose machinery that would allow it to respond quickly to changes in its envrionment, that is, changes in either wages, prices, costs, or demand. The mass production sector of the economy was the predominant sector, and the small business sector, while not disappearing, was expected to diminish in importance and was the least subject to change (Berger and Piore 1980). This view was intact as late as 1973.[1]

What happened to the macroeconomic environment that rendered the large corporation technologically "impotent" in terms of economic performance and catapulted small business into a position of national attention in a matter of years? This question has been especially difficult to explain in manufacturing because it was here that the large corporation had its strongest foothold in the ideology of mass production.[2]

As a result of the economic crisis of the 1970's, American firms and policymakers were no longer able to maintain the conditions necessary to preserve mass production—economic stability of prices. Just as the Organization of Petroleum Exporting Countries (OPEC) precipitated energy price spikes, the demise of the Bretton Woods Agreement in 1971 led to price and demand volatility by substituting flexible exchange rates for fixed. No longer could prices, input costs, and output be stabilized vis-á-vis those government and corporate policies that had been so effective during the previous three decades.

Because of the inability to stabilize the economic environment on the one hand, and the emergence of computer technologies on the other, more flexible technologies have emerged in the last fifteen years. These craft technologies, with the aid of the computer, require much less capital, are less dedicated, have a shorter payback period, and can be utilized to produce a wider range of products. But most importantly these dynamic technologies can compete with the older mass production technologies in terms of both price and quality. Indeed, in some instances these technologies can quite literally outperform the older technologies (Acs 1984).

It can be argued that the emergence of the new flexible specialization technologies is one of the engines that has catapulted the small business debate into the forefront of national attention. Flexible specialization technologies cut from the Gordian knot that wedded technology to the large corporation. These new technologies could be housed in smaller businesses in part because of the much lower capital costs. It was the obstacle, both perceived and real, of bringing new business on line that precipitated the national debate on small business (Acs 1985).[3]

The hypothesis is that recent changes in the economic environment—the breakdown of the pricing process—has confronted society with a choice between technological modes and business organizations, a choice between mass production and flexible specialization technologies, and a choice between large or small business. (For more complete discussion, see Acs and Audretsch 1986.)

Although large corporations using mass production technologies have experienced increasing economic difficulty over the past fifteen years (between 1970 and 1985 the Fortune 500 lost about 5 million jobs), smaller firms have been successful in the areas of both job creation and innovation (Birch 1979).

A recent study covering 635 product innovations in the United States during the period 1970-1978 for 121 four-digit SIC (Standard Industrial Classification) industries found that of the 563 firms studied, 226 were classified as small. Small businesses were identified as those with fewer than 500 employees. Moreover, the study found that the incidence of innovation among the employees of small and medium firms is significantly higher than among those in large firms. Small firms produce 2.5 times as many innovations per employee as large ones. In addition, the time necessary to bring an innovation to market averaged 2.22 years for small firms compared with 3.5 years for large firms (Gellman Research Associates 1982).

A study recently completed for the Office of Advocacy of the Small Business Administration examines the relationship of firm size to innovation in the U.S. economy and confirms the results of the previously mentioned study. A total of 8,074 innovations in 362 industries were identified from forty-six technical journals in 1982. About half of the innovations were from firms with more than 500 employees. The study found evidence that small firms are more innovative than large firms. The principal findings were as follows (Edwards 1984):

- The innovations of small firms per employee were 2.4 times those of large firms.
- The greater propensity of small firms to innovate was true regardless of the importance of the innovation.
- The average period of time between invention and innovation was the same for both small and large firms—4.3 years.

Exploring the process of innovation in the steel industry in conjunction with the concept of flexible specialization technologies is useful in determining their importance for small business. The steel story has been told many times. However, some believe that the wrong story is told over and over (Hogan 1983). The steel industry offers a particularly good example of an industry in which process innovation has been used to produce flexible specialization technologies by small businesses. These flexible specialization technologies are then capable of producing steel in a less stable environment and are able to adapt quickly and with minimal cost to a changing environment.

THE NEW STEEL INDUSTRY

Until recently, the mass production sector dominated the steel industry. Although the steel industry has always included a fringe of nonintegrated firms, these small firms traditionally existed only by the tolerance of the integrated producers. According to our analysis, the purpose of these periphery firms was to absorb the slack in steel production, leaving the integrated companies to enjoy a more steady output. As demand increased, marginal costs, along with prices, rose so that these smaller firms could meet the demand (Acs 1984: Ch. 5).

The share of production claimed by nonintegrated firms is not much different today than it was in 1950 (Federal Trade Commission 1977). However, this aggregate conveniently masks a complete restructuring of the industry's nonintegrated sector. During the 1950's, nonintegrated firms were small, inefficient, and declining. Lacking the financial resources of their integrated counterparts, they used the same technology—the open hearth—but without the benfits of mass production, captive sources of raw materials, extensive marketing networks, and so forth.

Today, the nonintegrated sector is made up of small, efficient, and aggressively expanding firms, the mini-mills. They rely on a different technology than their integrated counterparts—flexible specialization technologies—and their technology eliminates many of the advantages that formerly accrued to integrated operations. Mini-mills have established more or less complete dominance in several product lines, and, in these markets, the integrated firms now exist by the will of the mini-mills rather than the reverse. The former fringe of the industry is now the principal focus of the restructuring forces that have been generated by overall secular decline.[4] *Far from being an appendage to the mass production sector, the nonintegrated sector has become its dynamic force* (Crandall and Barnett 1985). Indeed, a recent study found that in industries showing declining employment—like steel—the ratio of sales to employment was 4.2 times higher in small firms than in large firms (Edwards 1984:4).

The mini-mills' total share of industry shipments does not convey the great strength that these producers have in their markets. At the present time, mini-mill techniques are widely used for only a few commodities such as wire rods, concrete reinforcing bars, and hot rolled bars. Since the mid-1960s and especially during the 1970s, mini-mills have gradually pushed their integrated competitors out of these product lines. Integrated firms have thus either given them up completely or have retreated to the higher quality ranges that have been difficult for mini-mills to produce. However, the pace of technological progress in the mini-mill sector is so rapid that they are already moving into higher quality products. Two examples are the North Star Steel Company in bar production and Raritan River Steel Company in wire rod. The eventual elimination of integrated producers from such product categories now seems inevitable, barring fundamental changes in the operating practices of the integrated sector.

More surprising perhaps, the mini-mills have enjoyed similar success against foreign producers (Crandall 1985:11). For example:

- Markets in which mini-mills have a substantial share also tend to have a lower than average import share.
- The trend of imports in mini-mill product lines has contrasted sharply with the overall trend toward an increasing import share.

This supports the view that the expansion of the mini-mill sector has not been a consequence of poor performance by domestic integrated firms.

Spectacular growth has made it possible for mini-mills to enjoy the types of advantages that have accrued to other steel industries in high-growth markets. Rapid expansion of capacity has been accompanied by continuous process innovation. Each new facility has thus served as a prototype and laboratory for its successors. This sort of technological ferment has produced a steady stream of innovations. Water cooling of the furnace, the use of ultra high power, oxygen enrichment, and ladle metallurgy have all been pioneered by mini-mills and have significantly improved electric furnace technology. Mini-mills have also made dramatic gains through the use of continuous billet casting in lieu of ingot casting. Other refinements have gradually lowered operating costs, simplified operations, and lowered capital costs. Direct rolling of finished shaped—long a goal of steel producers—has been pioneered by mini-mill firms, partcularly Nucor Corporation in Charlotte, South Carolina (U.S. Office of Technology Assessment 1980).

Rapid technological progress and rapid expansion have ensured that mini-mill facilities are generally quite new, suggesting that their technology is correspondingly up to date. The age of the facilities in the mini-mills compared with the integrated sector clearly indicates that the pace of modernization has been radically superior for mini-mills.

- The mean age of facilities for the mini-mills is 6.3 years as compared to 22.0 for the integrated mills.
- The median ages of facilities for the mini-mills is much more uniform than for the integrated mills.

This reflects a consistent process of modernization for the mini-mills, whereas the integrated firms have followed a patchwork approach (Barnett and Schorsch 1983:Table 4.2:91).

The advantages of newer facilities are compounded by the benefits (in terms of capital costs, labor requirements, etc.) provided by the simpler configuration of the standard mini-mill vis-à-vis its integrated "rival." Mini-mills are indeed newer, but they are also different. In spite of what the term implies, mini-mills are not miniature versions of an integrated plant. Their smaller size does not imply that they do not attain the economies of scale associated with large-scale integrated production. This issue is complicated by the fact that patterns of economies of scale differ between mass production and flexible-production specialization technologies. At any rate, both their choice of technologies and the newness of their facilities provide the mini-mills with a significant advantage over their integrated competitors as long as attractively priced scrap is available and as long as we restrict the comparison to characteristic mini-mill products. Superior management from an entrepreneurial perspective is a third advantage. While difficult to quantify, this is an important advantage (Drucker 1985).

INNOVATION

The distinguishing feature of flexible specialization technologies is the return to technology as the focal point of competition. Innovation once again carries a premium as the focus of innovation shifts from the refinement of existing products to the production of new products (Abernathy et al. 1983:28).

The effect of innovation by mini-mills can best be illustrated by looking at a typical mini-mill product: wire rod. A cross-sectional and international comparison will illustrate the point. In 1981 the cost of wire rod (per ton shipped) was $393 for an integrated producer in the United States and $284 for a mini-mill. For international comparisons, the cost for a Japanese integrated mill (the most efficient in the world) was $304 and for the West Germans it was $336. The lower cost of the mini-mill shows that the U.S. industry is not inherently noncompetitive internationally (Barnett and Schorsch 1983:Table 5-9:135). One result of the shift to flexible specialization technologies by the mini-mills is that U.S. Steel Company had to close a large wire rod mill at its South Chicago Works in the early 1980's, forcing it out of the wire rod business. The plant had been rebuilt in the early 1970's.

The productivity record of U.S. mini-mills is one of the strongest indications of the strength of flexible specialization technologies. Whereas the image presented by the integrated sector is a gloomy composite of lagging productivity in almost every process, U.S. mini-mills have a strong record. Between 1958 and 1980 absolute Man Hours Per Ton (MHPT) required for wire rod declined from 12.28 to 6.45 for the integrated mills. For the mini-mills, the comparable figures were 13.60 MHPT and 3.51 MHPT, respectively. Although both the integrated and the mini-mills improved their productivity during the period, the percentage change in MHPT was 47.48 percent for the integrated and 74.19 percent for the mini-mills (Barnett and Schorsch 1983:Table 5-10:136).

The mini-mills' advantage in productivity was 2.93 MHPT in 1980. Flexible specialization technologies are the sources of this comparative advantage. The largest single source is in primary processing where input uses 1.27 MHPT. This is because mini-mills rely on scrap and do not need blast furnaces. However, this advantage is less than half of the total—43 percent. In steelmaking, the mini-mills lose 0.20 MHPT because the electric furnace cannot meet the efficiency of the Basic Oxygen Furnace. In continuous casting, the mini-mills gain 0.23 MHPT because of better performance and 0.63 MHPT because of more continuous casting. In the rolling process, mini-mills gain 0.65 MHPT, and in packaging and overhead they gain 0.21 MHPT. The overall productivity improvement of 2.93 MHPT has been increased in the last five years, and the Raritan River plant in New Jersey can produce wire rod at below 2 MHPT (Barnett and Schorsch 1983: Table 5-10:136).

In an environment of price flexibility such as we have experienced since the early 1970's, the oligopolistic legacy of price maker continues to be a burden for the integrated producers. Competitive prices and oligopolistic costs make the mass production model incompatible, as is evident from the integrated sector of the steel industry. Mini-mills, using flexible specialization technologies, are able to adjust more easily to changing prices and, pricewise, can compete much more aggressively. The indirect effect of price taker status—responding to price changes—may be much more significant than we have just seen. *It forces firms to be more highly conscious about reducing costs.* Greater cost consciousness on the part of the mini-mills is evident on several fronts.

First, it involves their attitudes toward new construction. Although vertical integration was an asset during the era of mass production, it becomes a liability in an era of flexible production (Acs and Audretsch 1985:39). In contrast to integrated producers, mini-mills adhere to a set of principles inherent in flexible specialization technologies—that is, build tight, build quick, and build cheap. Building in this fashion involves elimination of round-out options, redundancies, and crutches such as additional cranes, furnaces, and rolls. As a result of the commitment to build quick, which is facilitated by the simplicity of flexible specialization technologies, a greenfield plant can be erected in less than two years as compared to more than five years for integrated plants. Finally, flexible specialization technologies mean that you build just enough capacity for the present. Integrated firms, both in the United States and Japan, would build for years in advance of the market, resulting in a loss of flexibility and profitablility.

Second, with flexible specialization technologies, operating costs are kept to a minimum. Mini-mills maintain a far leaner headquarters staff than do their integrated competitors. The smaller staff allows the mini-mill to be much more flexible as market conditions change. Because they are price takers and because they produce a relatively narrow product line, mini-mills are generally very aware of their cost structure for managerial decision making. Integrated firms using mass production technologies often have a less thorough grasp of their actual cost structure. This failing stems from their oligopolistic past, their intricate corporate hierarchies, and their extensive vertical integration. These factors make it difficult for even the best integrated firms to identify their cost structures, to target cost reduction efforts, and to price according to cost.

Third, flexible specialization technologies create the need for craft workers—people who are willing and able to perform several tasks in a plant (Piore and Sable 1984:Ch. 6). For the mini-mills, the managerial advantage of a nonunionized labor force lies not so much in lower wages, but in greater flexibility and higher productivity of its labor force. Whereas the structure of work rules is a significant obstacle to productivity growth for firms using mass production technologies, greater efficiency is constantly stressed in the mini-mill environment. Productivity gains are realized constantly through the creation of a team-oriented labor practice where workers learn a broad range of skills instead of narrowly defined jobs. Use of the worker as a "craft" worker rather than as a semiskilled worker is a necessary condition for the use of flexible specialization technologies.

In the mini-mills, flexible specialization technologies have fostered a paternal relationship with the workforce (Piore and Sable 1984:400). The welfare of all is dependent on the competitiveness of the firm. This message is continuously stressed. Profit-sharing plans, employee stock plans, scholarship programs for dependents, and the like are all employed to develop the same type of corporate culture and identity that is so striking in Japan. This corporate culture is not a luxury, however; actually, it is necessary for the employing of flexible specialization technologies. By tying a part of the employees' compensation to the health of the company, the firm can exist in an environment of flexible prices.

CONCLUSION

The emergence of flexible specialization technologies as a response to the breakdown of the pricing system and the subsequent need for craft workers has been one important element in the emergence of small business in the United States. We have seen that even in the steel industry, when certain products are examined, small business has made an important contribution to productivity through process innovation that has eclipsed the mass production sector of the industry. This narrow but concrete example offers evidence that fits the broader set of statistics on small business innovation. Of course, much more research is needed on the subject of policies that will foster the spread of flexible specialization technologies in an economy where the rules of the game have been set up to promote the growth of mass production.[5]

NOTES

1. Suzanne Berger and Michael Piore offer a theoretical explanation as to why the small business sector of the economy continues to exist in advanced industrial countries.

2. See Michael Piore and Charles F. Sabel (1984). This book follows Piore's earlier work and gives a reason as to why the small business sector of the economy may actually increase.

3. In the steel industry, the growth of the mini-mills took place without government help. Indeed, during this period, the govenment was actually supporting the mass production sector of the industry.

4. By secular decline we mean that the consumption of steel as a percentage of the gross national product (GNP) will continue to decline in the future.

5. For a good discussion of the policy choices to promote flexible specialization technologies, see Piore and Sabel (1984:Ch. 10).

REFERENCES

Abernathy, William J., Kim B. Clark, and Alan M. Katrow. 1983. *Industrial renaissance.* New York: Basic Books.

Acs, Zoltan J. 1980. *Price behavior and the theory of the firm in competitive and corporate markets.* New School for Social Research. Dissertation. Ann Arbor, Mich.: University Microfilms International.

———. 1984. *The changing structure of the U.S. economy.* New York: Praeger.

———. 1985. A case study of the financing of mini-mills in the U.S. steel industry. *Policy Studies Journal* 13 (June):747-755.

Acs, Zoltan J., and David B. Audretsch. 1986. The restructuring of the U.S. markets. Working Paper. International Institute of Management, Berlin, West Germany.

Barnett, Donald F., and Louis Schorsch. 1983. *Steel: Upheaval in a basic industry.* Cambridge, Mass.: Ballinger Book Co.

Berger, Suzanne, and Michael Piore. 1980. *Dualism and discontinuity in industrial societies.* Cambridge, Mass.: Cambridge University Press.

Birch, David. 1979. *The job generation process.* Cambridge, Mass.: Program on Neighborhood and Regional Change.

Chandler, Alfred. 1977. *The visible hand.* Cambridge, Mass.: Harvard University Press.

Crandall, Robert W. 1985. Trade protection and the "revitalization" of the steel industry. Paper presented at the American Economics Association, New York, December.

Crandall, Robert W., and Stephen Barnett. 1985. *Up from the ashes: The U.S. steel mini-mills.* Washington, D.C.: Brookings Institution. (Draft.)

Drucker, Peter. 1985. *Innovation and entrepreneurship.* New York: Harper and Row.

Edwards, Keith L. (The Futures Group). 1984. Characterization of innovations introduced on the U.S. market in 1982. Prepared for the U.S. Small Business Administration under Contract # SBA-60500 A-82: March.

Federal Trade Commission. 1977. *United States steel industry.* Washington, D.C.: November.

Gellman Research Associates, Inc. 1982. The relationship betweeen industrial concentration, firm size, and technological innovation. Prepared for the Small Business Administration: May.

Hogan, William. 1983. *World steel in the 1980s.* Boston: Lexington Books.

Piore, Michael, and Charles F. Sabel. 1984. *The second industrial divide.* New York: Basic Books.

Reich, Robert. 1983. *The next American frontier.* New York: Times Books.

U.S. Office of Technology Assessment. 1980. *Technology and steel industry competitiveness.* Washington, D.C.: June.

II

PUBLIC POLICY IMPACTS ON SMALL BUSINESS

3 The Costs of Complying with Government Requirements: Are Small Firms Disproportionately Impacted?

PAUL SOMMERS and ROLAND J. COLE

Throughout the 1970s government requirements increased the cost of doing business in all industries. The expansion of the new "social" regulation in such areas as the environment, occupational and consumer safety, and energy consumption has been a frequent topic of public disussions. Government requirements may pose special problems for small businesses.[1] Complying with these requirements may cost small businessess more per dollar of revenue than it does medium- or large-sized firms. If this hypothesis is true, the disproportionate impact on small businesses places an additional competitive disadvantage on them vis-à-vis medium-sized firms.

Research to date has discussed, but not confirmed, the existence of the disproportionate impacts of government requirements on small businesses. John O. Davies (1969) finds that 46 percent of Connecticut small businesses surveyed regard government regulation as "a problem." Only one problem was more frequent for those businesses—that of finding capable employees. No comparisons with large businesses are available to establish whether the problems perceived by small businesses are different. Robert E. Berney (n.d.) goes further, suggesting that disproportionate costs for small businesses may be a pervasive effect of government requirements, but he offers no empirical tests of this hypothesis. Such a test is offered by Arthur Andersen and Company (1979), whose data show es-

---

The research reported here was performed with support from the U.S. Small Business Administration (SBA). Some of the preliminary results have been described previously in Sommers and Cole (1985). The authors benefited from comments by SBA staff, Fred Becker, and David Evans. Any remaining errors in this effort are the responsibility of the authors.

sentially uniform costs of government requirements over the range of business sizes in their sample. This finding may be due to the restricted class of requirements studied by Arthur Andersen and Company or to the fact that the smallest size class in their sample, 0-1500 employees, included no firms smaller than about 500 employees, a size not considered "small" by most definitions of small business.[2]

In this chapter, the results of two different surveys of small business compliance costs are discussed. The first survey was conducted in the state of Washington in 1980, and the second in the states of Georgia and Massachusetts in 1981. Both surveys were conducted by mail, by means of similar survey instruments. Details of the two surveys can be found in Roland J. Cole and Philip D. Tegeler (1980) and in Roland J. Cole and Paul Sommers (1981a).

THEORETICAL FRAMEWORK

We have presented the theoretical framework used here elsewhere (Cole and Sommers 1981b:143-53). Briefly, we hypothesize a tension for small firms between incurring the costs that full compliance with government requirements implies, and taking the risk of not fully complying or avoiding information about requirements, hoping to escape unnoticed or unchallenged by regulatory authorities. Larger businesses are able to spread the fixed costs of compliance over a larger number of production units, resulting in lower costs per dollar of revenue. However, their size also makes larger firms more visible, and thus easier for regulatory authorities to detect if they do not comply. Moderate-sized firms can also be successfully prosecuted, in contrast to very large firms that have significant political power and resources to resist successful prosecution for noncompliance. Thus, some small firms may avoid compliance, whereas larger firms are more likely to comply.

The major empirical implications of this theory are that small firms should report higher mean costs and greater variation across a sample than larger firms, owing to more frequent differences in compliance strategies among small firms. The empirical analyses reported below concentrate on the relative compliance costs of small and larger businesses. Analyses of variance are used to find the best dividing line between small and larger businesses; multiple linear regression is utilized to control for cost differences associated with particular industries and product/market characteristics.

Results from the Washington Survey

Early in 1980 a mail survey instrument was mailed to approximately 3,500 small- and medium-sized businesses in the state of Washington. The instrument requested information concerning the characteristics of firms and their costs of complying with various types of government requirements. A total of 361 firms mailed back usable survey instruments forming the sample for this survey. Although we cannot guarantee the statistical representativeness of this sample, because of the low response rate, the sample firms do resemble the distribution of the population of Washington firms by industry category.

In analyzing the survey data, we were interested in two questions:

1. Is there a size level at which "small" can be distinguished from "not small" with respect to the costs of complying with government requirements?
2. Do "small" firms report higher mean costs and more variable costs of compliance?

The issue of what constitutes a small firm for the purpose of assessing compliance costs was attacked through analyses of variance. Because our theoretical framework is not precise about what size should fall into the "small" category, we simply examined our data in a systematic fashion looking for some consistent pattern in the level of reported compliance costs by size of firm, choosing alternative breakpoints for the small and not-small categories. After examining upper limits on the small category ranging from 5 to 500 employees and several cost variables, we determined that an upper limit of 50 employees usually produced the maximum differentiation between the small and large firms. Analyses of variance on several cost measures, with the sample firms divided into alternative small and larger categories, yielded F-statistics measuring the between-group variation in the cost measures. This F-statistic was generally maximized by choosing fifty employees as the small/larger dividing line. In no case was an upper limit of more than 100 employees the best small/larger dividing line. Some of these analyses are summarized in Figure 3.1.

Thus, we concluded that very small firms are more likely to experience significant cost burdens in complying with government requirements. Depending on the cost measure, fifty or 100 employees is the small/larger firm dividing line that minimizes within size-group variance on reported compliance costs and maximizes between size-group. Firms with fewer than fifty employees face higher costs per dollar of revenue if they fully comply with government requirements. However, the data are also consistent with our hypothesis that small firms are more likely to respond with less than full compliance, resulting in wider variances of reported compliance costs among small firms.

Results from the Georgia and Massachusetts Survey

After completing the study in Washington, we decided to conduct a new study in two other states to replicate and extend our findings. By using an

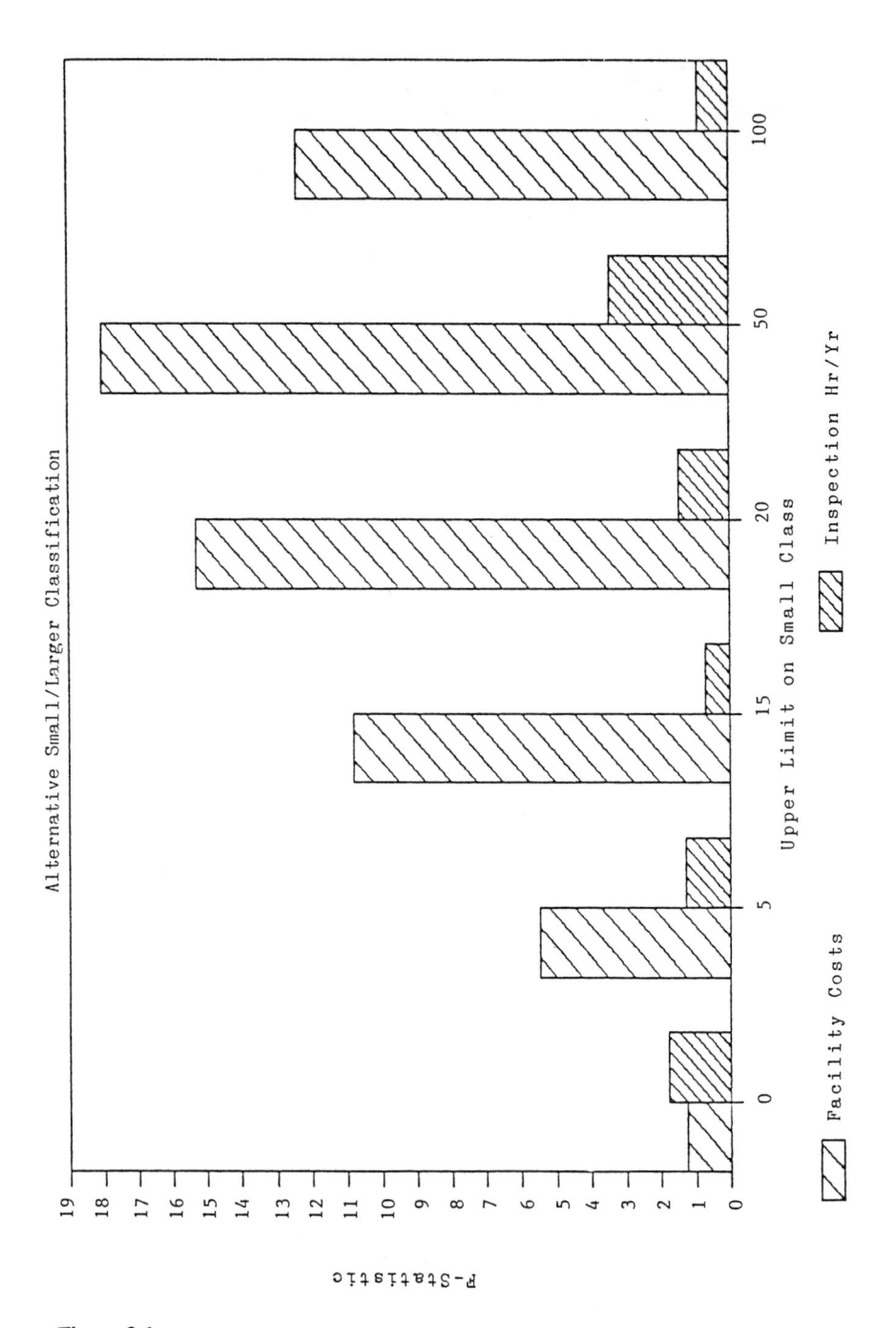

**Figure 3.1
Analysis of Variance (ANOVA) of Size on Cost Measures**

improved sampling strategy, we hoped to refine the findings concerning size of firm and to detect differences across major industrial groupings. We chose to study firms in Georgia, a development-oriented state in the Sunbelt, and Massachusetts, an older industrial state in the Northeast. We designed a stratified, random sample to detect both size and any industry effects on reported compliance cost. An equal number of small firms, and half as many larger firms, was chosen from each major Standard Industrial Classification (SIC) one-digit industrial catgory in Georgia and in Massachusetts. Dun and Bradstreet files were used to randomly select firms. Usable responses were received from 129 firms in Georgia (30 percent response rate) and 127 firms in Massachusetts (24 percent response rate). Details regarding the sample frame, sampling procedures, and survey instrument are presented in Cole and Sommers (1981a).

One measure of the overall costs of responding to government requirements is the number of different areas of requirement that impact particular firms. Table 3.1 summarizes the percentage of firms perceiving impacts in four general requirement areas: environment, goods and services, finance, and employee relations. A number of specific areas of requirements are listed under each of these broad requirement areas in the table. In all but five cases, a higher percentage of larger firms reported impacts in each area than did small firms. The anomalous cases were for consumer safety/health and noise requirements in Georgia, and for hazardous materials, air, and noise pollution requirements in Massachusetts. In each of these cases, a slightly higher percentage of small firms reported impacts than did the larger firms. The general pattern confirms our theoretical prediction that as firms grow larger, their activities become more diverse, bringing additional requirement areas into effect. In addition, some requirements have a size threshold, and as firms get larger they cross over these thresholds and begin to feel more regulatory requirements.

In Table 3.2, the responses are shown to questions relating to rating the three levels of government by their overall regulatory impact. A majority of sample firms nominated the federal level of government as having the greatest regulatory impact, the state level second, and the local level third. A higher percentage of larger firms cited the federal level as having the greatest level of impact than did the small firms in both states.

The survey yielded additional qualitative information which is summarized below. Government requirements cost larger firms more than small firms in absolute dollars. In some instances, the level of costs for larger firms was very close to that of small firms in absolute terms. This confirms the fixed cost nature of many compliance activities. On a proportionate basis, such requirements may cost small firms much more per dollar of revenue than larger firms.

Table 3.1
Areas of Requirements Affecting Sample Firms (Percentage of Firms Indicating Impacts)

	Georgia Small	Georgia Larger	Massachusetts Small	Massachusetts Larger
ENVIRONMENT				
Air Pollution	25.6	40.4	32.6	31.4
Water Pollution	22.0	44.7	26.1	37.1
Waste Disposal	30.5	46.8	30.4	31.4
Hazardous Materials	25.6	29.8	20.7	17.1
Noise Pollution	15.9	15.9	26.1	20.0
GOODS AND SERVICES				
Land Use/Zoning	26.8	44.7	50.0	57.1
Price of Goods/Services	26.8	61.7	25.0	48.6
Consumer Safety/Health	37.8	34.0	39.1	60.0
Product Safety	31.7	40.4	35.9	40.0
Product Performance/Reliability	17.1	36.2	25.0	28.6
Advertising/Marketing	19.5	31.9	17.4	42.9
Transportation	34.1	46.8	35.9	48.6
Energy Use and Rates	35.4	57.4	39.1	54.3
FINANCE				
Business Financing	28.0	38.3	29.3	54.3
Unemployment Compensation	59.8	95.7	67.4	100.0
Consumer Credit	17.1	40.4	23.9	42.9
Tax Reporting	80.5	100.0	80.4	88.6
EMPLOYEE RELATIONS				
Employee Safety/Health	53.7	93.6	58.7	85.7
Labor Management	22.0	59.6	21.7	54.3
Pensions	13.4	72.3	23.9	68.6
Equal Opportunity	41.5	93.6	44.6	85.7
N of Cases	82	47	92	35

As predicted by our theoretical framework, more requirement areas come into effect as firms grow. This is one reason why requirements cost larger firms more in absolute terms. No one agency is responsible for the majority of the requirements cost experienced by firms. A variety of federal, state, and local agencies are involved.

Administrative cost results show that some small firms report no staff days per year on government reporting, recordkeeping, and licensing requirements. These data can be taken as evidence of the noncompliance choices of some small firms as predicted by our theory.

A majority of sample firms feel they are adequately informed about government requirements, and a majority rely on accountants to deal with requirements. A few sample firms utilize lawyers to deal with government

Table 3.2
Ranking of Impacts by Level of Government (Percentage of Firms)

| Level of Government/ | Georgia | | Massachusetts | |
Impact Rating	Small	Larger	Small	Larger
FEDERAL				
Greatest	42.7	78.7	42.4	68.6
Second Greatest	8.5	14.9	21.7	11.4
Least	22.0	0.0	15.2	8.6
No Response	26.8	6.4	20.7	11.4
STATE				
Greatest	17.1	10.6	22.8	17.1
Second Greatest	53.7	72.3	40.2	68.6
Least	3.7	12.8	16.3	2.9
No Response	25.6	4.3	20.7	11.4
LOCAL				
Greatest	15.9	6.4	15.2	2.9
Second Greatest	12.2	6.4	16.3	8.6
Least	46.3	80.9	46.7	77.1
No Response	25.6	6.4	21.7	11.4
N of Cases	82	47	92	35

requirements, and some sample firms have attempted to avoid requirements by either influencing a requirement before it is passed or challenging it once it is imposed. Small firms are less likely than larger firms to obtain information on government requirements from business associations.

Sample firms were asked about broad areas of business impacts of government requirements. The judgments of small firms are consistently different from those of larger firms. For example, small firms tend to be much less affected by regulations, especially in such areas as business growth, competitive position, and managerial independence. Small firms in both states agreed that small firms are the most hampered by government regulations, whereas larger firms do not perceive greater impacts on any size group. Both size groups agree that larger firms are the most favored by government requirements.

These data provide considerable support for our theoretical framework. The data are consistent with some of our critical assumptions, which are as follows:

1. The number of requirements increases with size.
2. The number of challenges increases with size.
3. Noncompliance choices are seen only among small firms.

4. A disproportionate burden is placed on small firm management.
5. Small and large firms believe that large firms are most favored by government requirements.

The Effects of Size and Industry on Compliance Costs

Size may not be the only variable that affects compliance costs. It is possible that industry and product characteristics are also significant factors. To test these hypotheses, we estimated regression equations for six compliance cost measures constructed from the survey data. Regression equations of the following form were estimated: C=f(EMPL, PRINPROD, NONLOCAL, INTERSTATE, INTERNATL, STATE, D2, ..., D9). This regression specification embodies a number of hypotheses. We hypothesize that the cost to a particular firm will be:

Higher the larger the number of employees (EMPL). This hypothesis is discussed in some detail above. To capture the nonlinear effect of size, we used a log-log specification of the equation. Both size and the dependant variables were entered in logarithmic form.

Lower the higher the percentage of sales in one principal product (PRINPROD). Restriction of activity to a single product should bring fewer product-specific requirements into force.

Higher the percentage of sales sold nonlocally (NONLOCAL), interstate (INTERSTATE), and internationally (INTERNATL). The more jurisdictional boundaries spanned by a firm, the more regulatory agencies it may be subject to .

Different for the two states in the sample (dummy variable STATE=1 if Georgia, 0 if Massachusetts). States and localities may impose significantly different requirements, and federal requirements are sometimes implemented by states or localities, resulting in local variation in implementation.

Significantly different across industrial groups represented by industry dummy variables (D2 to D9. D1, Agriculture, omitted to avoid colinearity with constant term). Broad industry groupings are surrogate measures for industry-specific regulation.

Although we expect costs to increase in absolute value with the size of the firm, we expect that costs per employee will be higher for small firms than for larger firms. Thus, after estimating the equations for the various dependent variables, we calculate the predicted cost per employee for typical firms in the small and larger firm groups.

Initial regression runs revealed that the variables measuring concentration in a single product (PRINPROD), concentration in nonlocal area sales (NONLOCAL, INTERSTATE, and INTERNATL), and the dummy variable for state are insignificant in all equations. Table 3.3 shows the results of the regression analyses after the nonsignificant variables were dropped from the equation.

Table 3.3
Costs of Compliance: Estimated Regression Coefficients (*F*-Statistics in Parentheses)

Independent Variables	Log of Annual Cost of Licenses	Log of Cost of Physical Changes	Log of Staff Days for Inspections	Log of Staff Days for Govt Reports	Log of Staff Days for Licenses	Log of Staff Days for Recordkeeping
Constant	5.207 (234.000)***	2.363 (14.130)***	1.429 (64.900)***	1.211 (75.020)***	1.243 (70.126)***	1.569 (130.080)***
Log of No Employees	0.5557 (74.5200)***	0.9009 (57.0000)***	0.0605 (3.9600)*	0.1885 (54.7400)***	0.1329 (24.2100)***	0.1483 (35.8900)***
Industry Dummies						
SIC 2 Mining	0.7014 (0.1860)	2.9470 (8.6870)***	0.1439 (0.3840)	0.1801 (0.7860)	0.1281 (0.3280)	0.3288 (2.6410)
SIC 3 Construction	0.5579 (1.4710)	-0.2637 (0.9430)	0.3691 (2.5190)	0.4531 (6.1000)**	0.2842 (2.1000)	0.4057 (5.0410)*
SIC 4 Manufacturing	-0.8756 (3.4940)	-0.2818 (0.1110)	-0.4995 (5.1440)*	0.5842 (0.0940)	-0.2975 (2.1560)	0.0272 (0.0220)
SIC 5 Tran-Comm-Util	1.0160 (4.5600)*	-0.6115 (0.4950)	0.1459 (0.4080)	0.4980 (6.6370)**	0.1152 (0.3130)	-0.0460 (0.0600)
SIC 6 Wholesale	0.1418 (0.7750)	-0.1442 (0.0250)	-0.0132 (0.0023)	0.1776 (0.7640)	-0.0201 (0.0080)	-0.0761 (0.1510)
SIC 7 Retail	-0.2763 (0.5490)	-1.6270 (3.4200)	-0.2989 (1.7120)	-0.2180 (0.1440)	-0.3106 (2.6090)	0.0869 (0.2360)
SIC 8 Fin-Ins-RE	0.0917 (0.8580)	-2.2080 (5.4400)**	0.0993 (0.1760)	0.2691 (1.8760)	-0.0812 (0.1460)	0.2164 (1.2220)
SIC 9 Services	-0.5301 (1.6810)	-0.5314 (0.4981)	0.2337 (1.1810)	0.2400 (2.1570)	-0.1996 (1.2730)	-0.1328 (0.6820)
R2	.28	.26	.14	.20	.14	.18

Significance Levels

* .050
** .010
*** .001

The number of employees in a firm is a very strong predictor of the level of compliance costs. The employee variable is significant and positive in all of the six regression equations at a high level of significance. Compliance costs increase (absolutely) with firm size in every one of these equations. The predicted relative increase per employee is discussed later in this chapter.

Industry dummy variables are also significant in several of the equations. The dummy variable for the agriculture industry was omitted to avoid colinearity with the constant. Hence, all of these results must be interpreted as the impacts on a particular industry relative to the omitted industry, agriculture. The mining industry has a significant and positive coefficient in one equation: cost of physical changes. Because federal and state governments have imposed many safety-related requirements on mines, this result is not surprising at all. The construction industry has significant and positive coefficients in two equations: staff days for government reports and for recordkeeping. Again, the construction industry is required to obtain building permits and to meet a number of different codes. Higher costs than the omitted industry for reports and recordkeeping is a natural result. The manufacturing industry has significant and negative coefficients in one equation: staff days for inspection. The coefficients in all but two of the other equations, though nonsignificant, are negative as well. These results indicate that the manufacturing industry is, as a whole, less burdened by regulatory compliance costs than tne omitted industry. The transportation–communication–utilities sector shows positive, significant coefficients in two equations: annual cost of licenses and staff days for government reports. The finance–insurance–real estate industry has a significant, negative coefficient in the cost of physical changes equation.

Perhaps the most surprising aspect of these results is that there are no significant coefficients for the service industry. In prior work in Washington, we obtained significant, negative coefficients on service industry dummy variables in a number of equations (Cole and Sommers 1980). However that sample had an extraordinary number of very small service firms, making it impossible to separate the size and industry effects properly. These new results from a better structured sample indicate that smallness is the distinguishing characteristic.

Using the estimated regression coefficients, we can calculate the estimated impacts on typical firms of various sizes, abstracting from the specific industry effects. The results of such calculations are shown in Table 3.4 for five- and 100-employee firms. Estimated total costs and estimated costs per employee are shown in this table for each of the variables. Although total costs are higher for 100-employee firms than for five-employee firms, the costs per employee are higher for the smaller firms in all but one case. The difference in costs per employee ranges from

Table 3.4
Estimated Compliance Costs for Five- and 100-Employee Firms

			Staff Days For				
Firm Size	Cost of Licenses	Cost of Changes	Staff Inspections	Government Reports	Licenses	Records	Total Days
Small							
Total for Five Employees	447	45	4.601	4.546	4.292	6.096	19.536
Per Employee	89	9	0.920	0.909	0.858	1.219	2.107
Larger							
Total for Five Employees	2359	1062	5.515	7.997	6.391	9.506	29.409
Per Employee	23	10	0.055	0.079	0.063	0.095	0.294

about three times higher to sixteen times higher. Thus, in a relative sense, very small firms must devote a much higher percentage of managerial/administrative effort in complying with government requirements than do larger firms. As shown in the last column of Table 3.4, if one adds the total estimated staff days for various kinds of requirements for five-employee and 100-employee firms (on the assumption that these activities are independent and therefore additive), the total comes to over nineteen days per year for the five-employee firm, almost four working weeks, and to just over twenty-nine days for a 100-employee firm, about six weeks in total. Thus, the total staff days increase by a third as firm size increases twenty times. The proportional burden on the very small firm is therefore much greater.

RESEARCH CONCLUSIONS AND POLICY IMPLICATIONS

In this section, we summarize the major conclusions of our research and identify some of the policy implications. Surveys of small and larger firms in Georgia, Massachusetts, and Washington were conducted. Small firms were distinguished empirically from larger firms on the basis of analyses of variance. Based on these analyses, we chose fewer than fifty employees as the small firm class, and fifty or more employees as the larger firm class. This classification scheme for the purpose of studying requirement costs uses a much lower upper limit on the small class than do the SBA classification schemes derived for other purposes.

As predicted by our theoretical framework, the survey data show that larger firms are more likely to engage in frequent challenges of government requirements. Small firms are much less likely to use lawyers or other paid consultants in dealing with government requirements, and they are less likely to obtain information on government requirements from business or trade associations.

Because the costs of avoiding requirements are so high, small firms are left with the choice of complying, at very high costs per dollar of sales, or of choosing partial or noncompliance strategies, hoping that regulatory agencies will fail to detect their noncompliance. In our survey sample, only the small firms report spending zero staff days on several requirement types.

Although a few small firms report no compliance costs of certain types, on average the small firms in our survey sample report higher costs per employee than larger firms on all of the compliance cost measures subjected to regression analysis. The number of staff days used for various compliance activities is approximately nineteen days for five-employee firms and twenty-nine days for 100-employee firms in Georgia and Massachusetts.

Policy Implications

The broad range of government requirements affecting small business indicates that a very broad-scale effort would be required to make them neutral with respect to firm size. Several aspects of our research have implications for policy initiatives in this area. First, the level of firm size which discriminates between small and larger firm compliance costs is very small—somewhere between twenty and 100 employees depending on the specific requirement. This is much smaller than the size levels used for other purposes such as procurement regulations. Second, the compliance burden varies from industry to industry, a factor that should be taken into account in performing cost/benefit analyses of regulatory initiatives. Finally, despite the focus on paperwork costs, we conclude that purely information-gathering paperwork is often of benefit to business, whereas other paperwork burdens are means of demonstrating compliance with requirements. The choice in the latter case is not between paperwork and nothing, but between paperwork and other means of demonstrating compliance (Cole and Sommers 1982:554-56). The true purpose of many of the requirements underlying paperwork burdens needs to be considered in formulating policy initiatives.

This research has been conducted over a period of years in which considerable attention has been devoted to small business through White House Conferences on Small Business and various programs of the U.S. Small Business Administration. These programs have included the efforts of the SBA's Office of Advocacy which has sought to increase sensitivity to small business impacts of actions by the federal government. Progress has also been made at the state level. For example, in our home state of Washington, efforts have been made to coordinate and streamline the licensing and permitting processes, and a Small Business ombudsman has been established to help small businesses deal with the state government.

We think, however, that the basic thrust of the recommendations above has not been effectively implemented at the federal, state, or local levels of government. Federal size standards do not recognize the problems of the very small firm, nor has there been much discussion of the tradeoffs among paperwork burden, information collection, and alternative compliance strategies. The cost of complying with government requirements remains a salient issue with the small business owners of this country.

NOTES

1. We use the term *small* to refer to firms with fewer than fifty employees.
2. See size classes in U.S. Small Business Administration, *Economic research program announcement,* Washington, D.C., 1979, Appendix D.

REFERENCES

Arthur Andersen and Company. 1979. *Analysis of regulatory cost and establishment size for the small business administration.*

Berney, Robert E. n.d. *The cost of government regulation on small business.* Washington, D.C. U.S. Small Business Administration.

Cole, Roland J., and Paul Sommers. 1980. Costs of compliance in small and larger business. *Report for U.S. Small Business Administration by Battelle Human Affairs Research Centers.* Seattle.

———. 1981a. Complying with government requirements: The costs to small and larger businesses. *Report for U.S. Small Business Administration by Battelle Human Affairs Research Centers.* Seattle. BHARC -320/81/022.

———. 1981b. Business and government regulation: A theory of compliance decisions. *Journal of Contemporary Business* 10(1): 143-153.

———. 1982. Government paperwork: Not an easy villain after all. *Journal of Policy analysis and Management* 1(4): 554-556.

Cole, Roland J., and Philip D. Tegeler. 1980. *Government requirements of small business.* Lexington, Mass.: Lexington Books.

Davies, John O. 1969. Small business and legal services. *American Bar Association Journal:*172.

Sommers, Paul, and Roland J. Cole. 1985. Compliance costs of small and larger businesses. *Policy Studies Journal* 13 (June): 701-708.

4 Employment Disincentives and Small Business: A Pilot Study

HERBERT R. NORTHRUP and EVELYN M. ERB

Much of the government's efforts to encourage business is in the form of incentives (e.g., tax credits and job training programs). These incentives are often structured in such a way that they are most beneficial to large firms. Perhaps small business growth can be stimulated by removing the existing disincentives facing small businesses. The issue of disincentives to small businesses is a timely one, largely because jobs created by small businesses have accounted for two-thirds of all new jobs created in the past decade.

In late 1983 and early 1984 the U.S. Small Business Administration (SBA) commissioned the Wharton School's Industrial Research Unit (IRU) to conduct a pilot study of disincentives to small businesses resulting from government policies that hinder their growth and employment capability. The objectives of this study were to determine which government regulations affect small businesses, to what degree the impact of these regulations is beneficial or adverse to them, and how these regulations affect their employment practices. It was felt that the creation of jobs through small business would be extremely important during the 1980's because of the need to make up for the loss of jobs in basic manufacturing.

Chief executives of twenty firms were surveyed by personal interviews. The names of the companies and their management were obtained from, and cooperation assured by, members of the Small Business Committee of the American Institute of Certified Public Accountants (AICPA). All of the companies interviewed were in the mid-Atlantic region, specifically in New York, Philadelphia, Baltimore, and Washington, D.C. A "small business" was defined as a firm with fewer than 500 employees.

COMPANY PROFILE

The firms represented a cross-section of industries, including manufacturing, associations/services, retail, wholesale, and construction. The majority of the twenty firms have been established since 1960; one-half of the companies were staffed with fifty to 150 employees; their mean gross revenues were between $8 and $12 million; and nine of the twenty firms were unionized.

ACCESS TO INFORMATION

All the firms interviewed had access to good accounting and legal expertise. Accounting expertise seemed to be a well-utilized resource, but legal counsel was readily sought by only one-half of the firms. The prohibitive cost of legal fees was given as the reason why many firms hesitated to seek legal advice. Of the ten firms that consulted with their attorney regularly, four had attorneys on their staff, usually in a line-management position.

Only seven of the firms interviewed had a full-time person to handle personnel relations. Few of these individuals, however, were well versed in employment-related legislation. Most firms relied heavily on trade associations to keep them abreast of legislation and sought legal counsel when information or advice was needed on a specific employment issue. Whether a company had a personnel officer was related to its size. No company with fewer than 150 employees had a personnel department.

UNPROMPTED EMPLOYMENT-RELATED ISSUES OF CONCERN

Survey participants were asked what employment-related legislation had affected their businesses either in a positive or in a negative way. The three most frequently mentioned adverse concerns were issues involving the National Labor Relations (Taft-Hartley) Act (NLRA), the Equal Employment Opportunity Commission (EEOC) or the Office of Federal Contract Compliance Programs (OFCCP), and the Occupational Safety and Health Administration (OSHA). Issues relating to employment insurance, workers' compensation, and the Employment Retirement Income Security Act (ERISA) were also considered to be adverse by several of the companies. Legislation that was considered beneficial by the businesses included tax credits and job training programs.

PROMPTED PIECES OF EMPLOYMENT LEGISLATION

From a list of employment legislation items, each of the companies was asked to indicate which ones they had experience with and to what degree the legislation had been either beneficial or adverse. The items anticipated to be areas of concern are as follows: EEOC or OFCCP, the Age Discrimination in Employment Act (ADEA), minimum wage, OSHA, NLRA, ERISA, difficulties in reducing the labor force, recordkeeping, payroll taxes, and job training programs. Almost every prompted issue was considered adverse by more than 50 percent of the firms that had experience with it, with two exceptions—ADEA and minimum wage.

An employment legislation sensitivity index was developed to quantify the degree of impact which government legislation had on a particular firm. An index was determined for each of the twenty companies by assigning a point rating to the answer of each prompted item: Highly Beneficial, +2; Beneficial, +1; Neutral, 0; Adverse, -1; and Highly Adverse, -2. The impact of issues that were not included on the list of prompted items was also integrated into the index value. The index can be used to compare the effect of this legislation on one firm with that on another firm, even though the types of legislation that affect the two firms may be different. The more negative the employment legislation sensitivity index, the more adversely affected the company has been by government employment-related legislation. Table 4.1 shows the correlation between a firm's index and its industry.

Table 4.1
Index Values Correlated by Industry

	Individual Company Indexes								Industry Index Average
Manufacturing	-0.5	-7	-1	-2.5	-1	+2	-2	-5	-2.13
Service	+1.5	-3	-1	-1.0	-8	-1	-2		-2.07
Retail	-2.5	-3							-2.75
Wholesale	0.0	-10							-5.00
Construction	-10.0								-10.00

SURVEY RESULTS

Each prompted and unprompted item is discussed below.

EEOC. Of the seventeen firms that had experience with the EEOC, ten believed that antidiscrimination legislation has had an adverse or highly adverse effect on their businesses. In fact, this item of legislation was considered to be adverse by more companies than any other item. Although the president of one firm interviewed believed that "if a company doesn't like EEOC, it has something to hide," most of the companies surveyed reiterated three consistent concerns with the EEOC. The weakest argument was that "it is not fair for the government to tell me who to pick for my workforce." More importantly, companies gave many examples of how costly the hearings are and how much mangement time they consume. "[The] EEOC requires management to spend enormous amounts of time in terms of data gathering and preparation, then the case will be dismissed." This sentiment was echoed by all five of the firms that had experience with EEOC hearings. These firms had spent between $2,000 and $25,000 on litigation, and the cases were either thrown out of the courts or remain undecided. The companies also believed that they were guilty until proved innocent; that they could not countersue; and that the burden of proof was on the company and, therefore, firms must be careful to keep accurate documentation. One CEO explicitly said, "If EEO were rigorously enforced, it would be a limitation on hiring and growth."

Recordkeeping. Recordkeeping was the second most frequently adversely ranked issue. However, it is often difficult to separate the recordkeeping mandated by employment legislation from that which the firm chooses to do for its own records, for other government purposes (e.g., taxes), or for financial purposes. In addition to Internal Revenue Service (IRS) reporting, ERISA, EEOC, and Department of Labor reporting requirements were frequently mentioned as cumbersome. Government contract work was repeatedly pointed out as requiring unnecessarily voluminous records. One manager noted that "government work" was regarded as a "specialty" because of the paperwork required. Because of their recent growth, at least five firms had added personnel to handle the additional paperwork. One company president estimated that the government recordkeeping requirements added 20 percent more work to the personnel officer's workload.

OSHA. OSHA was perceived to be a disincentive by eight of the thirteen firms that had experience with it. The two main complaints related to the way the legislation was administered, rather than to the legislation itself. The firms complained of the adversarial attitude of OSHA inspectors. Some executives clearly believed that the charges and fines that OSHA assesses are inconsistently applied. In one firm's experience with OSHA, the inspector was very picky on one visit; on the next visit he concerned himself only with superficialities. The perceived focus of OSHA's inspections on the details, rather than on the gross safety hazards, was also noted. One small business manager summed it up by saying that they "miss the forest for the trees; the OSHA representative will be checking extension cord lengths in the basement, instead of making sure there are guard rails on the icy twelfth story of a building."

NLRA. The issue of union power was an emotional one for many firms. Twelve of the twenty firms had had some experience with the NLRA, and none considered the legislation beneficial. Most believed that the legislation empowered unions to do and say practically anything, while it restricted management's actions (or reactions) excessively. Four firms found the legislation highly adverse; four others rated it adverse; and another four considered it neutral. Managers from the three other firms, although they had no direct experience with the NLRA, were adamant that they would "rather shut the place down, than work with a unionized staff."

Most of the firms interviewed were clearly anti-union. One company president, although sympathetic to the original need for unions, said, "Unions are now as bad as the monopolistic powers they fought." Although these words may sound harsh, other executives interviewed expressed similar anti-union sentiments.

It was perceived that the NLRA also makes it difficult to fire someone. In the experience of many of these small businesses, arbitrators rarely uphold dismissals. Several managers noted that arbitrators often forced the company into a step-wise dismissal process beginning with suspension, regardless of the blatancy of the offense precipitating the desire to fire the employee.

ERISA. One-half of the firms that had experience with ERISA considered ERISA to have an adverse or a highly adverse impact. Two reasons for these ratings were given. First, it required considerable paperwork that was generally considered a "headache." Second, management had no discretionary ability to offer different types of pension plans to different groups of employees (for example, to offer a more generous plan to key managers, or to offer the managers a plan but not the staff). One manager believed ERISA was adverse to the employees as well. His company amended its profit-sharing plan recently. "It cost legal fees and involved paper work hassles." More importantly, the company "ended up reducing the benefits to employees because the company had originally been putting in 10 percent of pretax profit, but under ERISA it opted to make the contribution discretionary."

Difficulties in Reducing the Labor Force. Thirteen companies had experienced difficulties in reducing their labor force. EEOC, ADEA, and NLRA were all cited as contributing to the difficulties. According to one manager, "The attitude of the workforce is if you're laid off, sue before you apply for unemployment. A firm can't point blank fire an employee for showing up with alcohol or drugs. We can't accuse someone of being a thief even if they walk out with their pockets full of money. If we do, we get sued for defaming their character." Another owner noted that "dismissed employees have many avenues to appeal dismissal—they get money (if not their jobs) back." To avoid potential legal complications resulting from dismissals, some firms have hired personnel consultants to handle particularly difficult situations. Many of the firms have come to the conclusion that the only way to protect themselves against legal action is to document everything. The difficulty in dismissing employees also makes firms more cautious in terms of whom they hire.

Social Security Taxes. Almost one-half of the companies interviewed considered social security taxes to be either adverse or highly adverse. They believed that without the taxes either they could pay their employees higher wages or they could lower their prices, create demand, and hire more people.

Most of the companies that rated the impact of social security taxes neutrally seem to have resigned themselves to the fact that "it is a part of doing business." One company explained that "it's our social obligation." A government contractor said it was "recoverable overhead," but agreed with the other one-half of the firms interviewed when he noted that it is 'too expensive."

Several firms viewed social security taxes as a severe disincentive to hiring new employees. One company employs large numbers of part-time people because "social security taxes are a disincentive to hiring someone full-time." Another firm elaborated that, "without the taxes, we could generate more sales and, therefore, would have to hire more employees." The responses to this question regarding social security taxes were based more on business sense than on personal preference, and the effect of these taxes on small business was clear: social security is a disincentive to hiring more employees.

ADEA. ADEA was the only piece of legislation that received ratings in every category, ranging from highly beneficial to highly adverse. Two of the eight firms that had experience with the ADEA considered the legislation beneficial. Four considered it to be from slightly adverse to highly adverse. Two considered it neutral.

One firm that ranked ADEA's effect beneficial believed that the older employees on its staff were an asset to the company because of their extensive work experience. Another company was able to employ older people part time to accomplish the monthly envelope stuffing necessary for billing. "Even if there were a less expensive way to stuff those envelopes, I would hire those people. It is a social event for them and it helps company morale."

Some of the companies that considered ADEA to be adverse viewed it as another item that makes it more difficult to dismiss an employee without worrying about being sued. One manager elaborated, "We'd prefer to have mandatory retirement at age sixty-five. Previous to the ADEA, we tended to 'carry' people because we knew they'd be gone in a few years. Because of the ADEA, we terminated a guy with poor job performance that we might have otherwise carried," Also because of ADEA, the firm gathered an ample amount of documentation on this employee before dismissing him. The manager continued, "We now have two other people over sixty-five that we are not dismissing strictly because we'd risk being sued."

Minimum Wage. Less than one-third of the firms interviewed had employees working at minimum wage. Those employees paid at that level were mostly high school students. Of the six firms, four believed the minimum-wage requirement had a neutral effect on their hiring practices and two, an adverse effect. The minimum wage had little effect on firms that had only a few employees paid at that level. If the wage were increased, they claimed that they would not decrease the number of students employed (for social obligation reasons); if the wage were decreased, one of the firms would hire more students.

There was some disagreement about whether younger employees should be paid a lower minimum wage. Although two firms mentioned that the wage should be lower for those under eighteen, another firm thought that "paying younger people a lower minimum wage is not a good idea. The temptation to steal in the retail market is large enough as is."

Not all the employees currently working at minimum wage, however, are students. One company noted that "wages are correlated to the market and not directly to the minimum-wage level. If the minimum wage were decreased, we probably not get the same caliber of person at the lower wage—and caliber is important." Another company president believed, "The minimum wage contributes to unemployment." Without the minimum wage his company would hire more people.

Other Concerns. Unemployment insurance was raised as a concern by five companies because of its excessive cost. One manager in Washington D.C., believed that unemployment compensation was a disincentive to work, claiming that it "pays too much, it's too easy to get on, and it lasts too long." Another entrepreneur complained that the "ratings and policies seem exorbitant."

The Health Maintenance Act of 1973 was brought up specifically by two firms. It requires that, at anyone's request, the company offer a local Health Maintenance Organization (HMO) plan as an alternative to the company's regular health insurance coverage. This "increases recordkeeping requirements" and is discouraging in principle because the "rates keep going up while the service continues to fall."

The intent behind the Prompt Payment Act was to help government contractors by ensuring that the government would pay its bills on time. It requires that payments accrue interest if not paid within forty-five days. According to one firm interviewed, previous to the passage of the act, 67 percent of its receivables were paid within thirty days; within a month after the passage of the act, 100 percent of its receivables were paid on the forty-fifth day, and the company was forced to "double dip into the credit line."

Prevailing wage determinations, as required by the Davis-Bacon Act, were considered to be highly adverse by two construction firms whose growth had been restricted by the high cost of labor. The message of both firms was clear: "Without a doubt, without Davis-Bacon we would hire more people."

Four companies mentioned workers' compensation in their unprompted list of concerns. Two of these firms were predominantly concerned with the paperwork requirements. Another company that hires a large percentage of its workforce as part-time employees does so because "without having to pay workers' compensation or social security, they are less expensive." A fourth company complained about the money that it was paying because of the way job categories are defined. The company manager claimed, "I pay three times as much workers' compensation because my drivers are 'common carriers' instead of 'chauffeurs'."

Securities and Exchange Commission (SEC). Not all small businesses stay small. For those that eventually go public, the power of the SEC is an additional concern facing them. Three firms mentioned difficulties with the SEC. One firm believed that other firms can "bring suits too easily" and that "the antitrust structure should be reviewed." "A company can grow from $5 to $25 million in revenue, and go unnoticed, but over $25 million, especially if it is in a less competitive market, it becomes a target for antitrust suits brought on by competitors with a very small market share."

Another company had an acquisition attempt thwarted by the SEC which chose to "stonewall the request and didn't clear the acquisition before the agreements expired." This company is a publicly owned firm, with only 225 employees. The manager noted that it is unusual for a company of that size to be public, and that it faces certain disadvantages, one of them being the SEC. In addition to losing a half-million dollars in the acquisition attempt, the SEC is now conducting an investigation and the company is having to cover legal fees to clear itself. It's a situation of the company being guilty until proved innocent.

Tax Credits. Companies have been granted tax credits for a variety of reasons. Most commonly, companies had received investment tax credits or research and development tax credits. Tax credits are also given to companies for employing handicapped persons and, through the Neighborhood Assistance Act, for hiring disadvantaged employees.

Ninety percent of the firms questioned about tax credits considered them to be either beneficial or highly beneficial. A few noted that they were "beneficial but incidental." One company had applied for an employment credit through a Department of Labor program, but because of repeated modifications to the form, the company had to resubmit it numerous times. "After all the time spent, the cost was beyond the amount of the reimbursement." Another company that employed many young people recalled that tax credits formerly applied to people under the age of eighteen. This regulation has now been changed to include only those from a disadvantaged class. The company found this classification to be less useful, largely because it is not the kind of thing the company can ask on a job application.

Another important observation about tax credits and their benefit to small companies concerns the fact that small companies have less of a need to shelter their income, and that even though tax credits can generally be deferred, small businesses might be better served by a direct payback or grant.

Job Training Programs. The second most frequently mentioned item of beneficial legislation was job training programs. These, of course, come in many types and are administered at all levels of government from the county up. Nevertheless, of the nine firms that have had some experience with some type of job training program, five considered the programs beneficial, and the other four rated them neutral. The companies in the last-named category said that the programs just "did not work" or that they "did not attract the caliber of person that they needed." Of the companies with positive experiences with job training programs, one firm had achieved a documented $28,000 savings by using a county-run personnel development program. Another company staffed a new facility almost entirely with people from a similar personnel development program. One firm had taken advantage of the "old CETA programs" with success but believed that "there aren't enough job training programs; more need to be created through private industry."

Set Asides. Government-assigned set asides for minority-owned companies and for small businesses were considered highly beneficial by those companies that had been able to take advantage of them. Of those firms interviewed, two were minority-owned companies. Both had availed themselves of the special government contracts set aside for minority firms. In fact, on company's most significant difficulty was the transition from the 8-A set-aside program.

Two other nonrecipient companies, however, disputed the "fairness" of these programs. One manager was skeptical about the legitimacy of most of the organizations that take advantage of the 8-A set-asides. Another manager pointed out that the 8-A set-aside recipients often use government contracts as their sole source of work, and that too often "realistic or consistently administered graduation requirements have not been set."

The same manager noted that the small business set asides were also poorly administered. The "general small business standards are ridiculous." The maximum standards of gross revenues of $2.5, $4.0, or $7.5 million result in some small business–contract set asides being too large for small businesses to manage.

CONCLUSION

The interviewees seemed to be unwilling to rate an item adversely, even though the company may have had costly or time-consuming experience pertaining to the particular item. For example, although one firm had discharged two Puerto Rican employees, and, to avoid a threatened EEOC suit, replaced them with two Puerto Ricans, the firm claimed that employment legislation had no effect on its hiring practices. The phenomenon may occur for two reasons: (1) because firms have accommodated the legislation and may be unaware of the impact it actually has on them, and (2) because the personal opinion of the manager may be that the legislation is generally favorable. The second reason makes it more difficult for the manager to separate the effect of the legislation on his or her firm from its intent. For example, none of the four firms operated by women or minorities rated the EEOC adversely.

Two firms had a net rating of beneficial on the employment legislation sensitivity index. One was an association and hence had the option of simply passing on such costs as benefits packages, payroll taxes, and legal fees to the companies it served. The other was a manufacturing firm that had been operating at its present location for only a year. It was too new to have had many employment-related difficulties, and it has been able to make good use of a job training program by staffing its new facility almost completely with people from a personnel development project.

In general, there seemed to be a correlation between an understanding of the employment legislation, the availability of legal expertise, and the legislation index the company generated. Small companies without a legal staff to keep them informed of current legislation often do not have the information they need. This lack can result in costly mistakes. Many companies try to keep informed through information provided by trade associations. Others hire labor lawyers or personnel consultants as problems arise. A few just do not consider employment legislation or personnel matters much of a concern at all.

The companies' indexes clearly show that employment legislation is generally considered adverse by small business. But how does such legislation affect their employment practices? The companies mentioned both direct and indirect ramifications of the legislation. The EEOC, ADEA, and NLRA restrict what companies can ask on applications, what kind of policies they can set, and what they can say to their employees. Another specific effect mentioned was that the use of company-administered entrance tests has been reduced. One can argue that these items restrict the employee selection process and therefore increase the frequency of dismissing inadequate employees and training costs. Whether because of increased training costs resulting from higher turnover, increased legal cost because of dismissal-spawned lawsuits, or excessively picky safety requirements, the costs of complying with the EEOC, ADEA, or OSHA are real. More than 25 percent of the companies interviewed had been engaged in a legal dispute over at least one of these issues. The legal costs and the burden of proving one's innocence are the main complaints regarding them. On the other hand, recordkeeping requirements, as they become excessive, actually open up clerical-level positions but may restrict direct labor employment.

Direct out-of-pocket payments such as corporate taxes, payroll taxes, workers' compensation, and medical, life, and unemployment insurance are what the small business manager really feels. If the costs of complying with legislation could be reduced by screening potential suits more carefully, by enhancing the understanding of the law, by enforcing it more equitably, and, certainly, by reducing any of the above-mentioned expenses, the effect of the legislation would be less detrimental. Likewise, incentives could constitute a larger benefit to small businesses if they were in the form of direct dollar paybacks or grants, rather than in the form of tax credits. Most small businesses are concerned primarily with realizing a profit and maintaining a competitive edge. Although some small businesses recognize that some employment legislation is beneficial, most believe that minimum government involvement is best for achieving profits.

5 The Impact of Tax Reform on Small Business

THOMAS S. McCALEB

Reform of individual and business income taxation in the United States has been a major issue of debate in public policy circles for more than a decade. In 1977 the U.S. Treasury issued a report outlining the ingredients of two "pure" tax systems, the comprehensive income tax and the consumption tax, which have been proposed as alternatives to the existing "hybrid" system. In 1981, shortly after his inauguration, President Reagan proposed major reforms in the existing tax system, although he did not explicitly advocate adoption of either of the pure systems. Again in 1985, following his inauguration to a second term, the President introduced a comprehensive package of tax reform proposals. Although neither of the pure tax systems has been adopted, legislation to do so has in fact been introduced in the Congress. Furthermore, since 1981, Congress has enacted three major pieces of tax legislation that have substantially altered the federal tax system: the Economic Recovery Tax Act of 1981 (ERTA), the Tax Equity and Fiscal Responsibility Act of 1982 (TEFRA), and the Deficit Reduction Act of 1984 (DEFRA).

The changes that have been made in the existing tax system by this legislation have significantly altered the tax environment for all business firms, including small businesses. Adoption of any of the proposed tax reform programs would similarly affect the small business community. Nevertheless, the policy debates over tax reform have given little attention to the impact on small businesses of the proposed and actual changes in the tax system. This chapter attempts to redress that omission by considering the economic implications of tax reform for all small business. The focus of the discussion is on five major areas of concern: (1) the overall level of the tax burden on small business; (2) inventory accounting rules for tax purposes; (3) tax rules for depreciation accounting; (4) the impact of taxation on risky investments; and (5) the burden of the estate and gift tax.

In the first part of the chapter, the impact of the actual changes that have been made in the existing tax system since 1981 will be considered. The second section examines the implications for small business of the tax reforms proposed by President Reagan in 1985. The third section describes the treatment that would be accorded to small business should either of the pure tax systems be adopted.

Before proceeding, it is useful to have some sense of the average rate of tax imposed on small businesses before the recent changes in the tax system were enacted. Unfortunately, data available from U.S. individual income tax returns do not permit a clear separation between a given individual's business income and income from other sources. Nor do individual tax return data make it possible to disentangle income from several different businesses. Thus, studies of the burden of taxation on business have concentrated on the calculation of average effective tax rates on the income of corporations.

The evidence from these studies generally shows the tax burden rising with firm size up to about $1 million in assets. Above $10 million in assets, the rate structure becomes approximately proportional except for the largest size firms. In every case, the smallest firms (those under $1 million in assets) confront a lower effective rate than firms above $1 million in assets. Although estimates of the relative differential between small and large firms (that is, the degree of progressivity) vary from one study to another, the pattern is the same (studies reviewed in detail in McCaleb, 1984).

Several of these studies also calculated a measure of the absolute burden of taxation on all firms subject to corporate tax. The U.S. Treasury (1978), for example, estimated that in 1972 the average effective rate of corporate tax was 37.8 percent, while Randall Weiss (1979) calculated an average effective rate for 1979 of 30.9 percent. Thus, before the recent changes in federal tax policy, taxable corporations paid approximately one-third of their net income in corporate income tax. Furthermore, the corporate tax system was charaterized by a modest degree of progressivity, although it was not as progressive as the statutory rate structure would imply.

RECENT DEVELOPMENTS IN FEDERAL TAX POLICY

The most sweeping changes in federal tax policy since 1981, and those most favorable to all businesses, were enacted in ERTA (U.S. Small Business Administration 1982). The two subsequent revenue bills, TEFRA and DEFRA, represented primarily retrenchment in that they restricted or delayed implementation of many of the provisions of ERTA. Thus, whereas ERTA had a strong positive impact on the business sector, TEFRA and DEFRA have generally been negative.

This legislation affected small businesses in all five of the major areas of concern considered here.

- The average rate of tax on all firms and the average rate of tax on small corporations relative to large corporations has been reduced.
- Inventory accounting rules for small businesses have been simplified, thus alleviating the excess taxation of illusory inventory profits resulting from inflation.
- Depreciation accounting rules have been completely rewritten but in ways that are not necessarily favorable to small businesses relative to large corporations.
- Investment risk has been reduced by liberalization of the rules for incorporating without being exposed to the corporate tax penalty and by liberalization of the rules for obtaining tax benefits associated with business losses.
- The new legislation has eased the estate tax burden, a particularly important problem for closely held small businesses.

An analysis of these legislative changes in federal tax policy shows that the absolute level of taxation on all businesses, small and large, has been reduced. However, no definitive conclusions can be drawn about the burden of tax on small businesses relative to larger firms. Although some provisions have operated in favor of the small business sector, others are primarily beneficial to larger firms.

Reducing Tax Rates

ERTA reduced marginal individual income tax rates by 5 percent in 1981, followed by 10-percent reductions in 1982 and again in 1983. Thus, by 1983 the absolute burden of tax on the income of small business proprietorships and partnerships was 23 percent lower than in 1980. The burden of individual tax on dividend and interest income from both small and large corporations was also reduced. For individuals in the highest marginal tax brackets, the reduction in marginal rates was even greater as ERTA enacted an immediate reduction in the highest marginal tax rate from 70 to 50 percent.

The 1981 tax act also introduced more progressivity into the corporate income tax by reducing the marginal tax rates in the two lowest brackets. Before 1981 small corporations with taxable income of $0 to $25,000 paid a marginal rate of 17 percent and small corporations with taxable income of $25,000 to $50,000 paid a marginal rate of 20 percent. The corporate tax rates then rose to 30 percent for taxable income up to $75,000; to 40 percent for taxable income up to $100,000; and to 46 percent for taxable income above $100,000. ERTA reduced the marginal rate at the lowest bracket to 15 percent and the marginal rate in the next lowest bracket to 18 percent beginning in 1983, while leaving the rates applicable to higher income brackets unchanged.

The overall impact of the rate reductions has been to reduce the absolute burden of taxation on all businesses, large and small, thereby increasing the net return to saving and business investment and encouraging such investment. The increased progressivity in the corporate rate schedule has also reduced the relative tax burden on the smallest corporations, increasing their ability to compete with larger corporations for investment funds.

Accounting for Inventories

With inflation, tax accounting rules generate measures of business income that exceed the firm's real economic profits. This arises primarily from the use of historic cost as a basis for calculating depreciation and from the inclusion in profits of increases in the value of inventories held by the firm, even when these increases are no more than sufficient to compensate for the inflation. Because accounting profits exceed real economic profits and because the firm is taxed on its accounting profits, the measured average effective corporate tax rate is less than the true burden of tax imposed on the firm's real economic profits. Martin Feldstein and Lawrence Summers (1979), for example, estimated the extent to which corporate tax liability over the period 1954-77 arose from the inflation-induced reduction in the real value of depreciation deductions and inflated inventory profits. They found that, on average, these two factors alone accounted for 23.7 percent of annual corporate tax liability.

By simplifying inventory accounting requirements and by simplifying and accelerating depreciation schedules, ERTA has lessened the impact of inflation on small businesses. Firms are allowed to use either of two inventory accounting systems for tax purposes: first-in first-out (FIFO) or last-in first-out (LIFO). During periods of inflation, the use of FIFO results in the appearance of higher profits for tax purposes than does the use of LIFO, even though these taxable profits do not correspond to any additional real income to the firm. Nevertheless, the requirements for adopting LIFO have been sufficiently complex to confine its use to larger firms. By simplifying these requirements for smaller firms, ERTA has alleviated the excess taxation of illusory inventory profits owing to inflation. For those smaller firms that now elect to use the LIFO accounting method, the effective tax rate on their profits is more nearly equal to the rate of tax on the profits of larger firms.

Accounting for Depreciation

For all business investment that occurred after 1980, ERTA also provided a completely new method of asset depreciation, the Accelerated Cost Recovery System (ACRS). At the same time, a provision that allows full expensing (that is, a deduction from taxable income of the entire cost of the investment in the year of acquisition) of up to $5,000 of investment each year was adopted, and the eligibility life of the Investment Tax Credit (ITC) was shortened in order to conform to the new depreciation system. The limitation on the amount to be expensed was scheduled to rise to $7,500 in 1984 and to $10,000 in 1986. However, DEFRA deferred the scheduled increase to $7,500 until 1988 and deferred the increase to $10,000 until 1990. Furthermore, in 1982 TEFRA required that one-half of the ITC be deducted from the amount that could be depreciated under ACRS, thereby reducing the value of the ITC and partially offsetting the net benefit to be derived from the new system of depreciation.

Despite the reversal in TEFRA and DEFRA, the net effect of ACRS is to shorten the time periods over which business assets may be depreciated for tax purposes, to accelerate the depreciation schedules so that the largest deductions are taken in the early years, and to simplify the depreciation rules. Simplification of the rules will reduce the arbitrariness and uncertainties confronting businesses, large and small, when they decide to undertake investment. Reducing the depreciation periods and accelerating the depreciation schedules increases the value of the depreciation deductions, encouraging additional investment by all firms.

These new depreciation methods may be seen as more advantageous to large firms than to small and the adoption of ACRS as therefore increasing the *relative* burden of taxation on small businesses. In the first place, compared with larger firms, small businesses are, on average, less capital intensive and more labor intensive. Small businesses are often engaged in the provision of services or the sale of goods (see U.S. Small Business Administration 1984:7-19, for data). The service sector requires relatively little capital but much labor, whereas wholesale and retail trade tends to be labor intensive with investment concentrated in inventories rather than plant and equipment. Thus, relative to the volume of sales or the level of employment, the rate of investment in depreciable assets is lower, on average, for small firms than for large, and the tax benefits from the new depreciation deductions will accrue disproportionately to larger firms. For this reason, the simplification of inventory accounting requirements may provide greater stimulus to investment and capital formation for many small businesses than the more direct incentives embodied in the larger depreciation deductions.

Recent economic analysis suggests yet a second, and perhaps more important, way in which the adoption of ACRS has increased the relative tax burden on small business. The combination of the new accelerated depreciation and the investment tax credit has virtually eliminated the corporate tax on many new investments. In other words, it is often equivalent to full expensing on all new investment undertaken by taxable corporations after the date of enactment. Over time, as older capital is replaced by new capital which qualifies for depreciation under ACRS, the burden of the corporate income tax will become negligible.

The Council of Economic Advisers estimated that, under ERTA, the effective tax rate on new equipment and vehicles was on average *negative* (Council of Economic Advisers 1982: 122-25). In other words, the new depreciation system provides a net subsidy to investment in these short-lived assets. The estimated effective tax rate under the new system differs greatly across industries, depending on the distribution of new investment between equipment and structures in each industry. The industry rates calculated by the Council ranged from 37.1 percent for services and trade down to -11.3 percent for motor vehicles. Thus, the higher rates are imposed on the industrial grouping in which small firms are most frequently found.

Although the requirement in TEFRA that one-half of the ITC be deducted from the depreciation basis reduced the value of the depreciation benefits and therefore raised the effective tax rates above those calculated by the Council (Council of Economic Advisers 1983:91-95; U.S. Small Business Administration 1983: 419-36), the qualitative result remains the same: despite the uneven treatment of different assets and different industries, the overall impact of the new depreciation system is to reduce significantly, and in some cases even eliminate, the corporate tax on profits from new investments that qualify for ACRS treatment. The greatest number of small firms are unincorporated proprietorships or partnerships. Even the small corporations often avoid the corporate tax by electing to be taxed as partnerships under the provisions of Subchapter S of the Internal Revenue Code. Thus, the corporate tax is primarily a tax on size, and any policy action that reduces the corporate tax also reduces the cost of capital to the larger incorporated firms relative to small corporations and unincorporated firms.

Reducing Investment Risk

A primary advantage of doing business as a corporation is the limitation placed on an investor's liability for the firm's losses. All else being equal, then, the risk associated with equity investment in a firm will be lower if the firm is incorporated. There is a cost to incorporation, however, in the form of the additional corporate tax liability on the firm's profits. The recent changes in tax policy have attempted to reduce this tax cost to incorportion in two ways. First, as noted in the previous section, even after TEFRA, the overall thrust of recent tax policy changes has been to reduce significantly the burden of corporate taxation on all firms on which the tax is imposed. Second, both ERTA and TEFRA include provisions that have liberalized the restrictions on the maximum number of shareholders (up from fifteen to thirty-five) and on the kinds of income that a small corporation may have and still be exempt from corporate tax under Subchapter S. Although the new accelerated depreciation provisions favor larger firms, the changes in the Subchapter S provisions are of particular benefit to smaller businesses. The net effect is to reduce, perhaps substantially, the risk associated with equity investments in many small businesses and to make the risk of investment in small businesses more nearly equal to the risk of investment in large corporations.

Another approach to reducing investment risk is to make the tax treatment of business losses symmetric with the treatment of profits. Under the existing tax system, a firm is taxed on any net profit that it earns, but its ability to obtain credit for net losses is limited. A firm incurring a loss in a given year receives no payment from the Treasury. Instead, net operation losses must be offset against income derived form other business or nonbusiness sources. In the absence of other income, the loss may be credited against tax liability incurred in prior years (loss carryback) or, if this is insufficient to absorb the full loss, it may be carried forward and offset against tax liability in future years. Because of discounting, the carryforward provision reduces the value to the firm of each dollar of loss allowance below one dollar. Before 1981 the ability to carry losses back was limited to three prior years and the carryforward was limited to seven years.

Restrictions on loss offsets are less likely to be binding for larger firms than for smaller businesses. Larger firms are usually diversified, with other lines of business producing income against which the losses from any one line can be offset. In contrast, many small firms are single-line businesses. Larger firms are also more often well established with sufficient positive net income in prior years to absorb the losses incurred in any one tax year, whereas smaller firms, especially new ventures, often have insufficient prior-year net income to fully utilize the loss carryback provision. Smaller firms are therefore more likely to have to resort to the less valuable carryforward allowance, and even this may not permit the smaller firm to offset all of its net operating losses. A firm that lacks the ability to carry back all of its current net losses can obtain the full tax value of those losses only through merger with or acquisition by a profitable firm. These factors combine to increase the risk of investment in small business relative to investment in larger firms and to create incentives favoring the disappearance of small businesses.

ERTA attempted to deal with these problems in two ways. Under ERTA, the carryforward provision has been extended to fifteen years. This change can be of significant benefit to smaller firms, especially new ventures that, if successful, will have future profits against which to offset losses in the early years. Nevertheless, it remains true that one dollar of loss carryforward is worth less than one dollar to a firm.

In order to overcome this limitation and to give all firms the full value of tax credits for investment in new plant and equipment, ERTA established a tax device called "safe harbor leasing." Through the mechanism of a constructive lease, the tax benefits associated with acquisition of equipment (accelerated depreciation and investment tax credits) could be "passed through" from the loss company to a profitable company in whose hands they would have full value. The leasing provisions also permitted companies with positive taxable income to effectively purchase the net operating losses (negative taxable income) of other companies. By reducing the risk of investment in small businesses relative to large, the safe harbor leasing provisions preserved the incentives of small businesses to invest and to maintain their status as independent entities.

One year after enactment, however, the safe harbor leasing provisions were repealed by TEFRA and replaced by a liberalized version of the traditional "finance leasing," which is, nonetheless, much more restrictive than the safe harbor leasing. The liberalized finance leasing rules were scheduled to take effect in 1984, but their implementation has been delayed by DEFRA until 1988. Thus, the current status is essentially that which prevailed prior to 1981, with the exception of a longer carryover period. Unchanged are the differentially greater risk associated with investment in small businesses relative to large firms; the incentives toward consolidation of small, currently unprofitable firms with larger enterprises; and the disincentives for investment by small firms in plant and equipment.

Easing the Estate Tax Burden

The unified gift and estate tax poses two problems of particular significance to the owner of a small business or the holder of an equity interest in a closely held small business. First, the assets of a small business may have to be liquidated in order to acquire cash to satisfy the tax liability. Second, the absence of a ready market in the assets of closely held small businesses necessitates a subjective judgment by the authorities as to the taxable value of those assets. Because of these problems, the estate tax creates incentives for the sale to or merger with a larger firm of any small businesses whose assets are subject to estate tax liability.

Before 1981 taxpayers were allowed a unified credit against gross estate and gift taxes of $47,000 which, in effect, exempted from taxation all transfers by estate or cumulated lifetime gifts up to $175,625. ERTA increased the unified credit to $192,800, equivalent to an exemption of $600,000, by 1987. This provision was expected to exempt about 99.7 percent of all estates from federal gift and estate taxation. A second provision in ERTA reduces the maximum marginal tax rate applicable to estates from 70 to 50 percent by 1987. However, DEFRA has frozen this phased reduction in marginal tax rates at the 1984 level of 55 percent until 1987 when a one-time full reduction to 50 percent was expected to occur.

For an estate that has a small business as a major asset, the increased exemption and the rate reduction, if and when they take effect, will substantially decrease potential estate tax liability. This, in turn, should reduce the pressure on small business owners and their heirs to sell to or consolidate with larger firms in order to obtain liquid assets to satisfy gift and estate tax liability. Because the estate tax differentially affects small businesses, these changes reduce the relative burden of tax on smaller firms.

THE REAGAN ADMINISTRATION'S TAX REFORM PROPOSALS

Immediately following his reelection, President Reagan proposed an extensive set of tax reforms that were subsequently modified in May 1985. Although these reforms are unlikely to be adopted exactly as proposed, they will establish the agenda for discussion of tax reform for several years. The reform proposals do not significantly alter the effects of the tax system on investment risk, nor do they substantially change the tax treatment of estates. On the other hand, the reforms do provide for further reductions in individual and corporate statutory tax rates, and they do alter the tax rules for inventory and depreciation accounting in ways that have important implications for small businesses.

Reducing Tax Rates

The current individual income tax system has fourteen marginal tax rates. Under the President's proposal, these would be replaced by three rates—15, 25, and 35 percent. Thus, the maximum marginal tax rate on the income of small business proprietorships and partnerships would be reduced from 50 percent to 35 percent, and for many small business owners, the average rate of tax on their business income would also be reduced. The reductions in statutory tax rates would not be fully reflected in effective rates of tax, however, because the proposal would also limit deductions for entertainment and business meal expenses and for travel expenses.

The maximum corporate tax rate would be reduced from 46 to 33 percent, but this maximum would be applied to corporate income in excess of $75,000. The current system imposes the maximum rate only on corporate income in excess of $100,000. For income between $50,000 and $75,000, the marginal corporate tax rate would be reduced from 30 to 25 percent. At the same time, a new deduction from corporate income equal to 10 percent of dividends paid would by permitted. This would reduce the effective rate of tax on the income of those corporations that distribute earnings, and would also reduce the double taxation of dividend income that characterizes the current system.

On balance, these proposals would further reduce the absolute burden of taxation on all businesses. Their effect on the relative burden of taxation on smaller firms, however, would be quite small.

Accounting for Inventories

If the President's proposals were adopted, taxpayers would be permitted the option of using a new Indexed FIFO method of inventory accounting in addition to the current FIFO and LIFO methods. Under the Indexed FIFO method, the cost of inventories would be adjusted for inflation based on a federal government price index. Indexing would reduce or eliminate the excess taxation of illusory inventory profits resulting from inflation.

This proposal is particularly valuable to small firms that have found even the recently simplified LIFO rules too complex for their purposes. These smaller firms will now be able to continue using FIFO while nevertheless avoiding the payment of tax on the illusory profits arising from inflation. Like the earlier adoption of the simplified LIFO accounting rules, this proposal would promote more equal tax treatment of small and large firms.

Accounting for Depreciation

The Reagan administration's proposals include yet another modification of the ACRS depreciation system adopted in ERTA. The administration would establish a Capital Cost Recovery System (CCRS) that would lengthen, relative to ACRS, the time periods over which business assets may be depreciated for tax purposes; index the depreciation deductions to reduce the adverse effects of inflation; eliminate the investment tax credit; and permanently freeze the first-year expensing allowance at $5,000. On balance, these reforms would increase the cost of new investment by all firms, except perhaps during periods of relatively high inflation.

The increased cost of investment would discourage new investment and capital formation and would also increase the effective rate of tax on the income of all businesses, small and large. However, just as the adoption of ACRS was more advantageous to capital-intensive larger firms than to labor-intensive smaller firms, so the negative effects of the Reagan administration's reforms would have less impact on smaller firms as a group than on large enterprises.

COMPREHENSIVE TAX REFORM AND SMALL BUSINESS

In recent years, many economists and policymakers have advocated an even more radical restructuring of the tax system than has occurred. Several proposals have been put forward to replace completely the existing tax system with either a pure income tax or a pure consumption tax. Even if neither of these pure systems is ever adopted, they still are frequently used as benchmarks against which proposed reforms in the existing income tax are judged. For this reason alone, an understanding of the treatment of small business under each of these pure systems provides an important and useful perspective on the alterations that have or might be made in the current tax treatment of business income.

Comprehensive Income Tax (CIT)

A comprehensive income tax would be imposed on all income with virtually no exemptions, deductions, or credits other than deductions for legitimate costs of doing business. Because all income sources would be subject to tax, the statutory marginal tax rates would be lower than the current schedule of rates. In order to raise the same revenue, however, average effective tax rates would have to be essentially unchanged. Because the major business deductions would remain in place while most of the personal income deductions would be eliminated, the CIT would shift the tax burden from business to personal income.

Under a CIT, net income from the sale of inventories would be included in current taxable income. The cost of inventories would be calculated using an indexed FIFO system like the one proposed by the Reagan administration. Depreciation allowances would be determined by true economic depreciation—that is, the actual rate at which the market value of depreciable assets declines. For almost all types of depreciable business assets, economic depreciation would be less generous than either ACRS or the Reagan administration's proposed CCRS. Under the CIT, both the investment tax credit and first-year expensing would be eliminated. On the other hand, depreciation would be indexed for inflation.

The CIT would allow unlimited carryforward with interest of operating losses incurred by business. Thus, the tax system would treat losses exactly like business profits. This change would reduce the risk presently associated with business investments, especially investment in smaller enterprises that are more likely to utilize the loss carryforward provisions. On the other hand, the CIT would tax all capital gains at the same rate as other business income while indexing gains for inflation. Full taxation of capital gains reduces the return to investment in new ventures and thus could have a significant negative impact on this segment of the small business community. The adverse impact could be mitigated by the indexing provisions during periods of relatively high inflation.

The Reagan administration's proposals represent in effect a movement toward a CIT. Like those proposals, then, the CIT might be more favorable to small business than to larger firms.

Consumption Tax (CT)

The alternative pure tax system would impose tax only on that part of income that was consumed, exempting from taxation all income used for saving and investment. Because the tax base would be smaller under the CT than under either the CIT or the existing hybrid system, statutory marginal tax rates would be higher if the same revenue were to be raised. Again, however, average effective tax rates would be the same. Unlike the CIT, the CT would virtually eliminate any tax on business income per se. Instead, the income would be taxed only when it was distributed to individual business owners and used by them for consumption.

The cost of inventories would be deducted in full at the time of acquisition, whereas revenues from the sale of inventories would be included in taxable income at the time of sale. Investments in business equipment and structures would also be deductible in full, equivalent to full first-year expensing for all depreciable business assets, but there would be no investment tax credit. Proceeds from the sale of business assets would be taxed unless reinvested. Carryforward of net operating losses with interest would be allowed, and capital gains would be treated exactly like other forms of income.

The net effect of the CT on business is unclear because the income from business activity would for the most part be taxed as individual income. Because the CT allows full expensing of investment, however, it appears to be less advantageous to small business than to larger firms, and would therefore divert new investment away from the small business sector. In this regard, the effects of a CT are similar to the effects of the actual changes that have been made in the tax system since 1981, but are unlike either the CIT or the Reagan administration's reform proposals.

CONCLUSIONS

Major changes have been made in the tax treatment of business since 1981. As has been shown, these changes taken together have lowered the absolute burden of individual and corporate taxation on the net income of firms, large and small. No definitive statements can be made, however, concerning the impact of these changes on the tax burden on small businesses relative to larger enterprises. The new depreciation methods, although equally available to both small and large businesses, are on balance more favorable to the large corporations. On the other hand, measures such as the liberalization of the requirements for using LIFO inventory accounting, extending the loss carryforward period, and reducing the burden of estate taxation are of greater benefit to the smaller firms. By raising the net after-tax return to saving and business investment, the recent tax changes will encourage capital formation and economic growth, but it is unlikely that all firms will participate equally in the growth process.

Small business representatives often state that the current tax system contains numerous provisions that are detrimental to the continued good health of the small business sector of the U.S. economy. At the closing session of the 1980 White House Conference on Small Business, the delegates voted on sixty recommendations that had emerged from a series of regional caucuses and workshops held prior to and during the conference (White House Commission on Small Business 1980). Of these sixty recommendations no less than eleven concerned some aspect of taxation. Each delegate then voted for the fifteen recommendations that were deemed to be the most important. In the final ranking, the tax system was the subject of fully half of the first ten, including numbers two and three of the top five. To those attending the conference sessions, the most important way to promote capital formation for small business was through tax relief measures.

The recent changes in federal tax policy have in fact been partly responsive to these recommendations. For example, the top recommendation of the conference was for a more graduated rate schedule for corporate and individual income taxes, and indeed ERTA did increase the progressivity at the very bottom of the corporate tax rate schedule. The conference also recommended adoption of a new and simplified accelerated capital cost recovery system, including a limited expensing provision, and Congress responded by passing ERTA with the Accelerated Cost Recovery System, probably the most significant recent change in business tax policy, and with immediate expensing of small investments. Finally, the conference requested revision of estate tax laws to ease the tax burden on family-owned businesses and to encourage the continuity of family ownership, and Congress responded with higher exemptions and lower marginal tax rates on estates.

As has been shown, however, these changes in tax policy do not necessarily have an unambiguously positive effect on small business. Certainly, to the extent that tax rates have been reduced for all businesses, large and small, the rate of return on business investment has been increased. On the other hand, because so many of the tax policy changes, even those that follow the recommendations of the White House Conference, are more favorable to large firms than to small, not all smaller firms have benefited. Indeed, if investment is reallocated within the business sector from some smaller firms to larger enterprises, the recent tax policy changes will have had a negative impact on these smaller firms in spite of the reduction in tax rates and in their absolute tax burden.

On the other hand, the Reagan administration's tax reform proposals would probably on balance improve the tax climate in which small business operates. The benefits from lower tax rates and more favorable inventory accounting rules should outweigh the additional costs imposed by the less favorable depreciation accounting rules. The net effect would be a lower absolute rate of tax on small business income, and perhaps a lower rate of tax relative to larger firms as well. Although the Reagan administration's proposals represent a step toward a CIT, the actual changes in the tax system that were enacted by ERTA, even with the modifications adopted by TEFRA and DEFRA, represent a step toward a CT. Thus, should comprehensive tax reform ever be adopted, the CIT would appear to be more favorable to small business, at least relative to larger enterprises, than would a CT.

Whether the tax system should include provisions designed to promote investment and capital formation in the small business sector remains an open question in the realm of tax policy. It is clear, however, that not all the recent changes in tax policy have been consistent with such an objective. Instead, they have had an arbitrary and haphazard impact on small businesses, both relative to larger firms and among themselves. The evidence suggests that a full understanding of the economic impacts on small business has not characterized the recent changes in business tax policy. Nor has the discussion of further changes in the tax system given any substantial consideration to the effects of the proposed reforms on small business.

REFERENCES

Council of Economic Advisers. 1982. *Economic report of the President.* Washington, D.C.: U.S. Government Printing Office.

_____. 1983. *Economic report of the President.* Washington D.C.: U.S. Government Printing Office.

Feldstein, Martin, and Lawrence Summers. 1979. Inflation and the taxation of capital income in the corporate sector. *National Tax Journal* 32 (December): 445-470.

McCaleb, Thomas S. 1984. Tax policy and small business financing. In *Small business finance, part 1: Problems in financing small businesses.* ed. Paul M. Horvitz and R. Richardson Pettit. Greenwich, Conn.: JAI Press.

U.S. Congress, Congressional Budget Office. 1983. *Revising the individual income tax.* Washington, D.C.: U.S. Government Printing Office.

_____. 1985. *Revising the corporate income tax.* Washington, D.C.: U.S. Government Printing Office.

U.S. Small Business Administration. 1982. *The state of small business: A report of the President.* Washington, D.C.: U.S. Government Printing Office.

_____. 1983. *The state of small business: A report of the President.* Washington, D.C.: U.S. Government Printing Office.

_____. 1984. *The state of small business: A report of the President.* Washington, D.C.: U.S. Government Printing Office.

U.S. Treasury. 1977. *Blueprints for basic tax reform.* Washington, D.C.: U.S. Government Printing Office.

U.S. Treasury, Office of Tax Analysis. 1978. *Effective income tax rates paid by United States corporations in 1972.* Washington, D.C.: U.S. Government Printing Office.

Weiss, Randall D. 1979. Effective corporation income tax rates. *National Tax Journal* 32:380-89.

White House Commission on Small Business. 1980. *America's small business economy: Agenda for action.* Washington, D.C.: U.S. Government Printing Office.

6 Stages of Development and Stages of the Exporting Process in a Small Business Context

GEORGE S. VOZIKIS and TIMOTHY S. MESCON

Why have so few small businesses responded to years of government efforts to get them into international trade? The easy rationale is "they are too dumb" (Jacobs 1984:35). Recently, a federal advisory group on small and minority businesses, the Industry Sector Advisory Committee on Small and Minority Business for Trade Policy Matters, concluded that small business owners avoid exporting because they do not wish to expose their firms to the various risks and unknowns involved. According to the committee report, existing government programs directed at small business export assistance are grossly inadequate. The report states: "At the capitalist ground level of business risk-taking, the government has relentlessly opened up the maximum possible distance between itself and the small business" (Jacobs 1984:35). The committee recommends the following ameliorative actions:

1. Subsidization of start-up costs.
2. Outlays for marketing, product adaptation, and employee training.
3. Financing to overseas buyers with competitive rates.

Indeed, the committee report concludes with an emphatic assertion that the United States was more export oriented in 1776 than it is today!

A considerable number of research studies have investigated the obstacles or barriers to exporting. The apparent rationale is that the government could stimulate exporting by removing those obstacles that are usually institutional or infrastructural.

Many analysts regard a firm's size as critical for its propensity to export, yet empirical findings on this issue have been mixed (Bilkey

1978:36). The contradictory findings among analysts are attributed to the fact that exporting is essentially a sequential learning process, the coefficients of which tend to differ from one stage of the export process to another and from one stage of overall development to another.

This chapter investigates the relationships among internal, functional problems in the areas of general management, marketing, operations, and finance experienced by small businesses that have experimented with exporting. The purpose is to determine if a common set of functional problems occurs among small businesses at similar stages in their overall development or similar stages of the export development process. The literature published to this date is replete with inconsistent statements as to the kinds of problems a small firm is most likely to experience at each specific stage. In order to achieve this objective, the following relevant research questions will be answered:

1. What are the specific *functional problems* that small exporters experience?
2. How do these problems vary at each *stage of the development process*?
3. How do these problems vary at each *stage of the exporting process*?
4. Can a problem or set of functional problems be identified which is *common* to small exporters regardless of the export stage, and the stage of development?

SMALL BUSINESS PROBLEMS

Most field research and surveys have focused on the characteristics of the entrepreneur and the predictors of success or failure associated mainly with the starting venture stage.

Case studies and, to a lesser degree, field surveys form the basis of research on small business. The majority of the case studies emphasize isolated elements of the strategic planning process without reference to the total concept of strategic management. The case studies also seem to lack a cross-reference framework of different industries and different stages in the firm's development.

A. C. Cooper (1978) used the following typology to classify the small business literature:

1. *Discursive writings*—based on wisdom, observation, and general experience, usually prescriptive in character.
2. *Case studies*—based on intensive study of selected cases; data can be from secondary sources or field studies.
3. *Field surveys*—data gathered from many respondents through survey techniques.
4. *Field research*—based on comparative case studies, longitudinal studies, and field experiments.

In summary, the bulk of the literature is discursive and prescriptive, with emphasis on operating problems without support from research studies, and without reference to internal weaknesses in the sense of strategic disadvantage.

EXPORTING PROBLEMS

The manifold administrative problems associated with foreign trade have often been obscured by the broader problems of international relations. Less attention has been paid to the problems of the business managers who must try to carry on their business whether or not political, financial, or economic conditions are entirely to their liking. Although knowledge of these conditions and of the progress of political and trade development is essential for the greatest success, the immediate problems of a business enterprise are those involved in attaining the purposes of every business enterprise—that is, making a profit.

STAGES OF DEVELOPMENT

Just as living organisms, business organizations are subject to a life cycle: they experience a period of youth, a period of growth, a period of maturity, and a period of decline. The life cycle of a company is often depicted as the familiar "S" curve. Cooper (1978) presented a simple but sensible typology of the stages of development of the small firm:

- *The start-up stage,* including the strategic decisions to found a firm and position it within a particular industry with a particular competitive strategy.
- *The early growth stage,* when the initial product–market strategy is being tested and when the president maintains direct contact with all major activities (many firms stabilize at this stage).
- *The later growth stage,* often characterized by multiple sites for retail and service businesses and by some diversification for manufacturing firms; organizationally, the firm usually has one or more levels of middle management and some delegation of decision making.

In a critique of Cooper's paper, J. C. Susbauer (1978) classified the small business in a "success" continuum:

1. The survival firm
2. The attractive growth potential firm
3. The underachieving firm
4. The high success growth firm

The characteristics of each stage, ranked by frequency of citation by the small business theorists, are as follows.

Stage I

General Management

1. One-man show
2. Nonroutine, informal decisions
3. Good communication

Operations

1. Reliance on unique personal skills, unique product, or unique market
2. Limited resources
3. No cushion to absorb bad luck
4. Emphasis on historical cost

Marketing

1. Risk limited to a few products, markets, and people
2. No reputation outside the immediate vicinity
3. Stable market environment

Stage II

General Management

1. Delegation of operating decisions to "lieutenants" or "assistants to"
2. Formal consideration of growth
3. Direct control and direction

Operations

1. Improvement of skill, method, or market niche
2. Production problems
3. Technical specialization

Finance

1. Attention to industry standards

Marketing

1. Attention to competition
2. Attention to market feedback

Stage III

General Management

1. More management levels and more delegation
2. Utilization of staff analysts
3. Increased emphasis on management, skills, and techniques
4. Formal written policies and procedures
5. More planning time

Operations

1. Economies of scale

Finance

1. Lower rate of return
2. Emphasis on future costs
3. Emphasis on short-run performance measures

Marketing

1. Heavy investment in product and market development
2. Discontinuance of unprofitable products
3. Increased dependence on marketing distribution
4. Greater ability to fight competition

THE STAGES OF THE EXPORTING PROCESS

A basic theoretical question is whether a firm's export behavior should be considered a multi-activity development process keyed to the firm's position and perspective in this learning process, or whether it should be considered in terms of a single activity model at any given point in time. Most empirical studies have explored this question by analyzing export data without consideration for possible differences in the firm's export stages.

The research findings lead to two major conclusions regarding the export behavior of firms. First, exporting is essentially a developmental process which may be conceptualized either as a learning sequence involving feedback loops or as export stages. Second, equation coefficients tend to differ from one stage of the export process to another, suggesting that export profiles *can* be formulated for each stage of exporting development, with potentially great usefulness, both theoretical and practical. For example, government programs designed to encourage exporting could be tailored to the export development stage of the firms to be stimulated (e.g., experienced exporters versus nonexporters). Export management should also be keyed to the firm's position in the export development process which, from the firm's perspective, is a learning process. For example, a firm that has never exported should first concentrate on gaining basic export experience.

The following illustrative model involving export stages is derived from E. U. Rogers' (1962:81-86) stages of the adoption process.

1. The firm is unwilling to export. It would not fill an unsolicited export order because it is apathetic, it dislikes foreign activities, it is busy doing other things, and so on.
2. The firm fills unsolicited export orders but does not explore the feasibility of exporting.
3. The firm explores the feasibility of exporting. (This stage may be omitted by the receipt of unsolicited export orders.)
4. The firm exports experimentally to one or a few markets.
5. The firm is an experienced exporter to those markets.
6. The firm explores possibilities of exporting to additional markets. And so on.

The literature on the stages of the exporting process supports the following classification for the purposes of this study:

Stage I

1. The firm does *not* explore the feasibility of regular exporting.
2. The firm fills unsolicited export orders (if any).

Stage II

1. The firm explores the feasibility of regular exporting.
2. The firm fills exports experimentally to one or few markets.

Stage III

1. The firm is an experienced exporter to some markets.
2. The firm explores the possibility of exporting to additional markets.

RESEARCH DESIGN

The population of exporting small businesses used in this study was drawn from the files of the University of Georgia's Small Business

Development Center (SBDC). These Georgia firms received in-depth consulting services from the SBDC between May 1977 and October 1979. New ventures and/or feasibility studies were excluded because of the uncertainty of the enterprises' future.

The criteria for selecting exporting small firms for this study were: (1) the conclusiveness of the consultants' final report, and (2) the assignment to the case of two or more staff consultants from different functional fields to avoid "tunnel vision" and individual reporting bias owing to one-sided training and/or background. Thirty-two firms met both criteria. Their categorization in the three stages of overall development resulted in the frequency distribution shown in Table 6.1.

This research also focused on the stages of development of the exporting process. Export Stage I firms comprised the majority of the sample (see Table 6.2).

A study encompassing three phases was designed and implemented. The first phase consisted of literature research to identify and define the small exporters' problems and to construct a framework for analysis of empirical data. The second phase consisted of the identification by a panel of three independent judges of the overall weaknesses as well as exporting management and marketing weaknesses of small exporters. Inter- and intra-rater reliability assured the validity of the research design. The range of the inter- and intra-rater reliability scores was 12.34 and 7.5 percentage points and the mean was 83.95 percent and 84.18 percent, respectively.

The third phase consisted of hypotheses testing and statistical analysis through chi-square tests, exact partitioning of the overall contingency tables of the chi-square tests, and the Cramer's statistic (C.s.) to identify *whether* there are significant differences in overall exporting functional problems among the stages of overall and exporting development, *where*

Table 6.1
Frequencies of Surveyed Firms by Stage of Development

Stage	Frequency	Percent
I	5	15.6
II	9	28.1
III	18	56.3
	32	100.0

Table 6.2
Frequencies of Surveyed Firms by Stages of Export Development

Stage	Frequency	Percent
I	17	53.1
II	11	34.4
III	4	12.5
	32	100.0

these differences are, and *how strong* these differences are. The results are as follows:

Hypothesis 1. There will be significant differences in the *overall functional problems* which small exporters experience depending on their *stage of overall development*. From Table 6.3 the hypothesis is *accepted* for Marketing (Overall Stages I and III); Operations (Overall Stages I and III); and Finance (Overall Stages I and III). The hypothesis is *rejected* for Management. The smaller the organization, the more complex the functional problems of marketing, operations, and finance. No statistically significant differences are noted in management problems as related to organizational size.

Hypothesis 2. There will be significant differences in the *exporting functional problems* which small exporters experience depending on their *stage of overall development*. From Table 6.4, the hypothesis is *accepted* for Export Marketing (Overall Stages I and III); Export Operations (Overall Stage I); Export Finance (Overall Stages I and III). The hypothsis is *rejected* for Export Management. Once again, the primary functional problem areas are noted in export marketing, operations, and finance. *No* statistically significant differences are noted in export management. The results indicate that the smaller the firm, the greater the exporting obstacles.

Hypothesis 3. There will be significant differences in the *overall functional problems* which small exporters experience depending on their *stage of exporting development*. From Table 6.5, the hypothesis is *accepted* for Marketing (Exporting Stages I, II, and III); Operations (Exporting Stages I and II); and Finance (Exporting Stages I, II, and III). The hypothesis is *rejected* for Management. Management problems remain consistent regardless of the size of the small business exporter. As the small business exporter grows, however, there are significant differences in the types of problems encountered in the marketing, operations, and finance areas.

Table 6.3
Results of Chi-square Analyses for Differences of Overall Functional Problems of Small Exporters in Stages I, II, and III of Overall Development

Problem Area	% Problems Stage I	% Problems Stage II	% Problems Stage III	Overall Development Stages	x^2	df	p	C.s.
Overall Management	65.00	38.89	45.83	IxIIxIII	3.59	2	ns	.168
Overall Marketing	80.00	30.56	18.06	IxIIxIII	27.97	2	<.001	.467
				Ix(II+III)	25.80	1	<.001	.449
				IIx(I+III)	0.23	1	ns	.001
				IIIx(I+II)	13.04	1	<.001	.319
Overall Operations	60.00	19.44	8.33	IxIIxIII	26.58	2	<.001	.456
				Ix(II+III)	24.76	1	<.001	.440
				IIx(I+III)	0.01	1	ns	.001
				IIIx(I+II)	13.26	1	<.001	.322
Overall Finance	60.00	33.33	9.72	IxIIxIII	23.82	2	<.001	.431
				Ix(II+III)	16.76	1	<.001	.362
				IIx(I+III)	2.26	1	ns	.133
				IIIx(I+II)	18.96	1	<.001	.385

Table 6.4
Results of Chi-square Analyses for Differences of Exporting Functional Problems of Small Exporting Firms in Stages I, II, and III of Overall Development

Problem Area	% Problems Stage I	% Problems Stage II	% Problems Stage III	Overall Development Stages	x^2	df	p	C.s.
Export Management	75.00	66.67	68.06	IxIIxIII	0.45	2	ns	.059
Export Marketing	71.77	58.02	50.62	IxIIxIII	6.21	2	<.020	.147
				Ix(II+III)	4.97	1	<.050	.131
				IIx(I+III)	0.21	1	ns	.027
				IIIx(I+II)	4.18	1	<.050	.120
Export Operations	53.33	18.52	16.67	IxIIxIII	9.35	2	<.010	.312
				Ix(II+III)	9.30	1	<.010	.315
				IIx(I+III)	0.42	1	ns	.066
				IIIx(I+II)	2.77	1	ns	.170
Export Finance	73.33	48.15	29.63	IxIIxIII	9.87	2	<.010	.321
				Ix(II+III)	7.07	1	<.010	.271
				IIx(I+III)	0.45	1	ns	.068
				IIIx(I+II)	7.12	1	<.010	.272

Table 6.5
Results of Chi-square Analyses for Differences of Overall Functional Problems of Small Exporting Firms in Stages I, II, and III of Exporting Development

Problem Area	% Problems Stage I	% Problems Stage II	% Problems Stage III	Overall Development Stages	x^2	df	p	c.s.
Overall Management	47.06	52.27	31.25	IxIIxIII	2.08	2	ns	.128
Overall Marketing	51.47	9.09	6.25	IxIIxIII	27.65	2	<.001	.465
				Ix(II+III)	27.35	1	<.001	.462
				IIx(I+III)	15.10	1	<.001	.343
				IIIx(I+II)	5.11	1	<.050	.199
Overall Operations	29.41	9.09	6.25	IxIIxIII	9.07	2	<.010	.266
				Ix(II+III)	8.96	1	<.010	.265
				IIx(I+III)	4.66	1	<.050	.191
				IIIx(I+II)	2.01	1	ns	.125
Overall Finance	39.71	9.09	0.00	IxIIxIII	19.49	2	<.001	.390
				Ix(II+III)	18.99	1	<.001	.385
				IIx(I+III)	8.36	1	<.010	.256
				IIIx(I+II)	5.86	1	<.010	.214

Hypotheses 4. There will be significant differences of *exporting functional problems* which small exporters experience depending on their *stage of exporting development.* From Table 6.6, the hypothesis is *accepted* for Export Marketing (Exporting Stages I and III). The hyphthesis is *rejected* for Export Management, Export Operations, and Export Finance. Export marketing is the most important aspect of exporting regardless of the size of the small business exporter. Consistent with the conclusions derived from the first three hypotheses, marketing in exporting is a functional area deserving special attention. On the other hand, export management problems are experienced in all three stages, without any specific stage claiming the lion's share of managerial problems.

The results of this study confirm that different sets of overall and exporting problems emerge at different stages of overall and exporting development. This held true particularly for Marketing and Export Marketing functional problems and especially for Stages I and II of both overall and export development. Functional problems relating to operations and finance on both the overall and exporting level exhibited the same tendency, though to a lesser degree. Management and export management problems do not seem to differentiate among different stages of overall and export development.

The partitioning of the overall contingency table also revealed that Stage I seemed to account for most of the differences, with especially low probabilities and strong values of the Cramer's statistic. It may therefore be concluded that overall and exporting operations problems are closely associated with any kind of "beginning," whether it is the beginning of a venture or the beginning of development exporting transactions.

IMPLICATION OF THE STUDY

Managerial Implications. Through this study, it is possible to develop a no-nonsense, practical checklist that can be put to immediate use by the businessperson who wants to identify and pick the stage of the business life cycle and the stage of the exporting process that most closely describes his or her present situation. This practical checklist will include the characteristics of each stage of development, the characteristics of each exporting stage, the most likely problems that are usually encountered, a "what to do" section, and finally, a highlight of "keys to survival" tips.

Policy Implications for Congress. Congress should consider legislation that would design and implement specific statutory guidelines to ensure the "quality" rather than the quantity of exporting–small business, with more permanent and positive results for the U.S. balance of trade. By giving serious consideration to the need for different types of instrumental legislation at different stages of development, Congress can play a vital

Table 6.6
Results of Chi-Square Analyses for Differences of Exporting Functional Problems of Small Exporting Firms in Stages, I, II, and III of Exporting Development

Problem Area	% Problems Stage I	% Problems Stage II	% Problems Stage III	Overall Development Stages	x^2	df	p	c.s.
Export Management	69.12	70.45	62.5	IxIIxIII	0.36	2	ns	.053
Export Marketing	61.44	55.56	33.33	IxIIxIII	9.34	2	<.010	.180
				Ix(II+III)	4.03	1	<.050	.014
				IIx(I+III)	0.01	1	ns	.004
				IIIx(I+II)	8.47	1	<.010	.171
Export Operations	27.45	21.21	8.33	IxIIxIII	2.09	2	ns	.148
Export Finance	50.98	36.36	16.67	IxIIxIII	5.29	2	ns	.235

role in ensuring a bright future for America's small businesses. To this end, on March 1, 1984, the Senate passed the "Export Administration Act Amendments of 1984" (S. 979) which included a special section on small business export assistance.

Policy Implications for the SBA. Comprehensive and specialized export assistance as well as management and financial development for specific stages of their export potential development should be provided. This specialized aid should go beyond the typical "I need money" request of the small businessperson through custom-made programs and allocation of financial and consulting resources appropriate to the firm's stage in the life cycle and export process.

REFERENCES

Alexandrides, C. G. 1971. How the major obstacles to expansion can be overcome. *Atlanta Economic Review* (May): 12-15.

Alves, R., Jr. 1978. The prediction of small business failure utilizing financial and nonfinancial data. Ph. D. dissertation. University of Massachusetts.

Anderson, D. C. 1970. Factors contributing to the success of small service-type business. D.B.A. dissertation. Georgia State University.

Bilkey, W. J. 1978. An attempted integration of the literature on the export behavior of firms. *Journal of International Business Studies* 9(1): 33-46.

Bilkey, W. J., and G. Tesar. 1975. The export behavior of smaller sized Wisconsin manufacturing firms. Paper presented at the European Meeting of the Academy of International Business, Fountainebleau, France. July.

Cooper, A.C. 1978. Strategic management: New ventures and small business. (Mimeographed.)

De La Torre, J., Jr.1972. Marketing factors in manufactured exports from developing countries. In *The product life cycle and international trade,* ed. L. T. Wells, Jr. Boston: Graduate School of Business Administration, Harvard University.

Doyle, R. W., and N. A. Schommer. 1976. The decision to export: Some implications. Motivation study commissioned by the Minnesota District Export Council.

Edmister, R. O. 1970. Financial ratios as discriminant predictors of small business failure. Ph. D. dissertation. Ohio State University Press.

Filley, A. C. 1962. A theory of small business and divisional growth. Ph. D. dissertation. Ohio State University Press.

Glueck, W. F. 1974. An evaluation of stages of corporate development in business policy. Paper presented at the Midwest Academy of Management Annual Meeting, Kent, Ohio.

———. 1976. *Business policy: Strategy formation and management action.* New York: McGraw-Hill.

Gru, L. G. 1973. Financial ratios, multiple discriminant analysis and the prediction of small corporate failures. Ph.D. dissertation. University of Minnesota.

Jacobs, Sanford L. 1984. Group urges U.S. to subsidize firms' entry into exporting. *The Wall Steet Journal* 24 (September): 35.

Klatt, L. A. 1973. *Small business management: Essentials of entrepreneurship.* Belmont, Calif.: Wadsworth Publishing Co.

Myrick, F. L. 1977. Successful small business managers. *Journal of Small Business Management* 15 (3): 19-21.

Potts, A. J. 1977. A study of the success and failure rates of small businesses and the use or non-use of accounting information. Ph. D. dissertation. George Washington University, Washington, D. C..

Rao, C. P., and D. D. Weinrauch. 1974. External problems to export expansion: Perceptions of exporters and potential exporters. Paper presented to the Midwest Meeting of the Academy of International Business, Chicago. Spring.

Rogers, E. M. 1962. *Diffusion of innovations.* New York: Free Press.

Simpson, C. L., Jr. 1973. The export decision: An interview study of the decision process in Tennessee manufacturing firms. Ph. D. dissertation. Georgia State University.

State of Minnesota. Department of Economic Development. 1975. *Minnesota export survey summary.* St. Paul, Minnesota.

Susbauer, J. C. 1978. Commentary. (Mimeographed.)

Tesar, G. 1975. Empirical study of export operations among small- and medium-sized manufacturing firms. Ph.D. dissertation. University of Wisconsin.

Thain, D. H. 1969. Stages of Corporate Development. *Business Weekly* (Winter): 33-65.

U. S. Small Business Administration. Office of Advocacy. 1977. *The study of small business.* Washington, D.C.: U.S. Government Printing Office.

Vesper, K. H. 1978. Commentary. (Mimeographed.)

7 Economic Development Programs of State and Local Governments and the Site Selection Decisions of Smaller Firms

**WILLIAM L. WAUGH, JR., and
DEBORAH McCORKLE WAUGH**

Governments, like individuals, are susceptible to promotions and fads and the bandwagon effect of popular causes. The very nature of democratic government requires the development of consensual bases for major policy decisions. Whether precipitated by crises or popularized by "policy entrepreneurs," ideas seem to take off, gain momentum, peak, and slowly dissipate over time. This cycle is no less true of the current interest in the issue of public–private cooperation that has become the focus of economic development efforts and the impetus behind the present interest in deregulation of the business sector or, at a minimum, regulatory reform. The "policy window" created by a business-oriented national leadership, including those leaders who promote the notion of a national industrial policy and a comprehensive program of planned economic development and similarly oriented governorships,[1] has fueled interest in seeking out new industries and facilitating the expansion of indigenous businesses.

That the economic development movement has gained momentum is evident from the number of states and localities actively pursuing new industries. M. Ellenis (1983:116) estimates that there are nearly 7,500 economic development agencies in the United States. The initial interest of the development agencies seemed to be the large industries. Most recently, the focus has decidedly been on "high technology" firms, but there seems to be a growing interest in small firms, whether "high tech" or "low tech."

In this chapter we will examine the differences between large and small firms in terms of the factors they consider in selecting new business sites when they are relocating or expanding. We will study this question in the context of the inducements that state and local governments are offering to businesses to choose their jurisdictions for new sites. In doing so, we will analyze the following: (1) the reasons why state and local governments may find small firms attractive; (2) the factors that are assumed to affect site selection decisions and how state and local governments have tried to tailor their incentive packages to fit those factors; and (3) how small firms may differ from large firms in the value they place on the incentives offered. In the course of those analyses, we will develop a set of expectations concerning the differences between small and large firms. Propositions will be tested with data collected from a survey of firms with relatively high research and development expenditures as a percentage of gross sales.

WHY ARE SMALL FIRMS ATTRACTIVE?

The interest that state and local governments are now showing in small firms is understandable given the intense competition among governments for the favor of large firms, the need to diversify economic bases to insulate communities against macroeconomic fluctuations and crises, the greater potential for jobs created by small businesses, and the political influence of small firms. Small firms with 100 to 500 employees represent the fastest growing sector of the economy (*CPA Journal* 1984:68-69). However small businesses are defined, they are responsible for generating most of the new jobs in the United States each year (*Business Week* 1982a:40). Those reasons, however may be less important than the political clout of small firms with state and local policymakers (*Nation's Business* 1982b; *Journal of Accountancy* 1983; Thoryn 1982). Small firms are major sources of campaign funds and assistance for incumbent and aspiring public officials (Tomaskovic-Devey and Miller 1982:57-63).

The literature on what motivates small firms to move from one location to another or to choose particular sites for expanded facilities is not extensive, however. Public programs to lure new industries to states and localities first focused on large industries—often manufacturing firms—because of the prestige factor of "industrialization." Those programs now tend to focus on "high tech" firms because of the prestige of "postindustrialization" and "progress" and the appeal of clean products and services and attractive, campus-like facilities that many of the firms establish. The smokestacks of manufacturing firms might create more problems, political as well as social and economic, and the relatively low employment potential of high tech firms would not alleviate the known problems of unemployment and underemployment (Peterson et al. 1984: 56-62). Moreover, state and local officials were accused of "giving away the store" to lure large firms into their jurisdictions. Tax breaks to cover startup costs and to stimulate investment, regulatory reforms to reduce overhead and to encourage the generation of venture capital,[2] and expensive promotional programs, to mention but a few of the incentives offered, were costing taxpayers substantial sums of money and promised to cost even more in the future as the real impacts of tax expenditures and public debt were realized.

Small firms, however, require much less capital for startup, are generally more willing to take risks to assure success, and often are so sensitive to regulatory requirements that even the smallest reforms may have major impacts (Berney and Owens 1984:49-58). In short, small firms promise to provide a quicker return for the investment of economic development dollars (*CPA Journal* 1984:69). Moreover, the owners of small firms may be more susceptible to personal approaches and, thus, easier to seduce with the amenities that states and localities have promoted to attract the high tech industries. It has been suggested that small firms simply cannot compete with the large benefit packages that large corporations provide for employees and that the small firms have to pay more attention to the tangible and intangible "perks" that employees may find attractive (Waugh and Waugh forthcoming). The importance of amenity factors will be one of the major issues which the analysis to follow will address. A diversified economy is also an attraction. Single-industry economies are too vulnerable to market fluctuations, and single industries may exercise too great a sway over local politics.

The impetus behind the new efforts to attract small firms, however, may be due to the political influence of small businesses in general. Those who have helped put together the economic development schemes of most states and cities would likely agree that the programs have given many interest groups and individuals an opportunity to address more parochial concerns than simply economic development itself. Regulatory reforms include everything from liberalization of liquor laws to changes in banking regulations to promotions of parimutual betting and dog racing. Tax advantages, too, are given to indigenous businesses as well as to new businesses. This is not to say that the efforts have been entirely self-serving. Actually, the efforts have created opportunities to get rid of nuisance laws and regulations, and community and business leaders have frequently taken advantage of their influence in economic development programs (Fellar 1984:463).

The attractiveness of small firms, then, may be due to the political benefits associated with such programs. Small businesses are politically safe in the sense that each city and state has a very large small business constituency which will support programs designed to aid small firms, and the programs are less controversial if only because small firms are less obtrusive. The responsiveness of small firms to regulatory reforms, tax incentives, amenity factors, and other government-sponsored efforts encourages targeting them. Moreover, small firms may alleviate the problems of high unemployment—particularly among low-skill workers—and single (or few) industry locations. Dozens or even hundreds of small firms may be economically preferable to one or two large industries, even though the mortality rate among small businesses tends to be quite high.

SITE SELECTION DECISIONS AND THE SMALL FIRM

The literature on site selection decisions is generally of two types. First, there is a growing literature on the factors that should be important to businesses choosing sites for new or expanded facilities. Some of that literature deals primarily with the location of businesses within a relatively small area. Among the factors listed in that literature are trading area size, competition, volume of traffic, demographic characteristics, space for expansion, parking facilities, and quality of life. A number of those factors obviously would be considered by firms choosing among locations scattered across the nation or a region, but they largely relate to site selection within a rather small area such as a metropolitan area. Nonetheless, the weights which I. Burstiner (1979) assigns each factor in one proposed model for selecting locations for small retail firms, in fact, give greater importance to the macro-level factors—for example, quality of life and demographic characteristics, as well as the volume of traffic in an area—than they do the micro-level factors.

The second part of the literature attempts to tell government officials what businesses consider important factors when selecting new sites so that they can design their incentive packages accordingly. There is an apparent dichotomy between the two strands of literature, which will bear examination later in this chapter.

Clearly, certain factors are crucial to firms selecting new sites. Firms normally look for suitable locations with potential for expansion; adequate transportation networks for moving raw materials and finished goods or for providing access to customers seeking services or taking services to customers; an adequate labor force with appropriate skills; adequate utilities to support the firm; adequate capital for startup and expansion; and a regulatory environment that will not unduly inhibit business operations. The cost of labor, transportation, utilities, and other necessary production/service ingredients is also considered, and there may be some willingness to trade off one item for another if no ideal site can be found.

Additional factors are to be considered, including the political and social climate in the area under consideration. Quality-of-life factors were given considerable weight in the Burstiner (1979:65) and the Rudd, Vigen, and Davis (1983) models for small firm site selection.[3] Those and other models also assign great value to such factors as the availability and cost of housing, educational facilities available to the firm's employees and their families, the climate of the region, cultural activities, and the general aesthetic qualities of the community or region.

The quality-of-life factors have, in fact, received much greater attention in recent years. A study by K. R. Student (1976) includes the sociocultural, health, educational, and residential characteristics of potential sites. A survey (Lynch 1973) of executives in industrial firms found that quality-of-life considerations were considered most important, followed by labor supply and quality. N. Welles' survey (1981) of professional site selection consultants found selection criteria to include everything from local attitudes toward business and the "work ethic" and the level of unionization in the labor force to local environmental regulations and "everthing from hiking trails to the ballet." A study by Conway Data, Inc. (1983) found that the following factors were important to high tech firms making site selections:

1. Intellectual base, including educational programs throughout the graduate level.
2. Nucleus of scientific activity, to stimulate professional interaction and interest.
3. Accessibility, especially good airline connections.
4. Aesthetic appeal, including climate and schools and the physical beauty of the area.
5. Supporting services for research laboratories.
6. Suitable sites, with preference for campus-like parks.

A study by the U.S. Congress (1982) found that high tech firms gave the highest ranks to labor force availability, tax structure, and other factors directly related to production, in that order. Amenity factors were judged significant, but were only ranked as high as seventh or eighth on the listing (depending on whether educational facilities were considered a job-related or an amenity factor). Other studies have had similar results except in terms of the impact of taxes. The National Association of Manufacturers, for example, judged that taxes were not determining factors in site selections for manufacturing firms; two other studies, one by the U.S. Department of Housing and Urban Development (HUD) and the other by the Joint Center for Urban Studies, concluded that taxes are not decisive factors in small business site selections (U.S.GAO 1982:10). The impact of tax incentives on "free enterprise zone" projects has demonstrated much the same thing. Tax incentives only attract local businesses to move into the designated zones. In most cases, however, taxes only serve as tie breakers when all other factors are equal. A director of Coopers and Lybrand reached this same conclusion at an urban enterprise zone conference in 1981, as have studies by the U.S. General Accounting Office (1982) and others (Welles 1981; Schmenner 1979).[4]

The discrepancies among the rankings may be due to the different types and sizes of firms surveyed or studied. The importance of particular charcteristics of the labor force, such as skilled technical and scientific workers, would likely be industry specific, and the relative unimportance of such factors as raw materials for high technology research firms is understandable given the nature of their products. Tax breaks appear to be popular (such incentives are usually included in development programs sponsored by governments at all levels), but there is very little evidence that they are important. Interestingly, utility executives have reported that they use tax factors in the marketing of development sites to firms, although taxes were not rated that highly relative to their other selling points (Lynch 1973).

The types of incentives offered by state and local governments generally include programs that will [5]

1. encourage research, development, and technology transfer—usually meaning private sector–university linkages;
2. develop human capital through training programs and special eductional programs at all levels;
3. facilitate management training and assistance;
4. generate venture and expansion capital through tax breaks, industrial revenue bonds, loan guarantees, and other devices;
5. build physical capital by setting out zoning and building code easements, establishing industrial parks, and improving infrastructure; and,
6. establish information-gathering and dissemination capacities to actively recruit new firms.

These programs, as described, relate more directly to the stimulation of high technology development, but they are also indicative of the efforts now underway in states and cities. It is also instructive that the efforts rely heavily on regulatory and tax reform and emphasize university–private sector linkages. Government officials may perceive that the amenity factors, for the most part, are not as subject to "reform' as are taxes or regulations.

Notwithstanding those apparent discrepancies, we would expect that tax advantages might have more of an impact on small firms than they would on the larger ones. In terms of the other factors mentioned, some only in passing, we would also expect that amenity and quality-of-life factors, including connections with universites, would be even more important to small firms. As indicated earlier, small firms may have to rely on the more personal "perks" or rewards to attract and retain high-quality employees. Capital, particularly venture capital for startup, would be more of a problem for small firms, and, thus, programs to facilitate capital formation would be particularly useful. In fact, the degree of flexibility that managers of small firms have in terms of allocating resources would suggest that external factors, those they have the least control over, may be the largest concerns (*CPA Journal* 1984a; Peterson et al. 1984)[6] and, thus, may be crucial considerations in selecting new sites.

THE SURVEY OF FIRMS

Methodology

During the fall of 1984 and the winter of 1985, questionnaires were mailed to 200 of the approximately 800 firms listed by *Business Week* (July 1984 issue) as having large research and development expenditures relative to gross sales. The listing, "R&D Scoreboard," uses Standard and Poor's categorizations by firm type. We eliminated those categories of firms that would not be concerned with site selection or would have too many subsidiaries or divisions to make a definitive judgment about site selection criteria. The firms eliminated were those categorized as conglomerates and food industries. Most of the food industries were located in the Midwest and were closely tied to regional agribusiness; thus were not likely to be seeking new locations. A few other firms were removed from the listing, including one dealing with gambling devices, because they would not be considering site selections. A random sample was made of the remaining firms.

The initial mailing was made in October 1984, the second in late November, and the third in February 1985. Adjusting for erroneous addresses and duplications (when holding companies and their subsidiaries received questionnaires, only the subsidiaries were included in the survey), there were ninety-three responses to the questionnaire. Twenty-eight firms indicated that the information requested was proprietary and would not be released or, according to a few, that company policy precluded participation in surveys. The response rate, then, was approximately 50 percent.

The questionnaire itself was modeled on that used by the Joint Economic Committee of Congress, Subcommittee on Monetary and Fiscal Policy, for the 1981-82 study cited earlier. The only distinction was that the rating of site selection criteria was done on a ten-point scale, rather than in terms of whether the factors were considered "significant" or "very significant" by the respondents. Additional criteria were also factored in.

The sample of firms was not intended to be representative of small or large firms in general. The "R&D Scoreboard" listing was chosen because the firms would have similar orientations, although products and services were so diverse (even within the same firm in a few cases) that comparisons would be problematic and would likely be, as one respondent put it, in an "expansion mode." The listing was also chosen because it is based on several factors related to the "high technology" orientations of firms.

The literature on small firms was of little assistnce in developing a framework for analyzing the differences between small and large firms. The arguments against a categorization based on the number of employees were persuasive (Lippett and Oliver 1984; Miller 1982), and the categorization used here is based on gross sales rather than on employees. Beyond that, the easiest course, given the rather specialized firms in the survey, was to divide the high R&D firms into small, medium, and large groups. The "smaller firms" were those with gross sales of less than $140 million which, for some high tech firms, still meant rather small numbers of employees; the "medium firms" were those with gross sales between $140 million and $800 million; and the "larger firms" were those with gross sales in excess of $800 million.

The Propositions

The discussions of the importance of small firms in economic development schemes suggested that smaller firms would be more responsive to regulatory reform (or deregulation) because compliance costs represent larger proportions of their operating budgets. Much the same was suggested for tax incentives. Even small gains through tax credits would be of more benefit to smaller firms than they would be to larger firms. Programs to generate or encourage the in-migration of venture capital would also be of more benefit to smaller firms that need relatively little to get started.

One would also expect the intrinsic, product- or service-specific factors, such as markets and raw materials, to be of greater importance to smaller and less diverse firms. Size is usually accepted as an indicator of departmentalization, division of labor, and task specializaton; smaller firms would be less likely to have highly developed functional or product divisions. That assumption may not be strictly accurate given the categorization of firms utilized here, but we can hazard that assumption for purposes of investigation.

Finally, it was suggested that smaller firms will be more sensitive to quality-of-life or amenity factors because they may be important satisfaction factors for management and because management and technical personnel themselves may have more freedom to express their own location preferences, particularly when they are the ones being moved to the new site. Proximity to universities may fit into either category, as an amenity factor or as an intrinsic factor, and we would expect smaller firms to be influenced more than larger firms to locate near universities.

On the whole, we would expect the responses of smaller firms to be more intense, that is, exhibiting stronger preferences for particular criteria and, perhaps, indicating that other criteria are important. In that respect, smaller firms should be more responsive to government-sponsored incentive packages.

Data Analysis

The firms included in the survey were almost exclusively national in terms of their markets; only a few considered themselves to be primarily international, and only one considered itself largely regional. The overwhelming majority had relocated all or some of their facilities in the past two years, and a clear majority had plans to open more facilities in the next two years.

In terms of the criteria considered the most important, the mean responses by firm size given in Table 7.1 indicate significant differences among the rankings of selection criteria. Although the factors judged to be the most important are similar, the rankings are more dissimilar in terms of the middle-range criteria. If anything, the medium-sized firms show a greater concern for the intrinsic factors—labor availability and cost, taxes, regulatory practices, transportation, and markets—than do the smaller and larger firms. All three groups rate the quality-of-life factors, particularly climate and cultural and recreational facilities, relatively low. Proximity to universities, too, was not a major consideration for any of the groups.

In terms of the intensity of the responses, the medium-sized firms gave the strongest responses (i.e., lower average means) and the smaller firms gave the weakest responses. The expectation was just the opposite. One possible explanation is that larger firms have clearer preferences among the criteria listed. In addition, the high level of importance assigned to tax and regulatory considerations certainly runs counter to expectations.

The low score for university linkages or proximity also did not fit the expected pattern. Table 7.2 indicates how important each group of respondents or firms judged transfers of scientific knowledge from universities to their firms. More of the larger firms found the transfer to be "very important" or "important." Transfers do not necessarily require proximity, however. Table 7.3 suggests that smaller firms, in fact, have the strongest preference for locations near universities. The question is raised as to why

Table 7.1
Site Selection Criteria: Mean and Rank by Firm Size
(1 = very important; 10 = not important)

Site Selection Criteria	Smaller Firms	Medium Firms	Larger Firms
Labor: Skills and Availability	2.24 (1)	1.95 (3)	2.15 (1)
Potential for Expansion	3.00 (2)	2.29 (8)	2.45 (5)
Community Business Atmosphere-Receptiveness	3.14 (3)	2.52 (9)	3.15 (8)
Tax Climate Within Area/State	3.14 (3)	1.90 (2)	2.40 (4)
State/Local Regulatory Practices	3.19 (5)	1.71 (1)	2.20 (2)
Labor Costs	3.19 (5)	2.10 (4)	2.65 (7)
Transportation Facilities	3.43 (7)	2.14 (5)	2.55 (6)
Cost of Land and/or Construction	3.57 (8)	2.90 (10)	3.35 (10)
Energy Costs and Availability	3.86 (9)	2.29 (7)	2.30 (3)
Cost of Living	3.90 (10)	3.67 (13)	4.35 (14)
Community Social Climate-Pleasantness	3.95 (11)	3.90 (14)	4.20 (13)
Proximity to Customers	4.76 (12)	3.14 (12)	3.20 (9)
Access to Markets	4.85 (13)	2.19 (6)	3.35 (10)
Access to Raw Materials and Component Supply	4.86 (14)	3.05 (11)	3.50 (12)
Recreational Facilities	4.86 (14)	5.29 (17)	5.00 (16)
Proximity to Academic Institutions	5.05 (16)	4.86 (15)	5.15 (17)
Cultural Amenities (Parks, Museums, etc.)	5.67 (17)	5.33 (18)	4.60 (15)
Climate of Region	6.10 (18)	5.19 (16)	6.05 (18)

Table 7.2
Importance of Transfers of Scientific Knowledge from Universities by Firm Size (in Percentages)

Level of Importance	Smaller Firms	Medium Firms	Larger Firms
Very Important	14	9	21
Important	19	29	26
Slightly Important	38	43	26
Not Important	24	19	21
Respondent Did Not Know	5	0	5
Totals	100	100	99*

*Total less than 100 due to rounding

Table 7.3
Preference for Locations near Universities by Firm Size (in Percentages)

Level of Importance	Smaller Firms	Medium Firms	Larger Firms
Usually Important	43	9	27
Sometimes Important	19	62	45
Not Important	33	24	27
Respondent Did Not Know	5	5	0
Totals	100	100	99*

*Total less than 100 due to rounding

that preference is so strong given the relatively low importance of transfers of knowledge. This question may be answered by Table 7.4. According to this table, contrary to the numerous economic development programs built around university-private sector cooperation, firms attach marginal importance to such things as part-time teaching opportunities for employees, access to university laboratories, faculty consulting and research, and access to libraries and other facilities. Since 5.5 is a "marginal" mean on the ten-point scale used, only a few means would be considered high. Firms of all sizes, but particularly the smaller, are most interested in hiring university graduates and in having their own employees pursue degrees of additional training. Universities were not highly rated in terms

Table 7.4
Factors Affecting Importance of University-Related Sites, Mean and Rank by Firm Size (1 = very important; 10 = not important)

University-Related Factors	Smaller Firms	Medium Firms	Larger Firms
Employment of Graduates	2.90 (1)	3.79 (1)	3.90 (1)
Degree Programs for Employees	3.95 (2)	4.58 (2)	4.45 (2)
Access to Libraries and Information Systems	4.80 (3)	4.89 (3)	5.40 (3)
Faculty Consulting	5.65 (4)	5.84 (4)	6.80 (7)
Cultural Activities on Campus	5.65 (4)	6.58 (7)	5.70 (5)
Faculty Research	5.80 (6)	6.11 (6)	6.00 (6)
Access to University Laboratories	5.95 (7)	5.84 (4)	5.40 (3)
Part-Time Teaching Opportunities for Employees	7.50 (8)	8.42 (8)	7.90 (8)

Table 7.5
Use of Professional Site Selection Consultants or Firms in Decision Making by Firm Size (in Percentages)

Use of Consultant	Smaller Firms	Medium Firms	Larger Firms
Usually Use Consultants	14	5	9
Sometimes Use Consultants	14	38	27
Do Not Use Consultants	52	57	64
Respondent Did Not Know	19		
Totals	99*	100	100

*Total less than 100 due to rounding

Table 7.6
Involvement of Personnel Being Moved to New Site in Site Selection Decision by Firm Size (in Percentage)

Level of Involvement	Smaller Firms	Medium Firms	Larger Firms
Usually Involves Personnel to Be Moved to New Site	43	48	50
Sometimes Involves Personnel to Be Moved to New Site	43	33	36
Usually Does Not Involve Personnel to Be Moved	5	14	14
Respondent Did Not Know	9	5	0
Totals	100	100	100

of their contribution to the quality of life, although several respondents did indicate that proximity was important because of educational opportunities for family members. Even more respondents indicated that the training of employees by universities or trade schools was a high priority.

The low rating given quality-of-life factors generally would suggest that they are not of great importance in selecting new sites. As Tables 7.5 and 7.6 show, few firms use professional site selection consultants on a regular basis, and the overwhelming majority involve their own personnel who will be moving to the new site. That, in itself, would suggest that personal preferences would influence the selection of sites.

CONCLUSION

There is no evidence that small firms have special preferences or needs as regards site selection decisions. In fact, medium-sized firms appeared to be more emphatic about their preferences and more concerned about the intrinsic factor or factors related to product/service. None of the groups appeared to assign greater value to quality-of-life considerations relative to other concerns, although the mean averages, with 5.5 being a "marginal" response, suggest that most of the factors were considered at least somewhat important by all three groups.

Rather than substantiate or fail to substantiate the propositions, the data give lukewarm confirmation to the conclusions of the site selection consultants and analysts menioned earlier, with the possible exception of the tax and regulation issues. Relative to other concerns, taxes and regulatory practices were considered important factors by the firms with high R&D expenditures. The most important factor in selecting a new site, however, was the availability of labor with appropriate skills and at reasonable cost. For small firms, perhaps, that concern with labor also means proximity to universities to facilitate the hiring of graduates. Larger firms can recruit from afar.

NOTES

1. I. Feller (1984) concludes that high technology programs are particularly suited to sponsorship by governors because they normally crosscut policy areas and offer unusually attractive political rewards because of their "progressive" nature.

2. R. A. Peterson et al. (1984) argue that regulation has a greater impact on small businesses. We make the reverse argument, that deregulation will also have a greater impact on small businesses than on larger.

3. H. F. Rudd, J. W. Vigen, and R. N. Davis (1983) take the model several steps further than Burstiner (1979) from simple weights to weights calculated from multiple rankings of site selection criteria.

4. The analysts are certainly not unanimous, however. See, for example, D. W. Rasmussen, M. Bendick, and L. C. Ledebur (1982). The authors assess the value of tax and other incentives to firms.

5. U.S. Congress (1984a). The report is also summarized in *Research Management* (1984). Also see U.S. DOC (1984); U.S. Congress (1984b); National Governor's Association (1984); and Kansas DED (1982).

6. The logic is that small firms have a geat deal of flexibility as to how resources are allocated internally and very little control over external factors.

REFERENCES

Berney, R. E., and E. Owens. 1984. Small business policy: Subsidization, neutrality, or discrimination. *Journal of Small Business Management* 22 (July):49-58.

Burstiner, I. 1979. *The small business handbook.* Englewood Cliffs, N.J.: Prentice-Hall. Cited in H. F. Rudd, Jr., J. W. Vigen, and R. N. Davis. The LMMD model: Choosing the optimum locale for a small retail business. *Journal of Small Business Management (April 1983):48.*

Conway Data, Inc. 1983. Development opportunities for high tech: A meeting of the minds is in view. *Site Selection Handbook/83;* 28 (September): 532-536.

Ellenis, M. 1983. Six major trends affecting site selection decisions to the year 2000. *Dun's Business Month* (November): 116.

Fascinating facts about small business. 1984. *CPA Journal* (Fall): 68-69.

Feller, I. 1984. Political and administrative aspects of state high technology programs. *Policy Studies Review* 3 (May): 460-466.

Kansas Department of Economic Development (DED). 1982. *Strategy for the eighties: High technology industrial development.* Topeka, Kan.: KDED.

Lippett, J. W., and B. L. Oliver. 1984. The productivity, efficiency, and employment implications of the SBA's definition of "small." *American Journal of Small Business* 8 (January-March):46-48.

Lynch, A. A. 1973. Environment and labor quality take top priority in site selection. *Industrial Development* 142 (March-April):13-15.

Making time for politics. 1982. *Nation's Business*(September): 64-65.

Miller, E. 1982. Productivity and the definition of small business. *American Journal of Small Business* 7 (July-August): 17-18.

National Governors Association, Task Force on Technological Innovation. 1984. *State initiatives and federal policy.* Discussion Paper for Winter Meeting, February 26.

Peterson, R. A., G. Kozmetsky, and N. M. Ridgway. 1984. Opinions about government regulation of small business. *Journal of Small Business Management* 22 (January): 56-62.

Profile of small businesses. 1982a. *Business Week* (May): 61-90.

R & D Scoreboard. 1984. *Business Week* (July): 65-78.

Rasmussen, D.W., M. Bendick, Jr., and L. C. Ledebur. 1982. Evaluating state economic development incentives from a firm's perspective. *Business Economics* (May): 23-29.

Rudd, H. F., Jr., J. W. Vigen, and R. N. Davis. 1983. The LMMD model: Choosing the optimal locale for a small retail business. *Journal of Small Business Management* (April): 48.

Schmenner, R. W. 1979. Look beyond the obvious in plant location. *Harvard Business Review* 57 (January-February): 126-132.

Small business: The courtship by political and academic circles. 1983. *Journal of Accountancy* (November): 170-172.

State and local programs encourage high technology. 1984b. *Research Management* 27 (September October): 4-5.

Student, K. R. 1976. Cost vs. human values in plant location. *Business Horizons* 19 (April): 5-14.

Thoryn, M. 1982. Small business speaks, government listens. *Business Weekly* (May): 38-42.

Tomaskovic-Devey, D., and S. M. Miller. 1982. Can high tech provide the jobs? *Challenge* (May June): 57-63.

U.S. Congress. 1982. *Location of high technology firms and regional economic development: A staff study of the subcommittee on monetary and fiscal policy of the Joint Economic Committee of Congress.* Washington, D. C.: U. S. Government Printing Office.

U.S. Congress, Office of Technology Assessment. 1984a. "OTA releases study of state and local programs to encourage high-technology development." News Release, February 24.

U.S. Congress, Office of Technology Assessment. 1984b. *Technology, innovation, and regional economic development.* Washington, D. C.: OTA, Background Paper #2.

U. S. Department of Commerce (DOC). 1984. The Stevenson-Wydler Technology

Innovation Act of 1980. *Report to the President and the Congress.* Washington, D.C.: DOC.

U. S. General Accounting Office (GAO), Comptroller General. 1982. *Report to the Congress: Revitalizing distressed areas through enterprise zones.* Washington, D.C.: U.S. GAO. GAO/CED-82-78.

Waugh, W. L., Jr., and D. M. Waugh. Forthcoming. The political economy of seduction: Business relocation in nonindustial states. In *Public Policy and Economic Institutions,* ed. J. Anderson, M. Dubnick, and A. Gitelson. KAI Press.

Welles, N. 1981. What site selection consultants are saying now. *Institutional Investor* (November): 163-182.

8 Small Business Challenging Contemporary Public Policy: A Coalition for Action

DONALD F. KURATKO

No business, large or small, can operate without obeying a myriad of government rules and restrictions. Costs and profits can be affected as much by a directive written by a government official as by a management decision in the front office or a customer's decision at the checkout counter. Fundamental entrepreneurial decisions—such as what lines of business to go into, what products and services to produce, which investments to finance, how and where to make goods and how to market them, and what prices to charge—are increasingly subject to government control (Murray L. Weinbaum, quoted from Buchholz 1982).

As indicated by this quotation, government has become a new partner to business in America. Therefore, understanding and communicating with government is a key not only to success, but also, in the case of small business, to survival.

Although the subject of public policy affecting America's business environment is now being explored, the differential impact of public policy issues on small business is also surfacing. We have finally entered a decade of small business realization and revitalization.

The government and President Ronald Reagan's administration are beginning to establish new "ground rules" by which small business has an equal chance to survive and prosper in a world of corporate giants. New legislation has already been adopted.

Small businesspersons/entrepreneurs are becoming noticed and respected in Washington and on university campuses. They answer certain economic needs that are desperately plaguing America. While the legislators take notice, a coalition is building to advocate the interests of small business. A new network of state commerce departments, trade and professional associations, the National Chamber of Commerce, the Small

Business Administration (SBA), and certain universities is developing a stronger voice across the states and in Washington for the small businessperson/entrepreneur.

GOVERNMENT RECOGNITION OF SMALL BUSINESS IN AMERICA

To revitalize the nation, we must stimulate small business growth and opportunity. Small business accounts for over 60 percent of our jobs, half of our business output, and at least half of the innovations that keep American industry strong. The imagination, skills, and willingness of small business men and women to take necessary risks symbolize the free enterprise foundation of the American economy and must be encouraged.

I urge all Americans who own or work in a small business to continue their resourcefulness and successes, for these efforts contribute so much to the entrepreneurial spirit which made this nation great. It is with justifiable pride that the American small businessman can point to himself as the backbone of our nation.

Ronald Reagan
President of the United States

This statement by the President characterizes the importance not only of the realization of the impact small business has today, but also the federal government's stimulation to answer the voice of small business.

During the last few decades our legislators concentrated only on "big business" and simply waited for the little guy to fall into line. Although the area of aid and benefits was slight, it was the regulatory environment that truly spelled out a survival need for small business.

Over the past twenty years, public regulation of business has increased at an exponential rate. Too many times the plight of a small business, in terms of compliance, was *never* considered. What was demanded from the large corporate environment was simply expected from the small businesses in that same industry. It appears that the tide has now turned. Washington has taken into consideration this wrongful expectation placed on small businesspersons. The last four years have witnessed a shift in the attitudes and considerations of our legislators.

"Entrepreneurial Economics" is becoming a hot topic in Washington for a variety of reasons. First, a shattering recession in the late 1970s and early 1980s shackled our economy and stymied most economists. Second, in 1980 President Ronald Reagan shifted the nation's economic plan away from the public sector (Keynesian approach) to the private sector (supply-side approach). Whether right or wrong in economic theory, this shift brought about a revitalization and hope that working through business was our answer for long-range recovery. The entrepreneur could play a most vital role in this process. Third, the rapid rise in unemployment triggered a search for new business opportunities that were surfacing only in the smaller scale businesses. Fourth, a belief developed that the larger corporations were busy trying to regain their market position, while many small businesses were searching to start, expand, or internationalize. Finally, the growing domination of foreign economies that continually demonstrate greater productive and qualitative capabilities has unleashed a renewed pride in America's innovative and entrepreneurial spirit.

Small businesses tend to dominate the business structure of the United States (Figure 8.1).

Everywhere you look in America there is a small business—the corner drugstore, the auto dealer, the barber shop, the dry cleaners, the grocers; and every small business person you meet will rail against the same problems—pernicious inflation, restrictive regulation, burdensome taxes, lack of capital, flagging innovation.

Many economists and government officials at all levels have debated the remedies for the ills of small business.

Despite conflicting theories and policies, everyone agrees on one thesis: Unless something is done to help small business survive successfully as an American in-

Figure 8.1
Percentage Distribution of Employment and Establishments by Employment—Size Class

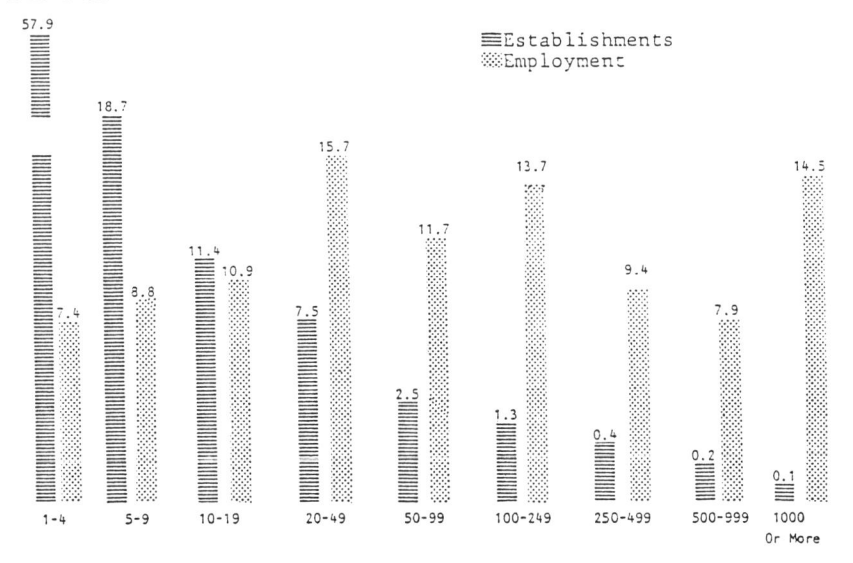

Size Class	Establishments	Employment
1-4	57.9	7.4
5-9	18.7	8.8
10-19	11.4	10.9
20-49	7.5	15.7
50-99	2.5	11.7
100-249	1.3	13.7
250-499	0.4	9.4
500-999	0.2	7.9
1000 Or More	0.1	14.5

SOURCE: "Small Business in America." 1987. Washington, D.C.: The Institute for Enterprise Advancement. June. (Renamed The National Federation of Independent Business, June 1987).

stitution, it will become as rare as the buffalo, with effects as severe on the American economy as the vanishing of that species had on the American Indian (*Nation's Business* 1980:22).

Small business is needed for America to stay competitive and strong. Articles, similar to the previous quote, have been filled with urgent statements concerning the survival of small business.

PROBLEM AREAS OF SMALL BUSINESS

The five main problem areas faced by small businesses today are:

1. Inflation and cash flow (liability)
2. Taxes (new tax reforms)
3. Sources of capital (seed and growth)
4. Innovations
5. Government regulation

Small businesspersons and researchers alike agree that these problem areas inherently revolve aroung the impacts of government policy. Number five may be the most obvious, yet the other four areas do rely on the continuous legislative policies that emanate from the public sector.

The first two, inflation and taxes, result directly from the economic plan the government is pursuing. Although all businesses—large or small—are beset with these economic problems, the small business suffers most from the inequitable distribution of its effects.

The third category deals with sources of capital. Agencies such as the SBA, Small Business Investment Corporations (SBICs), the Small Business Development Center (SBDCs), Certified Development Corporations (CDCs), or banks may feel pressure as a result of monetary policy changes inflicted through governmental action. (Note: The Federal Reserve System attempts to monitor its monetary policy to fit the fiscal actions of the administration.)

With regard to the fourth category, innovations are suffering in America. The Office of Management and Budget reports that small business accounted for over half of the nation's innovations from 1953-1973. Yet, private research and development has dropped 13 percent in the last ten years. Patent improvements, tax incentives, and direct government aid seem to appeal to businesses as the viable solutions for our innovation problem. Again, government policies directly influence these solutions.

Finally, government regulation is the largest, most visible factor affecting small businesses today (cf., Weidenbaum, 1986). Because it encompasses so many regulatory acts and agencies, the regulatory environment is the first problem small business must convince government to consider.

Government regulations affect small business in a variety of ways. Some examples are as follows:

- *Prices.* Small businesses are forced to raise their prices to absorb the costs of regulatory compliance.
- *Cost Inequities.* Small companies feel the financial brunt of regulatory burdens more than large corporations.
- *Competition Restriction.* Putting a greater burden on small business tends to favor big business and thus subtly encourages big while discouraging small.
- *Paperwork Burden.* Most small businesses cannot afford to hire a person to handle the paperwork involved in regulations. So, the small businessperson often takes on this time-consuming duty.
- *Managerial Restriction.* Because so much of their time is spent on paperwork-imposed duties, the small businessperson must sacrifice valuable managerial time in order to comply with government regulations.
- *Mental Burden.* Postponed projects, wasted time, and managerial failure owing to lack of available time and energy, all begin to take their toll on the psychological aspect of a businessperson. Frustration leading to depression will spell failure for the business.

THE REGULATORY ENVIRONMENT OF SMALL BUSINESS

This myriad of regulations causes businesses to re-evaluate, reassess, and sometimes shift entire resources into new dimensions. Big businesses may feel the strain and then adjust. Small businesses may simply fail. According to K. Chilton and M. Weidenbaum (1982:9), one of the most serious consequences of federal regulation of business is the threat to the continued existence of the small firm.

These regulatory burdens may surface not only in compliance costs, but also in the paperwork burden that becomes the ancillary aspect of government policies.

The small firm, unlike its large firm counterpart, does not have a professional staff to respond to heavy paperwork and reporting requirements. Often the owner/entrepreneur is the only individual with sufficient knowledge to respond to an agency's requirement for information. Reporting costs, like the other more severe burdens of federal regulation, are not proportioned to the size of the firm (Chilton and Weidenbaum).

Small businesses are turning to the public sector for aid in easing their regulatory burden. They cannot simply ignore the compliance orders, as some may suggest. The penalties are stiff and the consequences too great to pay (Buchholz, 1982). The legal penalties for noncompliance are too great to risk an entire small business.

In 1981 the Commerce Department set up a special toll-free hot-line which small businesses can use to voice complaints. In that year, over 800 calls registered the need for regulatory reform.

NEW TRENDS IN POLICY FORMATION

The Reagan administration attempted to set up a "tiered" mechanism, that is, a flexible regulatory system that would consider the differences and consequences of the small businessperson. Previously, in the late 1970s, President Jimmy Carter's administration realized the need to seriously examine this flexible idea. Some of the existing regulatory exemptions from the Carter and Reagan administrations are:

Agency

Environmental Protection Agency (EPA)	Exempts most companies from keeping records of disposal of hazardous waste if it totals less than 1,000 kg. per month.
	Exempts some flame-retardant producers from reporting rules if sales are less than $1 million and planned production less than 10,000 pounds per year.
Federal Trade Commission (FTC)	Requires no advance notification of some small mergers or acquisitions.
Occupational Safety and Health Administration (OSHA)	Exempts retail gasoline stations from its benzene-exposure standard.
	Exempts companies with ten or fewer employees from reporting illness and injury.
Securities and Exchange Commission (SEC)	Imposes less stringent disclosure and auditing standards on stock offerings of less than $5 million.

Peter J. Petkas, director of the U.S. Regulatory Council, stated in 1980: "the political influence of small business is growing. Any regulator or congressman who ignores that group does so at his peril. This appears to be *the* growing trend in our political structure today." *Venture Magazine* (1983:33) reported that politicians of every stripe are rushing to get out in front on the entrepreneurial issue: "New companies are being formed at record rates even without federal involvement, and a partisan debate revolves around the degree to which government should encourage new business activity." New regulatory reform legislation has set up "milestone" laws that now offer small businesses some objective considerations.

The Regulatory Flexibility Act (Reg Flex) passed in 1980 recognizes that the size of a business does have a bearing on its ability to comply with federal regulation. It puts the burden of review on government to ensure that legislation does not impact small business unfairly. According to the SBA (1982), the major goals of the act are as follows:

1. To increase agency awareness and understanding of the impact of their regulations on small business.
2. To require that agencies communicate and explain their findings to the public.
3. To encourage agencies to provide regulatory relief to small entities.

The Chief Council for Advocacy in the U.S. Small Business Administration monitors the agencies for compliance.

The Equal Access to Justice Act, also passed in 1980, offers a greater balance between small business and regulatory bodies. According to this new act, if a small business challenges a regulatory agency and wins, the regulatory agency must pay the *legal costs of the small business.* Equal Access has five main stipulations:

1. The government or the business may initiate litigation.
2. Bad faith by the agency does *not* have to be proven.
3. Substantially justified actions must be demonstrated by the agency.
4. To receive an award, the business does not have to prevail on all issues.
5. There is no dollar limit to the awards.

The Prompt Payments Act was developed to aid the small businesses involved in collecting from federal departments with which they have contracted to do business. It requires that bills be paid in thirty days with an additional fifteen-day grace period. If not respected, however, the penalty charges of interest will be retroactive from the thirty-day point. In addition, partial contractual disputes do not allow the federal agency to withhold the *entire* amount. The disputed section may be withheld while the remaining parts of the contract are paid. The penalties imposed (interest charges) are ordered out of the agency's present funds, and no allowance is made for additional appropriations to cover their late payment charges.

The federal government and presidential administrations appear to favor big business, yet they have opened the door to listen to and understand the small businessperson. Big business relies on, interacts with, and prospers by small businesses. Thus, the government must continue to be open to the needs and concerns of small business.

The White House inaugurated a special conference in 1980, followed by a breakfast series in November 1982, which was intended to analyze the unique problems confronting the small businesspeople of America. According to the President's special assistant for public liaison, these meetings included entrepreneurs, small businesspeople, and small business lobbyists brought together to help the Reagan administration to begin formulating an entrepreneurial policy stand.

In 1986 another White House Conference convened to reassess the policies over the last five years and to make reommendations for future policy decisions. These conferences have been successful because they have allowed informal exchange of ideas *before* policy is officially decided.

These newly instituted conferences and meetings could create an atmosphere of respect and understanding for the entrepreneur/small businessperson in future federal and state policies. This is the goal of small business in today's America.;

THE COALITION FOR ACTION

If government policy decisions are going to develop and enhance small business, various components must be networked. Three major categories must be developed to insure the success of this undertaking. First, in tax reform policies, incentives should be adopted to encourage entrepreneurship and the formation of new businesses. Second, federal, state, and local policies should be implemented to create a healthy entrepreneurial environment—funds for education. Finally, a reinvigorated and reformed SBA should aid, assist, and encourage new networks representing small business across the nation.

During the 1985, 1986, and 1987 budget revisions, SBA was under a threat of elimination. However, when proponents demonstrated that particular programs had provided value (SBICs, SBDCs, guaranteed loans, and management assistance), the agency gained support to remain in place. Yet, realizing drastic budget cuts would continue, the agency initiated a revamping process.

With a shift in emphasis to management assistance, the SBA has realized the importance of joining forces with other organizations. This "coalition" involves networking with the Department of Commerce in each state to increase the political impact when needed. In addition, this coalition permits a greater outreach to all aspects of business organizations—unions, professional societies, universities, associations, and so on. The state commerce departments provide the economical development connections that begin to formulate a strong coalition.

Banks and Weidenbaum (1982:10) pointed out that

> The variety of regulation calls for a variety of reforms. In some instances, information rather than standards are needed, as in product safety. In other areas, reorientation is required toward setting goals rather than promulgating detailed requirements such as those for workplace safety. Virtually all regulatory programs would benefit from a more reasonable approach to weighing their costs and benefits and to setting priorities among regulatory programs so as to maximize the benefits derived.

In order for small business to receive assistance in this varied manner, the "coalition" idea should be utilized as a networking force affecting all aspects of small business. Each state understands the particulars of its businesses; each trade association understands the unique problems of its members; each professional society seeks the specific solutions for the difficulties of its membership; and each major university researches specific entrepreneurial problems. Thus, the initiative for a network is motivated by a desire to unite all of these forces in a working relationship for a common cause—small business.

The state Chambers of Commerce are in affiliation with the National Chamber of Commerce of the United States which in 1978 established a Council of Small Business and a Center for Small Busines. The Council includes individual state councils and processes a continuous information flow to small business executives regarding policy development in Washington. Small business thereby gains an opportunity to remain updated on regulations, labor laws, taxes and overall economic policy changes.

The National Chamber's Council is made up of fifty-eight small business and professional association executives. Its goals are :

1. To identify issues and concerns important to small business and make recommendations on National Chamber policies.
2. To develop programs to meet the needs of small business.
3. To advise the National Chamber on communication with smaller enterprises.

In accomplishing these goals, the National Chamber of Commerce unites with other entities to offer assistance and to espouse the small business ideals of self-sufficiency. In other words, small businesses are given help to help themselves. The ideal is to inform small businesspeople, counsel them, advocate for them, and promote them, while allowing their business to work without government influence—or at least, with less influence.

CONCLUSION

In its description of the Reagan administration, *The Brookings Review* (1982) states, "The United States is so diverse that an administration limited by rigid ideology could neither govern well nor long survive. Ronald Reagan was the candidate of coalition." This coalition idea has gained momentum for greater representation and aid to small businesses. It is the only means by which Washington will hear a strong voice from small business. It is also the only means by which all diverse aspects of the nation's small businesses can be considered. This is the hope for an entrepreneur's future in America.

If new legislation, new flexible regulatory ideas, and new understanding in Washington for small business policy all take effect, the vitality of small business and the American economy could by well on the way to a new recovery and entrepreneurial growth.

Thus, a genuine network is now emerging from all the ideas being generated across America. This "coalition" of action can and will encourage those engaged in small business to continue their efforts to accomplish what they do so well: create new ideas and new companies, develop jobs, initiate innovations, and promote the drive for the spirit of enterprise in America.

REFERENCES

Armington, C., and M. Odle. 1982. Small business—how many jobs? *The Brookings Review* (Winter):14-18.

Banks, E. and M. Weidenbaum. 1982. Reforming regulation. *Journal of Small Business Management* 20(January):9-14.

Beset, bothered, and beleaguered. 1980. *Nation's Business* (February):22-30.

Bonuses for small bussinesses. 1980. *Business Weekly* (November): 100-102.

Buchholz, Rogene A. 1982. *Business Environment and Public Policy.* Englewood Cliffs, N.J.: Prentice-Hall.

Carbone, T. 1982. Helping hand for small firms. *Management World* (February):33-34.

Chilton, K., and M. Weidenbaum. 1982. Government regulation: The small business burden. *Journal of Small Business Management* (January):4-10.

Creating the right environment for small firms: Government regulations. 1981. *Finance and Development* 18(December):33-36.

Easing regulatory burdens on small business. 1980. *Business Weekly* (June 16): 156-157.

The empty jelly bean jar. 1982. *Forbes* (January 18): 70-71.

Entrepreneurial economics. 1983. *Venture* (January):32-40.

Finegan, Jay. 1986. Cleaning house. *INC.* (June):33-34.

Gatzinger, G. 1982. Federal small business assistance: Review and preview. *Journal of Small Business Management* (January): 38-43.

Gray, R. 1978. Small business shows big clout. *Nation's Business* (September):25-29.
Hanley, R., et al. 1979. Hidden cost of federal energy legislation. *California Management Review* (Fall): 13-22.
Hard times on main street. 1981. *Time* (October 26): 60-61.
Heated debate over the SBA. 1986. *Nation's Business* (June):180.
Kilpatrick, J. J. 1981. Small business vs. goliath. *Nation's Business* 69 (November):18.
Lamont-Brown, R. 1980. Small businessmen and the financial paperwork bogey. (Britain). *Accountancy* 91 (May): 167.
Ledvinka, J., and V. Scarpello. 1982. Surviving an EEO lawsuit. *S.A.M. Advanced Management Journal* (Summer):22-30.
Looser SEC reins on smaller companies. 1980. *Business Weekly* (October):47-48.
More banks give small firms a break. 1981. *Industry Week* (January 26): 93-94.
Pellegrini, M. 1983. Small business has got a friend in Pennsylvania. *Pittsburgh Business Journal* (January 17): 1-14.
SBA on the spot—again (The White House tries to eliminate the Small Business Administration). 1986. *Nation's Business* (April):15.
Schultz, Frederick N. 1981. Statement before committee on small business, U.S. House of Representatives. *Federal Reserve Bulletin* (April):3-17.
Schwartz, L. 1980. Government paperwork costs small business firms $10 billion a year; SBA finds. *Electronic* 26 (January): supp. 65.
Small business and government: A call to arms. 1980. *Entrepreneur* 8 (April): 22-25.
Small business: Fighting to stay alive. 1980. *Nation's Business* (July):33-36.
Small business: Major Senate compromise negotiated to retain SBA programs through 1988. 1985. *Journal of Accountancy* (July):18.
Solomn, George. Does the SBA satisfy the informational needs of small business? 1985. *Journal of Small Business Management* (October):67-70.
Taking the small firm into account. 1982. *Nation's Business* (December):30.
Taylor, R. A. 1981. Small businesses' turn for relief from red-tape. *U.S. News* 91 (October): 85.
Thoryn, N. 1982. A fairer shake for small business (Equal Access to Justice and Regulatory Flexibility Acts). 1982. *Nation's Business* 70 (February): 39-40.
Weidenbaum, Murray L. 1986. *Business, government and the public.* Englewood Cliffs, N.J.: Prentice-Hall.
When disaster strikes—wait. 1980. *Nation's Business* (August):65-68.
Whether small firms are sufficiently different from large ones to justify special policy treatment. 1981. *Three Bonds* (June):50-51.

Small Business Acts

Small Business Investment Act of 1978: report to accompany H.R.-11318. 1978-27096.
Small Business Administration and Investment Act: with amendments 1953. 1978-11949.

Small Business Administration and Investment Act: with amendments 1953-1976. 1979-18943.

The Regulatory Flexibility Act: report to accompany S. 1979-3420.

Small Business—Law and Legislation: H.R. 7739 and H.R. 10632, *Small Business Impact Bill:* hearings before the subcommittee on special small business, House of Representatives, 95th Congress, 2nd session. 1979-9137.

Small Business Innovation Act of 1980: report to accompany H.R. 5607/1980-17256.

Small Business Development Act of 1980: report to accompany S. 2698/1980-22492.

Small Business Equal Access to Justice Act: report together with additional views to accompany H.R. 6429/1980-19156.

Regulatory Flexibility Act: (An act to amend title 5, U.S. code, to improve Federal Rulemaking by creating procedures to analyze the availability of more flexible regulatory approaches for small entities, and for other purposes.) 1981-3561.

III

PUBLIC POLICY IMPLICATIONS FOR SMALL BUSINESS

9 Firm Size and Productivity Growth in Manufacturing Industries

STEVEN A. LUSTGARTEN

Growth of productivity is a major source of economic progress and rising living standards. An important area for public policy research is the impact of firm size on productivity growth. Are small firms or large firms more suited to rapid innovation and introduction of cost-saving techniques that contribute to economic growth? If firm size does affect productivity growth, then these effects must be considered in the formulation of public policy toward different-sized firms. If large firms are more able to generate productivity growth, then antitrust or antimerger policies that restrict the growth of firms can have potentially harmful effects. On the other hand, if small firms are more suited to advancing productivity, the policies that promote the number of small firms will have beneficial effects.

This chapter compares the long-term rate of productivity growth in industries with different average firm sizes. Comparisons are made between firms in different industries rather than between firms in the same industry. The reason is that differences in productivity growth between firms in the same industry cannot persist for long before the lower productivity growth firms become uncompetitive and are driven out of the industry. This chapter also computes labor productivity, a popular measure of productivity growth, with total factor productivity growth. Total factor productivity growth is a more accurate measure of technical progress.

Productivity growth in any short period of time is likely to be very small and subject to random forces. It may be unusually high in some years and unusually low in other years. In order to detect differences in productivity growth attributable to firm size, productivity must be measured over a very long period of time. This study examines productivity growth over the period 1947–1972. Although the data collected to perform this study are many years old, the attributes of small firms that have affected their productivity in the past are likely to continue to affect their productivity in the future.

MEASURING PRODUCTIVITY GROWTH: SAMPLE SELECTION AND DATA SOURCES

Productivity is the ratio of output to input. Productivity growth is the difference between the rate of output growth and input growth. If output increases faster than input, then productivity will be positive. In order to compute productivity growth, we must measure both output and input growth. This section discusses how measures of input and output were obtained. It then discusses the growth rate of output and several different inputs.

Sample Selection

A problem in constructing a sample of industries for measuring productivity growth is that industries whose definition is narrow enough to produce wide variations in average firm sizes (e.g., four-digit Standard Industrial Classification [SIC] codes) often tend not to be comparable over time. Because new products and industries appear and old ones die, the Census Bureau periodically revises the SIC system at the four-digit level. The use of four-digit industries thus limits the sample to those industries whose definitions are unchanged over the period of the study. Since productivity growth should be measured over a long period in order to capture the secular trend rather than cyclical or periodic influences, the investigator is usually forced to sacrifice a large sample size for a long time period.

The approach followed in this study was to measure productivity growth over time periods of moderate length and to pool these together. Specifically, productivity growth was measured for four-digit SIC industries for five time periods corresponding to consecutive census years from 1947 to 1972. Each industry which was consistent between any two consecutive census years was included in the sample even if the industry did not exist in prior or later census years. Thus, each sample observation was for an industry in one time period, and each industry could be an observation up to five times. Because the years between censuses were not always equal, all growth variables were expressed as annual rates of change. The sample contained data on 1,427 industry periods. These were five census periods (1947–54, 1954–58, 1958–63, 1963–67, and 1967–72) with an average of 285 industries per period.

Data Sources

Industry Output and Input. The measure of industry output used in this study is based on the benchmark indexes of production compiled for four-digit SIC industries by the Federal Reserve Board of Governors and the Bureau of the Census (1963; 1967; 1972) for those years in which a Census of Manufactures was conducted. The result represents constant dollar value added in each industry during census years.

Data on labor inputs and labor and nonlabor shares are derived from the four-digit industry statistics published in the Census of Manufactures for various years between 1947 and 1972. The census tabulates data on two types of labor inputs—production workers and nonproduction workers. The data on capital inputs were taken from the capital stock estimates compiled by the Bureau of Labor Statistics (1979) and are for two- and three-digit SIC industries. In using these capital stock estimates, the census assigned the growth rate of capital for a two- or three-digit industry to each of its component four-digit industries. This was done because data on the growth of capital inputs are not available at the four-digit level. Data on the share of capital were obtained from the *1963 Input Output Study for the U.S.*

Firm Size. Industry statistics at the four-digit level are assembled by the U.S. Census Bureau based on records from the individual establishments (i.e., plants) of each company. In the case of multiestablishment companies, each establishment is classified in an industry according to its primary product, regardless of where other establishments of the company are classified. The average firm size for each industry was computed by dividing the number of employees in the industry by the number of different firms who owned establishments. In each census period, the average of base and current year average industry firm size was used.

GROWTH OF INDUSTRY OUTPUT AND INPUT, 1947-72

Table 9.1 shows the mean rates of input and output growth for six firm size classes. The table shows that for all firm size classes there are dramatic differences between the rate of growth of different inputs. Specifically, there was almost no growth in production worker input (hereafter i_1), moderate growth in nonproduction worker labor input (hereafter i_2), and very high growth in capital input (hereafter i_3). In each size class, the rate of growth of capital exceeded the rate of growth of output, whereas the rate of growth of labor fell short of the rate of growth of output. The divergence between the growth rates of labor and capital inputs indicates that great care must be taken when labor productivity growth is used to assess economic performance. Growth in labor produc-

Table 9.1
Average Annual Percentage Rates of Growth[1] of Factor Inputs and Industry Output for Manufacturing Industries Classified by Industry Average Firm Size

Average Firm Size[2]	Number of Observations	Industry Output	Production Worker Man Hours	Non-Production Workers	Net Capital Stock[3]	Other Non-Labor Input
0 - 19	145	3.45 (5.41)	.41 (4.94)	1.25 (5.67)	3.79 (2.82)	1.34 (5.48)
20 - 49	380	3.31 (5.09)	.24 (4.39)	1.20 (5.85)	3.90 (3.03)	1.21 (4.90)
50 - 99	355	3.52 (5.34)	.15 (4.91)	1.59 (4.83)	4.73 (3.25)	1.47 (5.45)
100 - 249	290	3.80 (5.14)	.33 (4.51)	1.99 (4.90)	4.69 (3.21)	1.17 (4.91)
250 - 499	137	4.33 (4.73)	.60 (3.90)	1.61 (4.76)	4.45 (3.27)	1.76 (4.51)
500 & over	120	4.16 (7.13)	-.29 (6.25)	0.75 (6.84)	5.04 (3.64)	1.64 (6.55)
All	1427	3.65 (5.36)	.24 (4.25)	1.47 (5.38)	4.41 (3.20)	1.47 (5.22)

[1] Standard deviation in parenthesis.
[2] Based on establishment data, average firm size is total industry employment divided by number of firms in the industry.
[3] Adjusted for capacity utilization.
SOURCE: Output: Federal Reserve Board of Governors and Bureau of the Census, *Indexes of Production*.
Inputs: All inputs except for capital stock, U.S. Bureau of the Census, *Census of Manufactures*; capital stock, U.S. Department of Labor, BLS, *Capital Stock Estimates for Input Output Industries*.

tivity will reflect the substitution of capital for labor as well as technical change. Because the rate of growth of capital was nearly tenfold the rate of growth of labor, the potential impact of factor substitution is substantial.

Table 9.1 also reveals important differences between the rates of growth of capital and labor in the different firm size groups. Most significant is the fact that the rate of growth of capital input was 3.79 percent per year for the smallest firm size group and 5.04 percent per year for the largest. This represents a 25-percent difference in growth rates of capital. On the other hand, production worker labor declined by 0.29 percent per year in the largest firm size class. The rate of growth of capital increased nearly monotonically as firm size increased, whereas the pattern for labor input was more erratic. Although the growth of labor input was lowest for the largest firm size class, it was not highest in the smallest firm size class. Nevertheless, the substantially higher growth of capital for the larger firms indicates that, as a measure of economic performance, labor productivity will be biased against small firms.

Average Factors Shares

In order to further ascertain the magnitude of the potential bias against small firms inherent in labor productivity, it is necessary to compare the factor shares of labor and capital in each of the firm size classes. These are shown in Table 9.2. The table shows that small firms have a relatively high labor share and a relatively low nonlabor share. The nonlabor share is broken into two parts: capital and purchased services. The reason for the breakdown of nonlabor share is that the census definition of value added includes, in addition to payroll and capital costs, outlays for the purchase of business services such as advertising expense, insurance, patent fees, outside R&D, management consulting, maintenance and repair, and telephone as well as state and local taxes. Thus, the nonlabor share of census value added greatly overstates the share of capital. In order to correct for this problem, a part of each industry's nonlabor share was treated as additional purchased inputs. This was accomplished by computing the difference between the industry's value added according to the 1963 Census of Manufactures and its value added in the 1963 Input Output (I/O) Table. The I/O follows the national income concept of value added and excludes the above-mentioned business services. Capital's share was obtained by subtracting the difference between census and I/O value added from the nonlabor share of census value added.[1]

The rate of growth (plus one) of the purchased business service inputs (hereafter i_4) was computed by deflating the gross change in expenditure for these inputs by a price index for services (the Consumer Price Index

Table 9.2
Average Factor Shares Classified by Industry Average Firm Size

Average Firm Size[1]	Share of Production Worker Wages[2]	Share of Non-production Worker Salaries	Non-Labor Share Total	Non-Labor Share Capital	Non-Labor Share Purchased Service
0 - 19	.412 (.098)	.156 (.045)	.432 (.085)	.256 (.113)	.176 (.179)
20 - 49	.370 (.104)	.162 (.043)	.468 (.097)	.275 (.135)	.193 (.091)
50 - 99	.369 (.086)	.159 (.048)	.473 (.086)	.292 (.113)	.181 (.080)
100 - 249	.367 (.100)	.138 (.044)	.495 (.105)	.329 (.134)	.166 (.078)
250 - 499	.362 (.128)	.131 (.058)	.507 (.149)	.371 (.166)	.137 (.066)
500 & over	.361 (.080)	.133 (.068)	.506 (.121)	.365 (.137)	.141 (.070)
All	.372 (.100)	.151 (.050)	.478 (.105)	.305 (.174)	.173 (.082)

[1] Average number of employees per firm.
[2] Standard deviation in parenthesis.
SOURCE: U.S. Bureau of the Census, Census of Manufactures. Data are averages for 1947-72 for 4-digit SIC industries.

for services less rent services was used).² The mean rate of growth in this input is shown for each firm size group in the last column of Table 9.1.

The importance of accounting for the inputs represented by i_4 can be understood by noting that the benchmark indexes of output, which form the numerator of the productivity measures, are based on the census definition of value added. Therefore, increases in these inputs contribute to the measured growth in output, and they must be accounted for in measuring the growth of inputs in order to have a consistent measure of productivity.

Computation of Productivity Growth

Two estimates of labor productivity and two estimates of total factor productivity were computed. The first measure (*LP*1) is a geometrically weighted average of the rate of growth of production worker man hours (i_1) and nonproduction workers (i_2), where the weights are their respective shares of total payroll (a_1 and $1-a_1$). With Q as output growth, the first measure of labor productivity is thus:

$$LP1 = \dot{Q} / i_1^{a_1} i_2^{1-a}$$

The second measure of labor productivity growth (*LP*2) is simply output growth divided by total employment growth. Total employment includes the number of production workers plus nonproduction workers.

The first measure of total factor productivity growth (*TP*1) uses the capital stock estimates from *Capital Stock Estimates for Input Output Industries* (i_3) as discussed above (mean values shown in Table 9.1, col. 6) as well as the growth in purchased services (i_4) (mean values shown in Table 9.1, col. 7) It is computed as:

$$TP1 = \dot{Q} / i_1^{b_1} i_2^{b_2} i_3^{b_3} i_4^{1-b_1-b_2-b_3}$$

A second measure of total factor productivity growth (*TP*2) uses a measure of capital input (i_5) derived by taking the growth of total expenditures on nonlabor inputs (value added minus payroll) and deflating by the gross national product (GNP) implicit deflator for fixed investment. The weight for capital is the share of value added that is not production worker wages (b_1) or nonproduction worker salaries (b_2). Therefore, the computation of *TP*2 is:

$$TP2 = \dot{Q} / i_1^{b_1} i_2^{b_2} i_5^{1-b_1-b_2}$$

In computing *TP*1 and *TP*2, we adjusted i_3 and i_5 to reflect changes in capacity utilization.³ The reason is that the growth of capital should include not only additions to the stock of capital, but also capital in place that was utilized in the current period but not in the base period (or the reverse).

The logic of using two measures of total factor productivity growth is that each can compensate for a deficiency in the other. The deficiency in *TP*1 is that capital input is measured at the two-digit and three-digit level of aggregation rather than at the four-digit level as all the other inputs and outputs. A second problem with *TP*1 is the inaccuracies in measuring the share of capital because of peculiarities in the *Input Output Table*. *TP*2 on the other hand uses four-digit census data in measuring all the inputs but measures the growth of what can be viewed as "expenditures for nonlabor input services" rather than the growth of actual capital inputs. The logic behind *TP*2 is that all nonpayroll expenses represent purchases of nonlabor inputs (capital, business services, etc.) whose prices change at the same rate for all firms.[4]

RATES OF PRODUCTIVITY GROWTH BY FIRM SIZE CLASS

Analysis by Size Class Mean

The mean values for four alternative measures of productivity growth are shown in Table 9.3 for the six firm size classes. In terms of the growth of labor productivity, industries dominated by large firms outperform those dominated by small firms. In fact, both measures of labor productivity growth increase nearly monotonically with firm size. The difference in growth in labor productivity between the smallest and the largest firm size classes is 1.32 percent per year when we use *LP*1 and 1.49 percent when we use *LP*2. The rate of growth of labor productivity is roughly 40 percent higher among the largest firm size class as compared to the smallest firm size class.

Using total factor productivity gives a much different picture. Although the largest size class still had higher productivity growth, the difference between the largest and smallest is much smaller and the pattern of firm size and productivity growth among the six firm size groups is U-shaped rather than monotonically increasing. For both *TP*1 and *TP*2, the smallest firm size class had higher productivity growth than the next three firm size classes.

These results are consistent with the theory that labor productivity growth is larger for large firms mainly because they are more capital intensive and because the rate of growth of capital was greater than the rate of growth of labor for all firms over the period 1947–72. Larger firms as well as smaller firms were substituting capital for labor, but the effect was greater among the more capital-intensive firms.

Table 9.3
Average Annual Percentage Rates of Productivity Growth for Manufacturing Industries Classified by Industry Average Firm Size

Average Firm Size[1]	Number of Industries[2]	Output per Unit of Labor (LP1)	Output per Employee (LP2)	Output per Unit of Total Factor[3] (TP1)	Output per Unit of Total Factor[4] (TP2)
0 - 19	145	2.84 (2.43)	2.71 (2.42)	1.79 (2.54)	1.62 (2.56)
20 - 49	380	2.77 (2.67)	2.67 (2.39)	1.64 (2.63)	1.46 (2.59)
50 - 99	355	2.95 (2.65)	3.01 (2.69)	1.52 (2.96)	1.32 (2.78)
100 - 249	290	3.02 (2.44)	3.08 (2.50)	1.51 (2.72)	1.52 (2.67)
250 - 499	137	3.48 (2.92)	3.67 (2.92)	1.78 (2.86)	1.69 (2.99)
500 & over	120	4.16 (3.02)	4.20 (3.03)	1.95 (3.26)	2.11 (3.21)
All	1427	3.06 (2.67)	3.07 (2.64)	1.64 (2.75)	1.53 (2.75)

[1] Based on establishment data.
[2] 4-digit level.
[3] Uses capital stock data at 2- and 3-digit level.
[4] Using deflated nonlabor value added for estimating capital stock.
SOURCE: Tables 9.1 and 9.2.

150 / Public Policy Implications

Regression Equations

In order to determine whether the relation between productivity growth and firm size suggested in Table 9.3 is statistically significant, ordinary least square regression equations were estimated. In each equation, the dependent variable was productivity growth and the independent variables were as follows:

T_1 Time dummy equal to 1 for the 1937-54 period and zero otherwise.
T_2 Time dummy equal to 1 for the 1954-58 period and zero otherwise.
T_3 Time dummy equal to 1 for the 1958-63 period and zero otherwise.
T_4 Time dummy equal to 1 for the 1963-67 period and zero otherwise.
FS   Average number of employees per firm.
FS**2   Square of FS.
CS   Nonlabor share of value added.
DCS   Change in nonlabor share of value added.
CS*DCS   Product of CS and DCS.
DW   Change in average wage rate.
UT   Change in capacity utilization.

Time dummies are used because not every industry is used in each time period. If there are differences in the frequency with which different firm sizes appear in the sample in different time periods, as well as differences in economy-wide productivity growth between time periods, it is possible that some of the effect of time could be attributed to firm size. The use of time dummies will prevent the variable of firm size from exercising such a strong influence in the determination of economy-wide productivity growth. The square of firm size is included to allow for the quadratic or U-shaped relationship which Table 9.3 suggests. The variables CS, DCS, and CS*DCS are included in the labor productivity equations to adjust for differences in capital intensity and growth of capital. This represents an attempt to adjust LP for its bias which arises because capital is not considered. The variable CS is a proxy for capital's share, and DCS is a proxy for growth of capital inputs. Both CS and DCS are employed because the impact of capital input on productivity depends on the magnitude of capital's share as well as on capital's rate of growth. The interaction term (DC*CS) is included because the impact of capital input growth and capital share is expected to be nonlinear. The change in capacity utilization (UT) is included because each of the time periods is of moderate length and the reduction (increase) of excess capacity could represent an increase (decrease) in capital input. The change in the wage rate (DW) is introduced as a proxy for a change in the skill of labor input which should be viewed as a change in the amount of human capital. Because data on human capital are not available, human capital input was not included in the computation of either measure of productivity growth. The proxy is intended to compensate for this neglect.

If the relation between productivity growth and firm size has a U shape, there should be a negative coefficient on *FS* and a positive coefficient on *FS**2*. In Table 9.4, only the equation using *TP1* gives any support to the U shape, but the support is weak because neither coefficient is statistically significant. Using the other productivity measures yields a positive sign on *FS* and a negative but insignificant coefficient on *FS**2*. The other independent variables in Table 9.4 behave about as expected. The variables *CS* and *CS*DCS* are highly significant and indicate that the more capital-intensive industries had higher labor productivity growth. Since *DCS* alone was not significant, the regressions indicate that growth in capital's share increases labor productivity growth only in proportion to the average share of capital. This is also expected. But the significant coefficient on *CS* indicates that capital's share has an effect that is independent of its growth rate. *DCS* may therefore be a poor proxy for capital input growth, and *CS* may capture some of its effect. The dummies indicate that the highest productivity growth took place during 1947–54 and 1958–63.

The regression coefficients indicate that increased capacity utilization raises labor productivity growth but lowers total factor productivity growth. This difference is not unexpected. In the labor productivity equations, increased capacity utilization reflects additional capital input and should raise the productivity of labor.

However, since both *TP1* and *TP2* include capital that is already adjusted for capacity utilization, increased utilization probably indicates the use of lower quality or otherwise less productive resources. This could mean the use of less skilled labor or less modern machinery, both of which would lower productivity growth. The regressions also show that higher wage rates increase productivity growth. This effect is also as expected, since higher wages indicate that the level of labor skills is higher. However, only in the case of *LP1* are any of the dummies statistically significant.

The regression equations indicate that firm size has a statistically significant effect on raising productivity growth. However, the magnitude of this effect is modest. Note that the mean values of productivity growth were 3.06 percent per year and 1.64 percent per year for *LP1* and *TP1*, respectively. Now, on the basis of the regression coefficient of *LP1* in the first equation of Table 9.4, a difference in average firm size of 500 employees (which covers the range of Table 9.3) leads to a difference in *LP1* of 0.36 percent per year. When we use the coefficients of *TP1* in the second equation of Table 9.4, we see that a difference of firm size of 500 employees

Table 9.4
Regression Equations Relating Average Firm Size and Productivity Growth Using Continuous Variables for Firm Size (t Ratio in Parenthesis)

Dependent Variable	FS	FS**2	CS	DCS	CS**DCS	T1	T2	T3	T4	UT	DW	R2
LP1	.072 (4.160)		4.040 (6.140)	-.105 (1.010)	1.140 (4.600)	1.160 (4.520)	0.700 (1.950)	1.750 (6.040)	0.820 (3.230)	0.186 (2.900)	0.364 (6.080)	.219
TP1	.045 (2.560)					0.093 (0.327)	0.570 (1.950)	2.150 (6.580)	0.819 (2.850)	-0.045 (0.620)	0.218 (3.300)	.052
TP2	.067 (4.040)					1.360 (5.120)	0.430 (1.580)	0.067 (0.222)	-0.248 (0.925)	-0.277 (4.070)	0.070 (1.130)	.163
LP1	.095 (3.200)	-.0007 (0.8700)	3.970 (6.000)	-.107 (1.030)	1.140 (4.610)	1.160 (4.540)	0.697 (2.700)	1.740 (6.000)	0.810 (3.200)	0.187 (2.920)	0.362 (6.030)	.220
TP1	-.001 (.020)	.0010 (1.6300)				0.070 (0.260)	0.580 (1.990)	2.180 (6.650)	0.840 (2.920)	-0.048 (0.660)	0.226 (3.400)	.053
TP2	.100	-.0010				1.380	0.423	0.050	-0.262	-0.274	0.065	.163
Mean Values (SD)	1.920 (4.050)	20.1300 (148.7000)	0.478 (0.105)	0.760 (2.500)	0.333 (1.040)	0.203 (0.403)	0.131 (0.330)	0.227 (0.419)	0.235 (1.424)	0.401 (1.900)	4.350 (1.610)	

Critical t-value for the 0.05 significance level is 1.96.
Critical t-value for the 0.01 significance level is 2.58.
See Table 9.3 for mean values and standard deviations of the dependent variables.
Number of observations is 1,427.
FS is measured in hundreds (i.e., 1.92 = 192 employees).
Hypothesized Signs: CS > 0, DCS > 0, CS*DCS > 0, T1-T4 ≥ 0, UT > 0 for LP and UT < 0 for TP, DW > 0

leads to a difference in *TP*1 of 0.23 percent per year. In other words, an industry with an average firm size of 510 employees could be expected to have labor productivity that is 0.36 percent higher per year and total factor productivity 0.23 percent higher per year than an industry with an average firm size of ten employees.

CONCLUSION

This study found no statistically significant evidence that industries belonging to the smallest firm size class have had higher productivity growth than other industries. It did find some evidence that the largest firm size class of industries had moderately higher productivity growth than other industries.

Historically, public policies have been proposed that would limit the growth of firms. One type of policy is an antimerger policy that would prevent a merger between large firms, even if the merging firms were not direct competitors. Another type of policy that has been proposed is industrial deconcentration legislation which would restructure major segments of U.S. industry through divestiture. The results of this study suggest that such policies will have the effect of lowering productivity growth.

The results of this study also suggest that higher productivity growth and the falling output prices which they may ultimately generate may offset any tendency of large firms to monopolize industries when they gain a large market share. Thus, even if the large firms are able to earn abnormally high profits, consumers may still be better off in the long run if, in response to higher productivity growth, firms can raise their profits by lowering prices as production costs fall.

NOTES

1. Unfortunately, the share of capital is probably still overstated for many industries because the Input Output Table tends to overstate the value added in many manufacturing establishments by including excise taxes as part of value added. In a few four-digit industries, the result is that the value added, according to the I/O definition, exceeds value added in the Census of Manufactures. These industries were excluded from the sample. In computing the share of value added represented by purchased business services (b_3 in the equation for *TP*1 below), we must assume that the share computed for 1963 was constant for all other years. Inspection of the data indicates that for many industries this cannot be the case because the implied share of capital will be less than zero. These industries were also excluded from the sample.

2. Because business services were assumed to be a constant proportion of value added, the input i_4 is simply the change in industry value added deflated by the price index for services.

3. The Wharton Index of Capacity Utilization was used. The adjustment was to multiply the index of capital input growth by the index of capacity utilization with the same base year. The effect of this adjustment was to raise capital input when utilization increased and reduce capital input when utilization declined.

4. Another feature of *TP2* is that it treats business profit as a nonlabor input. Increases in profits, at a rate above the capital goods price index, are implicitly treated as increased capital input. A bias could arise here if the rate of profit (the price of capital inputs) rose or fell in large firms relative to small firms because cost savings owing to "true" total factor productivity growth were not completely reflected in the selling prices of industry output. But this is unlikely in the long run since it would require continuously rising profits.

REFERENCES

U.S. Bureau of the Census. 1975. *Census of manufactures and mineral industries, 1967, special report series: Indexes of production.* MC67(s)-6. Washington, D.C.: U.S. Government Printing Office.

U.S. Bureau of the Census. 1977. *Census of manufactures, 1972, vol. 4, indexes of production.* Washington, D.C.: U.S. Government Printing Office.

U.S. Bureau of the Census and the Board of Governors of the Federal Reserve System. 1968. *Census of manufactures, 1963, vol. 4, indexes of production.* Washington, D.C.: U.S. Government Printing Office.

U.S. Department of Labor, Bureau of Labor Statistics. 1979. *Capital stock estimates for input-output industries: Methods and data.* Bulletin 2034. Washington, D.C.: U.S. Government Printing Office.

10 Encouraging Small Business Startups: An Alternative to Smokestack Chasing?

BENJAMIN W. MOKRY

Scholars interested in urban economic development have long criticized the "smokestack chasing" policy as being an ineffective way of promoting economic growth (Ledebur and Hamilton 1986; Cornia et al. 1978). In response, a new orthodoxy appears to be emerging which makes it politically fashionable to propose that governments should concentrate more of their development resources on small, new, preferably high tech firms (Balderston 1986; *Governor's Weekly Bulletin* 1986). The argument is that young firms with fewer than twenty employees create most of the net new jobs in the country, are more likely to be in "sunrise" sectors, and are most likely to need and benefit from government help (Pierce and Steinback 1981; Harris 1984).[1]

This new model for development policy can be called "entrepreneurial" because it requires local governments to serve business in innovative ways and to do more than simply pick up the trash on time (Bearse 1976; Vaughan 1986). Included are activities such as encouraging the development of venture capital pools, organizing small business incubators, creating information clearinghouses on business services, appointing ombudsmen to cut red tape, and becoming advocates of small business (Litvak and Daniels 1979; Vaughan, Pollard, and Dyer 1984).

The existence of such policies may impress potential entrepreneurs in two ways. First, providing resources to businesses helps some get underway that might not have otherwise. More startups might therefore occur. Second, entrepreneurial policies may improve the general climate for entrepreneurship in a locality. Albert Shapero argues that if we are interested in renewing older industrial centers or in maintaining a strong economic base in any community, we should concentrate on "new and developing firms ... [on] diversity and reduced dependence in any community or region on one or a few sectors of economic activity ... [and] on creating the ecological conditions conducive to new company formations" (1981; see also Doctors and Wokutch 1983).

A number of writers assert that the nature of a community's policies creates a "business climate" that promotes or stifles investment (Butler 1981; Downs 1978). By offering policies helpful to small new firms, governments encourage more people to think of the area as a good place to do business. People on the verge of starting a firm but who are uncertain might be encouraged to go ahead if government and private interests are known to be actively working to improve conditions for small, young firms. If governments could improve the startup and survival rates of new businesses, they would increase the options available to economic developers. Instead of chasing after the relative handful of corporate plants built each year, developers could concentrate their efforts on assisting local entrepreneurs, with wider impacts on the local economy (Widner 1980; Vaughan, Pollard, and Dyer 1984). Although the idea of encouraging indigenous entrepreneurs by local policy efforts is appealing, one must be skeptical about the ability of local governments to change the balance of incentives facing potential entrepreneurs. The startup decision is the outcome of a long process (Shapero and Sokol 1982), and only a few of the variables are subject to government manipulation. Furthermore, the autonomy of local governments is limited, making it difficult for them to act innovatively (Zimmerman 1981). It is therefore worth examining how sensitive entrepreneurs are to changes in local public policies, especially when they are constrained by the legal and resource limits of existing state and federal development programs. Two studies have examined the impact of development policy on business startups and conclude either that policy has no impact on births (Carlton 1980) or that low-tax, low-service governments provide the best environment for births (Pennings 1982b). These findings contradict the expectations of the entrepreneurial model, but further research is needed. Both studies operationalized policy variables in a way that made it difficult to separate policy effects from those of other factors. In addition, neither study considered the impact of policies of the sort outlined above.

This study examines startup rates under different policy climates using data from counties in New York, Pennsylvania, and Michigan. The specific question addressed is whether policies helpful to small firms encourage more startups.

METHODOLOGY

To determine whether adopting entrepreneurial policies produces more business starts, we compared birthrates in a county that was helpful to young firms to birthrates in a similar county that offered little help to such firms.[2] Here these two counties are called the case study counties. To improve what Cook and Campbell (1979) call the external validity of the study and control for such events as business cycles, we compared births in these two counties to those in five similar counties, here called baseline counties, in the states of New York, Pennsylvania, and Michigan.

We identified the baseline counties by using a hierarchical clustering procedure to group case study and baseline counties on the variables identified above.[3] Because the baseline counties come from states with varying political and economic conditions, averaging birthrates across them produces a data series that reasonably summarizes birthrates in northern industrial counties as they are affected by national economic trends.

Information was collected on the development policies in use in the two case study counties,[4] and an effort was made to determine how fully each county addressed four needs of startup firms: access to capital, information on supplier and buyer markets, managerial assistance, and a positive political climate (Kieschnick 1979; Vaughan, Pollard, and Dyer 1984). A county was considered to be more entrepreneurial if it adopted more of the policies helpful to small firms. The policies defined as entrepreneurial are listed in Table 10.1.

Policies in the two case study counties are described below. The purpose is to show how policies in the high-effort site differ from those in the low-effort one.

DEVELOPMENT POLICIES

Of seven New York counties initially contacted, Oneida County in central New York proved to be the most innovative. Financing in the county is significantly more likely to go to younger and smaller firms than financing in the comparison county, Niagara, in western New York. Two types of financing were examined; revolving loan funds (RLFs) and industrial revenue bonds (IRBs). Oneida has four RLFs to Niagara's one; IRBs are the principal form of financing in Niagara, and they are used here to represent that county's financial assistance efforts. It is significantly more likely that firms three years or younger will receive financial assistance from Oneida's RLFs than from Niagara's IRBs (phi square = 0.29, $p = 0.001$).

It is also significantly more likely that Oneida's financing rather than Niagara's will go to firms with fewer than twenty employees (phi square = $0.36, p = 0.001$). Oneida's other loan programs (IRBs and SBA guaranteed loans) are also more likely to go to smaller firms than Niagara's IRB loans (phi square = $0.39, p = 0.001$). These figures show that Oneida is offering more financial help to young firms than Niagara is. The counties also dif-

Table 10.1
Operating Definition of Policy Entrepreneurship

Policy Innovativeness

    Availability of Equity or Equity-like funds

    Efforts to assemble public or joint public-private equity funds locally

    Willingness of local developers to risk some of their resources on small or new firms

    Creation of Incubator Facilities for new or young firms

    Availability and nature of small business technical assistance

Small Business Targeting

    Presence of an explicit small business component in the local development organization

    Amount of staff resources devoted to small firm concerns

    Percentage of capital funds channeled through development organizations into young ventures less than 3 years old

Policy Commitment

    Support of local governmental bodies for economic development
      -public monies channeled into loan programs
      -public monies supporting local development organizations

    Characteristics of public support
      -level of funding
      -stability and trends in public monies going to development matters
      -year in which programs first used locally

    Cooperation of county and municipal officials on economic development

    Working relations between economic developers and elected officials

    Working relations among economic developers

fer as to the amount of managerial assistance provided. Oneida County Industrial Development Corporation (OCIDC) created a position in 1979 which was responsible for organizing small business seminars, providing information and helping to arrange financing, and assembling business plans. OCIDC has been consulted by up to 120 individuals or small firms annually, as many as thirty of them being startup situations. Other development agencies in the county also provide such assistance. Niagara, on the other hand, had no staff devoted to helping small firms on management and financial matters between 1975 and 1982. The political climate in Oneida and Niagara also differed. A significant improvement in Oneida's climate occurred after 1977. Before then, the mayor of Utica (the largest city in the county) and the county executive feuded, and developers in the various public and private agencies in the county did not work together regularly. A new mayor and county executive elected in 1977 changed staff in several development organizations and channeled more funding into economic development projects.

Niagara's development apparatus was underfunded and poorly organized up to 1981. The county legislature was reluctant to put much money into development or to set up a strong development organization at the county level. Countywide efforts were carried out in an industrial development agency; its staff concentrated on placing IRBs which tended to go to larger, more established firms. The city of Niagara Falls was active in development but concentrated its efforts on completing projects begun under urban renewal rather than on new firm creation. A great deal of effort was spent on a large enclosed shopping mall downtown. This project had an innovative feature that provided seed money for new retail shops, but it was limited to mall tenants and did not get underway until after 1981, too late to have an impact during the study period.

EXPECTED POLICY IMPACTS IN THE CASE STUDY COUNTIES

Oneida has been energetic, fairly innovative, and risk oriented in its development promotion efforts. In contrast, Niagara has little to offer small new firms. If resources and political climate do influence business startup decisions, an increase in the rate of startups in Oneida after 1978 should be observed while little change occurs in Niagara.

EVIDENCE ON BIRTHRATES

Data were collected on business births in selected manufacturing and service industries. Twenty-four manufacturing SIC (Standard Industrial Classification) firms were subdivided into the following categories: high technology, small business dominated, and mature manufacturing. Twenty-seven service industry SIC firms were grouped into personal services, wholesaling, and business services. Each industry grouping contained between seven and fourteen three-digit SIC firms. (A list of the specific industries used is available from the author on request.)

The business birthrate was measured with the following formula:

$$\text{Birthrate} = \frac{\text{Firms 0-to-1 year old in SIC}}{\text{Employees in SIC}} \times 1000$$

Dun and Bradstreet records for the selected three-digit SIC firms in the years 1976, 1978, 1980, and 1982 were scanned to identify the number of firms in which the business age was less than or equal to one year. This number (which was used as the number of measured births) was divided by the number of employees in that three-digit SIC in 1975 (for 1976 and 1978 birth years) and in 1979 (for 1980 and 1982 birth years). The result was then multiplied by 1,000, giving the number of firms created per 1,000 employess.

Employment was used as a denominator to control for the size of an industry in an area and to take into account the fact that new businesses are most often started by individuals already working in the industry (Cross 1981).

Two outcome measures were examined: (1) differences in the mean level of births by industry grouping in 1980 and 1982, and (2) change scores calculated between mean 1978 and 1980 birthrates and mean 1980 and 1982 birthrates. These measures were evaluated using one-way analysis of variance (ANOVA) with type of county policy (high or low effort or baseline county) as the single predictor variable.[5]

FINDINGS

The entrepreneurial model would suggest that Oneida should experience significantly higher birthrates than both Niagara and the baseline in 1980 and 1982. To test whether this happens, the variance explained by location was partitioned into components associated with specific contrasts: Oneida-versus-Niagara, Oneida-versus-baseline, and Niagara-versus-baseline. Partitioning variance into components helps to determine which pair of locations had significantly different birthrates. The larger the difference between two sites, the more that pair would contribute to explaining the variance of the birthrate variable. If Oneida's birthrate was higher and significantly different from the one in Niagara and the

Table 10.2
Effect of Location on Mean Birthrates: First Location Compared to Second

F Value (p = .10)

	Oneida–Niagara 1980 1982	Oneida–Baseline 1980	Oneida–Baseline 1982	Niagara–Baseline 1980	Niagara–Baseline 1982
Business Services					
High Technology Manufacturing		3.2** (.08)	4.6** (.04)		
Mature Manufacturing	4.7* (.03)			12.2* (.001)	
Personal Services					
Small Firm Manufacturing		6.95** (.01)			
Wholesaling	9.7* (.003)		17.0* (.0001)	6.3* (.02)	

* Niagara's birthrate was higher
** Oneida's birthrate was higher

baseline, we could be more confident that policy effort was in fact affecting entrepreneurial behavior in these counties. (For a discussion of the partitioning procedure, see D. G. Kleinbaum and L. L. Kipper 1978:277-283; and SAS Institute 1982:146-47.) The contrasts are presented in Table 10.2.

Table 10.2 presents F values and significance levels for individual contrasts between the two case study counties and the baseline average. The greatest differences between Oneida and Niagara for 1980 occurred in wholesaling and mature manufacturing. The contrast between Niagara and the baseline counties was also significant in these same industries in 1980. Examining plots of birthrate values revealed that Niagara had much higher birthrates for these two industries than either Oneida or the baseline counties.

Table 10.2 also shows that the contrast between Oneida and the baseline was significant for small firm industries in 1980. Oneida's birthrate was not significantly different from Niagara's in this industry, however. In 1982 Niagara's birthrate in wholesaling was significantly different from the baseline but not from Oneida's.

The upshot of these findings is that Oneida's mean level of births was not significantly different from Niagara's in any industry or year, although it was different from the baseline average in two industries in different years. These findings fail to support the expectations of the entrepreneurial model. Oneida's more innovative efforts did not lead to significantly higher birthrates than Niagara experienced. The fact that Oneida's birthrate was higher than the baseline average in two industries while it was not significantly different from Niagara's probably indicates that New York State's economic climate was better than that of other northern states for these industries.

Oneida's births may be naturally lower than Niagara's, and comparing their mean levels of births is inappropriate. Another way to examine Oneida's performance is to compare the increase in Oneida's birthrate to that of Niagara. To test the hypothesis that Oneida's rate of increase is higher, we can employ a change score analysis (Reichardt 1979). Birthrates in 1978 and 1980 were subtracted from the rates for 1980 and 1982, respectively. The differences were then analyzed using one-way ANOVA.

Table 10.3 shows significant F values for the change score analysis. Values are listed when one location's increase in birthrates was significantly different from another's change in birthrates. The table also shows that Oneida had significant increases in births compared with both Niagara and the baseline counties only in high technology industries in 1978-80.

Table 10.3
Effect of Location on Change Scores (Where birthrates increased significantly more in one location)

F Value (p = .10)

	Oneida–Niagara 1978/80	Oneida–Niagara 1980/82	Oneida–Baseline 1978/80	Oneida–Baseline 1980/82	Niagara–Baseline 1978/80	Niagara–Baseline 1980/82
Business Services		4.1* (.05)				8.5* (.006)
High Technology Manufacturing	6.1** (.02)		5.4** (.02)			
Mature Manufacturing	6.8* (.01)	7.8* (.007)			19.3* (.0001)	
Personal Services						
Small Firm Manufacturing			7.5** (.008)			
Wholesaling					7.8* (.007)	

* Niagara's increase was steeper
** Oneida's increase was steeper

164 / Public Policy Implications

In mature manufacturing, Oneida experienced a significant increase in birth compared to Niagara in 1980-82, but its increase was significantly different from the baseline. Oneida had a significant increase in births compared with the baseline average in small firm manufacturing in 1978-80, but it was not significantly higner than Niagara's. It should also be noted that in 1978-80 Niagara's rapid growth in mature manufacturing outpaced that of both Oneida and the baseline.

We can summarize the change score results as follows. Of the three industries in which Oneida and Niagara experienced significantly different rates of increase in births, Oneida was higher in one and Niagara in two. These results indicate that the presence of entrepreneurial policies does not make individuals more likely to begin businesses in the area. The entrepreneurial model suggests that Oneida should have had higher birthrates in more industries than Niagara had.

CONCLUSION

The most innovative and entrepreneurial site in this study did no better at creating new firms than a similar site that offered almost none of the policies recommended by the entrepreneurial model. What are policy makers to do, given such a finding? How they should respond depends on what we think caused the negative findings.

The entrepreneurial model may simply be wrong in suggesting that there is a pool of potential entrepreneurs who are waiting for the right mix of policies and resources before springing into action. New businesses may indeed be troubled by insensitive government policies. This does not mean that the potential entrepreneur will actually notice policies intended to address these difficulties. The entrepreneur is by nature independent and antibureaucratic, and may spend little time watching government actions, especially at the local level. Local government policy is a minor source of uncertainty for the businesspersons when compared to other potential sources such as locating suppliers or identifying markets. They may devote so little attention to the local politicoeconomic climate that they do not notice when it changes for the better or may not perceive how it affects their operations. In short, this line of thinking suggests that local governments can do little to greatly change the thinking of potential entrepreneurs about starting a firm in the area because they are paying attention to other matters of concern to them.

Before we accept the verdict that local action is useless, we should consider another explanation for the weak results in this study. Even a cursory examination of the policies followed by the more innovative county in this study reveals that by the standards of the entrepreneurial model it was not as aggressive or as innovative as it might have been. Oneida had adopted only part of the entrepreneurial model. It did not, for example, provide true equity funding or an incubator facility. It is possible that startups did not increase in Oneida because its policies failed to reach a still-to-be-defined "critical mass" of resources and forms of assistance. Thus, if local governments want to increase business startups in their communities, they may have to address several aspects of the entrepreneurial model simultaneously, including capital, managerial assistance, physical facilities, and regulatory matters.

Note, however, that if the entrepreneurial model must be undertaken altogether rather than on a partial basis as in Oneida, its value to state and local governments will be limited. No local government on its own can be expected to undertake the full range of activities called for by the model, and few states are likely to be able to extend the approach beyond one statewide program (which would, of course, diminish its impact in any one community). The entrepreneurial model might only be feasible in selected (one might say privileged) locations where there is a combination of local initiative, flexible state legislation regarding local autonomy, and significant amounts of funding for operating and loan purposes.

More research is needed to establish whether communities that have undertaken more extensive programs of assistance to small firms than Oneida later experienced increases in startup activity. In the meantime, since we have seen that partial adoption is ineffective, policymakers should remain skeptical that entrepreneurial policies will do much to increase startup activity in their localities.

NOTES

1. This research received funding from the U.S. Small Business Administration under SBA contract no. SBA-8541-AER-84. Assistance was also received from the New York State Department of Labor which supplied figures on the number of new businesses in selected counties.

2. Similarity is defined on the basis of a number of economic and demographic variables which research has shown to be related to business starts (Fennell 1980; Pennings 1982a). The variables used in this analysis were:

Average employment growth, 1970-75 (business cycle declining)
Average employment growth, 1976-80 (business cycle rising)
Median family income, 1980
Population change, 1970-80
Dummy variable indicating if the county is a suburb of a large city
1980 population
Average unemployment rate, 1977, 1978, and 1980
Employment distribution across thirty-two two-digit SIC divisions

3. The baseline counties selected with this procedure were Kalamazoo and Saginaw, Michigan; and Lackawanna and Northampton, and Broome, New York.

4. The policy data come from interviews with economic developers, bankers, government officials, and Chamber of Commerce representatives. Agency records and newspaper articles also proved helpful.

5. We made several ANOVA runs using mean 1978 and 1980 birthrates as covariates, but the results differed little from the ANOVA results using only type of policy and so are not reported here.

REFERENCES

Balderston, Kris M. 1986. *Plant closings, layoffs, and worker readjustment: The states' response to economic change.* National Governors Association.

Bearse, P. 1976. Government as innovator: A new paradigm for state economic development policy. *New England Journal of Business and Economics* 2 (Spring):37-57.

Bryce, H. (ed.). 1979. *Revitalizing cities.* Lexington, Mass.: Lexington Books.

Butler, S. 1981. *Enterprise zones: Greenlining the inner city.* New York: Universe Books.

Carlton, D. W. 1980. Why new firms locate where they do: An econometric model. In *Interregional movements and regional growth,* ed. W. C. Wheaton. Washington, D.C.: Urban Institute.

Cook, T., and D. Campbell. 1979. *Quasi-experimentation: Design and analysis issues for field settings.* Boston: Houghton Mifflin.

Cornia, G., et al. 1978. *State-local fiscal incentives for economic development.* Columbus, Ohio: Academy for Contemporary Problems.

Cross, M. 1981. *New firm formation and regional development.* Westmead, Farnborough, Hants, England: Gower Publishing Ltd.

Doctors, S. T., and R. E. Wokutch. 1983. The importance of state and local government assistance to small business development. *Public Administration Quarterly* 7 (Spring):76-90.

Downs, A. 1978. Political interaction is a key ingredient for successful urban investment. *The Mortgage Banker:*62-65.

Fennell, M. A. 1980. The effects of environmental characteristics on the structure of hospital clusters. *Administrative Science Quarterly* 25:485-510.

Governors' Weekly Bulletin. 1986. States take lead in promoting economic change. September.

Harris, Candee S. 1984. The magnitude of job loss from plant closings and the generation of replacement jobs: Some recent evidence. *Annals of the American Academy of Political and Social Science* 475 (September):15-27.

Kieschnick, M. 1979. *Venture capital and urban development.* Washington, D.C.: Council of State Planning Agencies.

Kieschnick, M., L. Litvak, and B. H. Daniels. 1980. *Financing new business development.* Washington, D.C.: Council of State Planning Agencies.

Kleinbaum, D. G., and L. L. Kipper. 1978. *Applied regression analysis and other multivariate methods.* North Scituate, Mass.: Duxbury Press.

Ledebur, Larry, and William W. Hamilton. 1986. The great tax-break sweepstakes. *State Legislatures* (September):12-15.

Litvak, L., and B. Daniels. 1979. *Innovations in development finance.* Washington, D.C.: Council of State Planning Agencies.

Mokry, B. 1985. Public policy and the entrepreneur: The impact of capital, technical assistance and political climate. Ph.D. dissertation. Syracuse University.

Pennings, J. M. 1982a Organizational birth frequencies: An empirical investigation. *Administrative Science Quarterly* 27:127-144.

———. 1982b. The urban quality of life and entrepreneurship. *Academy of Management Journal* 25:63-79.

Pierce, N. R., and C. Steinbach. 1981. Reindustrialization on a small scale—but will the small business survive? *National Journal* (January 17):105-108.

Reichardt, C. S. 1979. The statistical analysis of data from nonequivalent group designs. In *Quasi-experimentation: Design and analysis for field settings*, ed. T. Cook and D. Campbell. Boston: Houghton Mifflin.

SAS Institute. 1982. *SAS users guide: Statistics.* Cary, N.C.: SAS Institute.

Schmenner, R. 1980. Industrial location and urban management. In *The prospective city,* ed. Arthur P. Solomon. Cambridge Mass.: MIT Press.

Shapero, A. 1981. Entrepreneurship: Key to self-renewing communities. *Economic Development Commentary* 7 (April): 19-23.

Shapero, A., and A. Sokol. 1982. The social dimensions of entrepreneurship. In *Encyclopedia of entrepreneurship,* ed. C. Kent et al. Englewood Cliffs, N.J.: Prentice-Hall.

Vaughan, Roger. 1986. *Financing economic development in the south: Public infrastructure and entrepreneurship.* 1986 Commission on the Future of the South, Southern Growth Policies Board.

Vaughan, Roger, Robert Pollard, and Barbara Dyer. 1984. *The wealth of states: Policies for a dynamic economy.* Washington, D.C.: Council of State Planning Agencies.

Widner, R. 1980. City development strategies for the future. *In cities and firms,* ed. H. J. Bryce. Lexington, Mass: Lexington Books.

Zimmerman, C. 1981. The discretionary authority of local governments. *Urban Data Services Report* 13 (November): 350-365.

11 Linking Small, Advanced Technology Firms and Universities

VICTOR LEVINE and DAVID N. ALLEN

Recognition of the critical role of small business in economic development has grown dramatically in recent years (Hansen 1981; Litvak and Daniels 1979; National Governors Association 1983; U.S. Small Business Administration 1983). Policymakers and practitioners have been particularly interested in the potential of small, advanced technology firms in job creation, innovation, and economic diversification.[1] Central to most advanced technology initiatives is the belief that universities and small, advanced technology firms can be brought into effective collaborative partnerships in research and training.[2] Examples of successful partnerships in California's Silicon Valley, Boston's Route 128, and North Carolina's Research Triangle encourage this belief. It has been observed, however, that there are fundamental differences in the culture and mission of these two institutions as well as structural and organizational obstacles to collaboration (Hoy and Bernstein 1981; Morgan 1974; Peters and Fusfeld 1983; Brodsky et al. 1980; Tornatzky et al. 1983; and Giamatti 1983).

Relatively little work has been directed at assessing the reported needs and perceptions of advanced technology executives as they pertain to the university. This chapter develops and tests a descriptive model of the way in which nine university roles might be important to small, advanced technology firms. Building on this model, we address four questions:

- Are universities actually perceived to be important by small, advanced technology firms?
- What is the relative importance of different university roles?

- Does the importance of the university (or of specific university roles) differ with firm characteristics?
- How much of the variation in importance can be explained by our model?

UNIVERSITY-FIRM INTERACTION: A CONCEPTUALIZATION

Universities are important to advanced technology firms because they engage in research and development (R&D) activity which is transferred to commercial application, and they train technical and professional employees (Office of Technology Assessment 1984:56). Within the R&D dimension, universities are important in two ways. First, firms need access to research faculty for consulting, collaborative projects, and so forth. Second, firms need access to university equipment and facilities, for example, laboratories, information systems, and libraries.

Advanced technology firms also value universities because firms need highly skilled employees. University students and graduates provide a source of full- or part-time employees. Access to skilled, relatively low-wage labor is valuable in itself; in addition, firms are able to obtain first-hand information about the characteristics of potential employees (Battelle 1982). In addition to providing a pool of new employees, universities provide training to current employees through degree and continuing education course offerings.

Universities help advanced technology firms meet personnel needs by attracting highly skilled workers to an area. Some evidence indicates that university-related recreational and cultural amenities are important for location decisions (Glasmeier, Hall, and Markusen 1983) and that importance is positively associated with firm size (Allen, Robertson, and Bailey 1983). Finally, for workers with advanced graduate training, the opportunity to hold an adjunct appointment or to teach part-time at a local university may be an important factor in choosing an employer.

The needs of small, advanced technology firms can be viewed as consisting of two major dimensions—research and employees. Each of these can be further divided into two components that reflect nine individual interaction activities (Figure 11.1).

Not all advanced technology firms are expected to attach equal importance to each dimension of activity. For example, smaller firms that are typically in early stages of product development with partially equipped research facilities should value the research and development dimension (Churchill and Lewis 1983). Firms that are more R&D intensive should value both the research and employee dimensions. The employee dimension should be important in firms that have difficulty attracting technical and professional personnel. Firms that use outside organizations in training new employees should value universities (Doeringer and Pannell

```
University ┬─ Research ┬─ Faculty ─── Faculty Research
           │           │              Faculty Consultants
           │           │              Joint Research Efforts
           │           └─ Facilities ─ Access to Libraries and Information
           │                           Systems
           │                           Access to Laboratories
           └─ Employees ┬─ Training ── College Graduates
                        │              Degree Programs for Employees
                        └─ Attracting ─ Part-time Teaching
                                        Cultural Activities
```

Needs of Firms | University Services and Capabilities | Interaction Activities

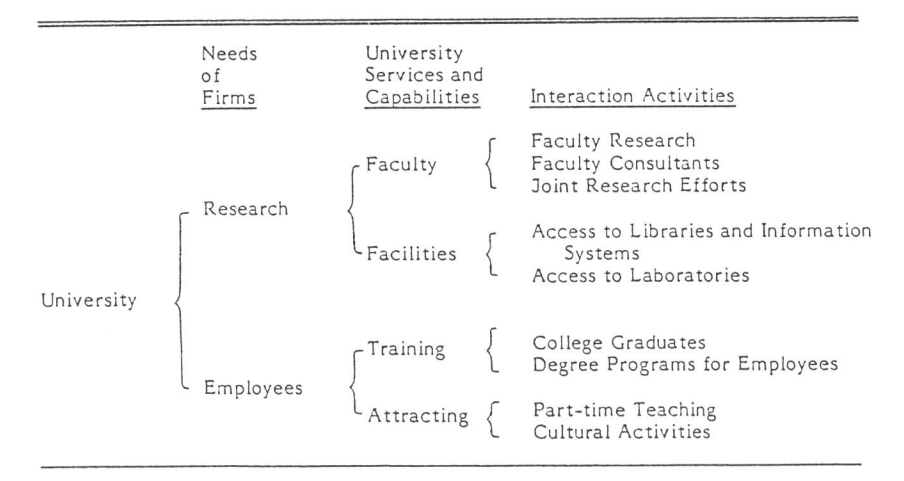

Figure 11.1
The Role of the University in the Activities of Advanced Technology Firms

1982). Rapidly growing firms in which product and job cycles are relatively short are likely to need employee capacity-building activities offered by universities.

Pennsylvania: An Economy of Transition

Pennsylvania provides an excellent setting for examining university/advanced technology firm interactions. The state has an extensive higher education system. With 200 colleges and universities, Pennsylvania ranks third in the nation in terms of number of institutions of higher education. The state has the fourth highest concentration of scientists and engineers in the United States (Stengel and Plosila 1982). It also has a high level of R&D ranking in the top five states in the nation in combined corporate and university R&D in science and engineering (Coy 1982). The state's basic economy, however, is substantially depressed. During the 1970s Pennsylvania's rate of employment growth was only one-third that of the national average and the rate at which new businesses were established was less than half the national rate (Erickson et al. 1983).

The decline of Pennsylvania's traditional industries provides the incentive for promoting advanced technology industry; the existence of a substantial education sector provides the opportunity. Pennsylvania has established a reputation as a leader in developing innovative policies to encourage the growth of advanced technology firms. A central element in state policy[3] is linking universities and other technological support organizations with advanced technology firms (Roberston and Allen 1983). Understanding the factors linking universities and advanced technology firms is of particular importance given these new policy initiatives in the state. Because university/industry interactions may, in part, be influenced by state-level policy, a cross-sectional analysis within a single state controls for the influence of such policy factors, allowing a clearer test of the influence of differences in the characteristics of firms.

UNIVERSITY-FIRM INTERACTION: AN EMPIRICAL DESCRIPTION

Data Collection

In December 1982 a four-page questionnaire was sent to the chief executive officers (CEOs) of 2,432 advanced technology firms in Pennsylvania. Firms were included in the sample based on primary SIC codes, as listed on the Dun and Bradstreet inventory of firms in the state.[4] Data were collected on an array of items including sales, size, labor force composition, projected growth, research and development commitment, training, finance, and perceptions about the business environment. One section of the survey instrument dealt specifically with the role of colleges and universities in these firms' business activities. A total of 459 questionnaires was returned (about 19 percent). Of these, 327 were completed by the executive managers of advanced technology firms with fifty or fewer employees.

Measures of University Importance

Executive managers of these firms were asked to rate the importance of the nine university activities (described in Figure 11.1) in their daily business activities using a ten-point Likert scale.[5] The scale was anchored with values of 1-3 representing minor importance, 4-6 moderate importance, and 7-9 major importance. The individual factors receiving the highest ratings were access to college graduates, followed closely by access to libraries and information systems (Panel A of Table 11.1). Over half the executives (58 percent) indicated that these two factors were important (rating 4 or higher) in their daily operations. The least important factors were faculty research, joint research, access to laboratories, and part-time teaching opportunities; fewer than one-quarter of the executives indicated that these were important.

Table 11.1
Importance of the University in Nine Roles (N=327)

PANEL A

Individual Roles	Mean Importance Rating	Pct. Indicating Role Important
1. Faculty Research Activities	1.80	21
2. Faculty Consultants	2.20	26
3. Joint Research Efforts	1.60	18
4. Access to Libraries and M.I.S.	4.17	58
5. Access to Laboratories	1.92	24
6. College Graduates	4.25	58
7. Degree Programs for Employees	2.57	35
8. Part-time Teaching Opportunities	1.82	21
9. Cultural Activities	2.70	42

PANEL B

Aggregate Measures	Mean Importance Rating	Pct. Indicating Role Important
University (sum of 9 roles)	23.31	80
Research (sum of roles 1 - 5)	11.09	63
Employees (sum of roles 6 - 9)	11.61	74

Three aggregate measures of university importance were constructed to reflect the major dimensions shown in the model (Panel B of Table 11.1). Measures of the research and employee dimensions were constructed as the sum of the ratings on the individual activities associated with each in Figure 11.1. An overall measure of university importance was constructed as the sum of all nine activities. An aggregate measure was classified as important if any of the activities associated with it was assigned a rating of 4 or above. Overall, firms assigned the university high importance. Four out of five firms indicated that at least one of the nine university-related factors was of moderate to major importance. Almost two-thirds of the executives (63 percent) reported that at least one of the five research factors was important, and almost three-quarters (74 percent) reported that one of the four employee factors was important.

Measures of Firm Characteristics

Eleven measures of firm characteristics and proximity to local universities were constructed from questionnaire responses (Table 11.2). Firms in this sample tended to be quite small (fewer than twelve employees on average), young (in operation for about twelve years), and evenly split between manufacturing and services.

A high-skill employee index was constructed as a measure of the proportion of total employees in technical or professional occupations; almost two-thirds of all employees were in this category. Two measures of labor scarcity were constructed. The first reflects the perceived attractiveness of skilled labor in the current location; the second measures difficulty in recruiting skilled labor in the local area.

Information on the policies of firms for training new employees was used to construct two dichotomous training variables. If outside training facilities were used for low-skilled workers, the first variable was coded "1." The second variable was similarly coded "1" if high-skilled workers were trained outside the firm. The probability of receiving outside training is substantially higher for high-skilled (0.75) than for low-skilled (0.32) entrants. The percentage of gross revenue devoted to research and development was used as a measure of a firm's research intensity. On average, a substantial share of gross revenues (over 10 percent) was reportedly allocated to R&D.

Two measures of the cultural/educational ambiance of the firm's present location were constructed. The sum of responses on four items (good schools for children, recreational activities, cultural activities, and proximity to a major research university) constituted the first measure. The second measure is a dummy variable, coded 1 if respondents picked any of these four items as being among the five most important items (from a list of thirty-one) that influenced their initial location decision. About one-quarter of the firms indicated that at least one of the four education-related items was among the top five influences on their choice of location.

Executives were asked to indicate the extent to which they agreed with the following statement: "Colleges and universities in Pennsylvania could be much more responsive in developing working relationships with advanced technology firms." Over half of the firms in the sample reported that they agreed with the statement.

A set of three dichotomous variables was constructed to measure each firm's proximity to universities. The number of 1982 degrees in five related academic disciplines (business administration, computer science, engineering, physics, and math) were used to construct indicators of the size of the local university at three degree levels. About half of the firms were located in counties where local universities granted over 300 bac-

Table 11.2
Firm Characteristics and University Importance—Stepwise Multiple Regression (N=327)

	Descriptive Statistics		Stepwise Multiple Regression		
Independent Variables	Mean (1)	Standard Deviation (2)	University Total (3)	Research Dimension (4)	Employee Dimension (5)
1. Size - number of employees in PA	12.55	11.73	.19**	.10**	.12***
2. Age - years in PA	11.45	12.24	.12*	.09**	-----
3. Sector — designated as primarily non manufacturing by Dun & Bradstreet (D)	.57	.52	-3.21**	-3.16***	-----
4. Growth - projected growth in employment next 2 years	.59	.49	-----	-----	-----
5. High Skill Labor Index - percent of total employees in technical or professional	64.11	30.60	.14***	.06***	.07***
6. Labor Scarcity - perceived importance of availability	5.93	2.68	.98***	.60***	.47***
- difficulty in attracting high skill workers	3.69	2.48	-----	-----	.39**
7. Training Policy - train low skill entrants outside firm (D)	.32	.47	3.21*	-----	-----
- train high skill entrants outside firm (D)	.75	.43	4.96**	2.41**	3.36***
8. Research Intensity - percent of gross sales allocated to R&D	10.16	15.21	.22***	.13***	.09***
9. Educational/Cultural Ambiance - attractiveness of university related items education/cultural factor on top five location factors (D)	22.56	8.43	.24**	.13*	.12**
	.29	.46	7.48***	4.72***	2.69***
10. Responsiveness - University related unresponsive (D)	.58	.49	5.03***	2.78***	1.94**
11. Proximity to University - over 300 local B.A. (D)	.52	.50	-----	-----	-----
- over 10 M.A. (D)	.40	.49	-----	2.90***	-----
- any Ph.D. (D)	.30	.45	5.32***	-----	1.92**
Adjusted R^2			.33	.24	.31

NOTE: Significance levels *** $p < .01$, ** $p < .05$, * $p < .10$.   Criterion for inclusion is stepwise regression is significance at the .10 level.

calaureates; almost 40 percent were in counties where over ten masters were granted; and fewer than one-third were in counties granting any doctorates in these five academic areas.

Multiple Regression Analysis

The three aggregate measures of university importance were regressed separately on sixteen measures of firm characteristics using forward stepwise multiple regression (Table 11.2). Both firm size and age were positively related to the importance attached to the university. As small firms in this sample increased in size, they attached increasingly greater importance to the university overall and to both dimensions. Older firms valued the university more but only in its research-related functions. Service sector firms valued the university less than did those primarily engaged in manufacturing. Firms that were more dependent on technical and professional workers valued the university more overall and in both dimensions. Those firms that rated labor availability as important rated both dimensions as being more important. Firms that reported difficulty in recruiting high-skilled employees also emphasized the employee dimension.

The firms' training policies for new entrants were also systematically related to the importance attached to the university. Those firms that reported greater use of outside facilites for training attached greater importance to the university; this was particularly true for high-skilled employees. Similarly, firms that allocated a larger share of gross revenue to research and development, or attached greater importance to educational/cultural ambiance, viewed the university more favorably.

An unexpected and distressing finding was that firms that viewed the university as unresponsive were the ones that valued it the *most* in both dimensions. Logically, perceptions of university responsiveness and university importance should be positively related; this was not the case. Finally, geographic proximity to universities is related to university importance only through post-baccalaureate programs.

Overall, one-third of the variation in the importance assigned to the university was explained by these characteristics. About one-quarter of the variation in the research dimension and one-third in the employee dimension were accounted for.

SUMMARY AND IMPLICATIONS

Bearing in mind that these data are cross sectional and that a specific definition of advanced technology was used, we can point out a number of interesting findings. First, the belief that universities are important to small, advanced technology firms is supported; 80 percent of the CEOs indicated that at least one university role was of moderate or major importance. The most important university function is its traditional one of producing graduates. This is followed by access to university libraries and information systems and the university's role as a source of cultural amenities.

Within the advanced technology sector, the importance of the university differs systematically with the firm's characteristics. In general, manufacturing, use of high-skilled workers, concern about labor availability, use of external training facilities, high levels of R&D, concern for the local educational/cultural ambiance, size, and age are all positively associated with university importance. These relationships are consistent with conventional wisdom and have face validity. They suggest that current policy initiatives directed at fostering university/advanced technology linkages are not misdirected; the characteristics of firms that are most prototypical of "advanced technology" in the abstract (R&D, high-skilled workers, etc.) are most strongly related to university importance.

Although both dimensions of university service are apparently important to small, advanced technology firms, greater emphasis is placed on the university's traditional role of producing and attracting high-skilled workers than on research. Of the three measures of geographic proximity, only the doctoral program is related to the employee dimension. It may be that the county is not the appropriate unit for measuring proximity. Urban and industrial concentrations do not follow county lines, and substantial interaction occurs between institutions in different counties.

Finally, an unexpected finding emerged. Firms that view the university as unresponsive tend to value the university most in both its research and employee dimensions. This relationship, in the context of the generally high levels of importance attributed to universities, suggests that factors within the university rather than the indifference of firms are the major obstacle to university/industry collaboration. Given the emphasis currently placed on university collaboration in many state and regional development plans (Office of Technology Assessment 1982; National Governors Association 1983), the issue of university responsiveness is critical. At the national level, recent propoals such as the Advanced Technology Foundation Act similarly presuppose that university/advanced technology interactions can be implemented through public initiatives.

Research on the origins of successful interactions suggests that, in most cases, interinstitutional arrangements were the outgrowth of prior personal or professional interactions of individuals with common interests, not of institutional or policy initiatives (Peters and Fusfeld 1983). This research suggests that clear indications of interest and opportunity exist, but collaboration obstacles also exist. Before implementing large-scale programs, policymakers would be well advised to invest resources in research directed at understanding the nature of university/advanced technology interactions.

NOTES

1. The terms *advanced technology, high technology,* and *new technology* are used interchangeably to refer to firms characterized by high levels of research and innovation, high concentrations of technical and professional employees, science-based processes, and high growth rates.

2. See L. S. Peters and H. L. Fusfeld, 1983, and Battelle, 1982, for a description and critique of this belief.

3. Many of Pennsylvania's advanced technology initiatives were not underway when the data used in this chapter were collected.

4. See D. N. Allen and G. E. Robertson, 1983, for a description of the study and listing of SIC codes classified as being in the advanced technology area.

5. Factor analysis of these nine activities yielded two nonorthogical principal factors reflecting research and employees. Results of the factor analysis are available from the authors.

REFERENCES

Allen, D. N., and G. E. Robertson. 1983. *Silicon, sensors and software: Listening to advanced technology enterprises in Pennsylvania.* University Park, Pa.: Institute of Public Administration, Pennsylvania State University.

Allen, D. N., G. E. Robertson, and C. M. Bailey. 1983. Worshipping at the shrine of advanced technology: Focusing state and local economic development policy. Paper presented at the Urban Affairs Association Meeting. March 25. Flint, Michigan.

Battelle. 1982. *The higher education system in New York and its potential in economic development.* Special Report III prepared for the New York State Science and Technology Foundation. Columbus, Ohio: Battelle Laboratories.

Brodsky, N. H., H. G. Kaufman, and J. D. Tookers. 1980. *University industry cooperation.* New York: New York University, Graduate School of Public Administration.

Churchill, N. C., and V. L. Lewis. 1983. The five stages of small business growth. *Harvard Business Review* (May/June): 30-50.

Coy, R. W. 1982. *Human and R & D resources for advanced technology in Pennsylvania.* Harrisburg, Pa.: Pennsylvania Milrite Council.

Doeringer, P. B., and P. Pannell. 1982. Manpower strategies for New England's high technology sector. In *New England's vital resource: The labor force,* ed. J. Hoy and M. Bernstein. Washington, D.C.: American Council on Education.

Erickson, R. A., J. H. Miller, and M. J. Wayslenko. 1983. *The competitive position of Pennsylvania business.* Harrisburg, Pa.: Business Council of Pennsylvania.

Giamatti, A. B. 1983. Free market and free inquiry: The university, industry and cooperative research. In *Partnerships in the research enterprise,* ed. Hackney et al. Philadelphia, Pa.: University of Pennsylvania Press.

Glasmeier, A., P. Hall, and A. P. Markusen. 1983. *Recent evidence on high technology industries' spatial tendencies: A preliminary investigation.* Working Paper No. 417. Berkeley, Calif.: Institute of Urban and Regional Development, University of California.

Hansen, D. 1981. *Banking and small business.* Washington, D.C.: Council of State Planning Agencies.

Hoy, J. C., and M. H. Bernstein. 1981. *Business and academia: Partners in New England's economic survival.* Hanover, N.H.: University Press of New England.

Litvak, L., and B. Daniels. 1979. *Innovations in development finance.* Washington, D.C.: Council of State Planning Agencies.

Massachusetts Division of Employment Security. 1981. *High technology employment: Massachusetts and selected states, 1975-1979.* Boston.

Morgan, R. P. 1974. *Science and technology for development: The role of U.S. universities.* New York: Pergamon.

National Governors Association. 1983. *Technology and growth: State initiatives in technology innovation.* Washington, D.C.

Office of Technology Assessment. 1984. *Technology, innovation and regional economic development.* Washington, D.C.: U.S. Government Printing Office.

Peters, L. S., and H. L. Fusfeld. 1983. Current U.S. university/industry research connections. In *University-industry research relationships.* Washington, D.C.: National Science Board.

Robertson, G., and D. N. Allen. 1984. From kites to computers: Pennsylvania's Ben Franklin partnership. Paper presented at the annual meeting of the American Society for Public Administration, Denver, Colorado.

Stengel, G., and W. H. Plosila. 1982. *Advanced technology policies for the Commonwealth of Pennsylvania.* Harrisburg, Pa.: Commonwealth of Pennsylvania.

Tornatzky, L. G., J. D. Everland, G. B. Myles, W. A. Hetzner, C. Johnson, D. Roitman, and J. Schneider. 1983. *The process of technological innovation: Reviewing the literature.* Washington, D.C.: National Science Foundation.

U.S. Small Business Administration. 1983. *The status of small business: Programs and activities.* Washington, D.C.: U.S. Government Printing Office.

12 Divergent Perspectives on Social Responsibility: Big Business versus Small

PHILIP M. VAN AUKEN and
R. DUANE IRELAND

It has been suggested that concentrating on enhancements of a firm's efficiency and its profitability discourages active commitment to social responsibility programs (Cook and Mendleson 1977). In turn, failure to display concerns for issues advocated by various constituencies may contribute to unfavorable perceptions of business firms. In considering this dilemma, managers have concluded that financial goals must remain a top priority (Weaver 1978). Nonetheless, it is important to recognize that the social effects of a firm's activities will likely continue as a critical issue for those operating business firms (Jaersbury 1977) and that demands for socially responsible corporate behaviors represent legitimate societal aspirations (Moskowitz 1977). With this understanding, it can be seen that the social responsibility of the business community is essentially a political concept.

Society makes numerous demands on the business community which are typically articulated by special interest groups. Complicating the firm's ability to respond to often conflicting demands is the reality that social responsibility is unavoidably a matter of degree and interpretation (Dalton 1982). Firms are sometimes surprised to learn that certain actions, which may have received a thorough examination, have been viewed by some constituency as socially irresponsible actions. Thus, through a complicated array of carefully orchestrated actions, the business must attempt to satisfy the concerns of its key constituencies. Failure to do so may result in a withdrawal of the firm's contract with society to provide products and/or services that are valued.

HISTORICAL EVOLUTION OF CORPORATE SOCIAL RESPONSIBILITY

Traditionally, society made almost exclusively economic demands of business relating to efficient mass production of goods and service. This was held to be virtually the only social responsibility of business. Indeed, "the business of America was business." One of the principal proponents of this view is Milton Friedman. He has argued that a firm's primary responsibility is to earn a profit. Achieving this objective, Friedman suggests, simultaneously satisfies the firm's social responsibilities. In this sense, one might believe that allocating portions of a firm's scarce resources to anything other than production-related investments is inappropriate.

With increasing affluence and social change bordering at times on upheaval, the United States experienced unparalleled institutional change in the 1960s and 1970s. The business institution went through a particularly turbulent era of change keyed to a redefinition of corporate social responsibility.

An increasingly pluralistic and politically liberal society, in the form of burgeoning special interest groups, had dramatically increased expectations for business performance. Efficient economic productivity was now viewed, not as the maximum social responsibility of business, but rather as the minimum responsibility.

New, unprecedented societal demands for corporate social activism evolved. The larger, more visible companies found themselves besieged with request/demands to financially and managerially support social activist and reform activities: educating and employing the hardcore unemployed, championing civil rights and feminist causes, underwriting urban renewal, combating drug abuse, and so on. Corporate social responsibility became synonymous with corporate social activism.

SURVIVAL THROUGH PROFIT AND SOCIAL RESPONSIBILITY

In order to maintain social legitimacy and continue to thrive economically, big business has institutionalized social activism. Corporate social responsibility officers are commonplace; companies now routinely speak out on controversial social issues; annual reports systematically itemize the nonprofit contributions of companies. Social responsibility is an entrenched part of today's business scene.

In a simpler historical era, business survived by making a profit. Today profit alone is not sufficient for most large companies; social activism in one guise or another has become necessary for business survival and prosperity. The almost volcanic eruption of business regulatory legislation during the tumultuous 1960s and 1970s serves as a sobering reminder of what happened to the business community as it struggled to redefine its social role. Despite occasional reactionary diatribes from some business leaders and social reformists, it appears certain that business will henceforth have to view social responsibility as mandatory for survival. Social responsibility has indeed become the other "bottom line" of corporate America.

Apologists for social responsibility have advanced several arguments in favor of corporate social activism, most of which are discussed from a big business perspective. For example, K. Davis, W.C. Frederick, and R. Blomstrom (1980) suggest that businesses should be socially active because of changing expectations among public constituencies, owing to stockholder interests in such actions, and because social proaction on the part of business is superior to responding to governmental mandates. Among the most interesting of the Davis et al. (1980) positions are the issues of responsibility and power and system interdependencies. In the first instance, it is argued that businesses control and/or influence a large percentage of the total resources available to society. As such, it is appropriate for business to accept the social responsibilities that are commensurate with the power represented by the resources acquired by particular firms. This position, though reasonable, is difficult to operationalize for the small business. The resources available to a firm like General Motors are extensive and somewhat easily documented. In recent years, Lee Iacocca has persuasively argued the breadth and depth of the social responsibilities of firms the size of General Motors and Chrysler. On a relative basis, the resources controlled by the small business are insignificant. As a result, it is difficult for the managers/owners of such firms to formulate reasonable social actions in terms of hard-to-measure social responsibilities.

The argument regarding system interdependencies is also difficult to operationalize in small business firms. It is rather obvious that the actions of large organizations have direct and/or indirect impact on numerous other organizations. In this regard, these firms should be socially active to verify that the consequences of both an intended and unintended nature are positive. In contrast, the impacts of the small business firm's operations on other agencies, groups, or individuals are typically minimal. More importantly, these inconsequential derivative effects are extremely difficult to measure. An inability to measure the effects prevents any rational social response by the small firm.

D.A. Hayes (1972) also argues for social activism. He suggests that socially responsible corporate actions are probably critical to a goal of long-term profit maximization. Whether firms do or do not attempt to maximize profits is certainly debatable (Donaldson and Lorsch 1983). However, the small business manager/owner rarely seeks this goal. The more typical goal for this individual is survival and gradual growth. Thus, the Hayes (1972) argument may be more appropriate in larger business organizations.

A DIVERGENT PERSPECTIVE FOR SMALL BUSINESS

Corporate social activism is a dangerous precedent for small business, that community of proprietorships, partnerships, and small corporations which numerically, if not financially, dominates the American business scene. If small firms were held to the same social responsibility expected of the "Fortune 500 set," the economic backbone of the United States would potentially collapse.

For many smaller firms, profit-making is an unsure, uncertain, unpredictable proposition. Survival is a daily struggle. The bottom line is typically a mighty tough taskmaster for the small business community. For society to expect small firms to join in social activism would be philosophical folly and economic suicide. Society cannot expect any firm, but particularly a small one, to undertake social programs that would seriously jeopardize its competitive position, or worse, its survival.

At best, small firms can only react to the ever shifting currents of societal change; they cannot have a significant role in actually molding such change. All the while, the vast economic network of small business forms the very foundation of our capitalist society.

Given the unique economic role of small business in America, what does society expect of these firms? What does society have a right to expect?

SOCIAL IRRESPONSIBILITY

The socially responsible firm does not necessarily avoid being socially irresponsible. This irony can be seen in light of equating social responsibility with social activism.

When seen as primarily social activism, corporate social responsibility is concerned with advancing societal change and placating special interest groups. This is in contrast to avoidance of social irresponsibility, which entails a company's efforts to conduct operations in a legal, socially acceptable manner. Social activism is a separate, more proactive dimension of corporate behavior.

To say the least, our society has not generated a common set of expectations for corporate social activism. This arena of business activity is much too novel and controversial for a public consensus to have emerged. However, expectations for avoidance of corporate irresponsibility are much more clearcut. Companies are clearly expected to avoid the following socially irresponsible activities:

1. Violating the law, including government regulatory legislation.
2. Taking advantage of consumers through deception, defective product design or performance, refusal to make good on terms of sale, and so on.
3. Deliberate damaging of the environment through pollution in any form.
4. Discrimination against individuals on the basis of age, sex, or ethnic group.

THE REAL BOTTOM LINE FOR SMALL BUSINESS

Small business is responsible for delivering quality goods and services to society in a manner that avoids social irresponsibility. Proactive social activism is not a legitimate responsibility for the small business community. Smaller firms are sufficiently hard pressed to meet the bottom line of long-term profitability. To expect small companies also to pursue a second "bottom line" of social activism would be dysfunctional to society. Small firms have enough problems of economic survival without shouldering another societal role for which they are ill equipped and poorly prepared.

Small firms must concentrate not on the vagaries of social activism, but rather on performing economically in a way that avoids negligence. When attempting to be socially responsible, those operating small businesses should remember that they are dealing with questions about social values; that is, individual and group preferences for the allocation of society's resources (Maskow 1976). For small firms, efforts should be made to avoid negligent actions in those areas that are personally relevant for the firms' constituencies. To facilitate these actions, they should develop guidelines for verifying that their actions are socially responsible (Smith 1976). Through adherence to this philosophy and these practices, the small firm can produce a quality product, sell it with the customer in mind, and avoid pollution and discrimination and other negligent acts. Through these actions, the small business community benefits society and is able to survive. This is true small business social responsibility.

REFERENCES

Cook, S., and J. A. Mendleson. 1977. Management: Key to social responsibility. *Advanced Management Journal* 42: 25–45.

Dalton, D. 1982. The four factors of social responsibility. *Business Horizons* 25: 19–27.

Davis, K., W. C. Fredrick, and R. Blomstrom. 1980. *Business and society: Concepts and policy issues.* New York: McGraw-Hill.

Donaldson, G., and J. Lorsch. 1983. *Decision making at the top.* New York: Basic Books.

Hayes, D. A. 1972. A case for social responsibility. In *Issues in business and society,* ed. G.A. Steiner. New York: Random House.

Jaersbury, R. 1977. Introducing corporate social responsibility. *Work and People* 3: 25-27.

Maskow, M. 1976. Environmental regulation and public values. *The Conference Board Record* 13: 47-50.

Moskowitz, M. 1977. The Bank of America's rocky road to responsibility. *Business and Society Review* 22: 61-64.

Smith, R. H. 1976. Make your code of ethics work through a program of education. *Association Management* 28: 44-48.

Weaver, C. 1978. Social responsibility in the corporate goal heirarchy. *Business Horizons* 21: 29-35.

13 A Geographic Structure for Black Small Business Research

DAVID B. LONGBRAKE and
WOODROW W. NICHOLS, JR.

Independently owned, small entrepreneurial businesses are the foundation of economic activity in the United States. Small businesses account for 48 percent of the nation's business output, 43 percent of the gross national product, over half of all industrial inventions and innovations, and over half of the labor force in private industry (Minority Business Development Agency [MBDA], Research Division 1982). David Birch (1979) has concluded that the establishment and growth of independent firms create more than half of all new jobs. Companies with twenty or fewer employees provide two-thirds of all new jobs in the private sector, and firms with 500 or fewer employees have created 87 percent of net new jobs.

MINORITY BUSINESS ENTERPRISES

With few exceptions, minority businesses are small businesses. The definition of small business recommended by the White House Conference on Small Business (1980) is 500 or fewer employees. These businesses represent 97 percent of all businesses in the United States (MBDA 1982). In 1977 fewer than twenty of the nation's 561,395 MBEs (minority business enterprises) had more than 500 employees, and only 10 percent of all MBEs had five or more employees (MBDA 1982).

Thus, minority business enterprises (MBEs) are a subset within the larger realm of independently owned small businesses. But they differ from other small businesses in a number of ways, not the least of which is the fact that they are greatly underrepresented in the American business population. A general business participation rate (firms per 1,000 population), which is one-fifth of the nonminority rate, suggests that minority businesses are not as numerous as they can or should be. In 1977 there were 13.9 nonfarm MBEs per 1,000 minority population compared to 62.9 nonfarm businesses per 1,000 nonminority population (MBDA 1982). Nor are MBEs equally distributed among minority groups; business participation rates in 1977 were 8.7 for blacks, 15.0 for persons of Spanish origin, and 22.5 for Asians and others.

MINORITY BUSINESS DEVELOPMENT AGENCY

The research reported here is a response to the Minority Business Development Agency's (MBDA's) Research Solicitation SA-83-RSB-0013. MBDA is the successor to the Office of Minority Business Enterprise (OMBE) which was charged with responsibility for "establishing, preserving, strengthening, and developing the United States' minority business community." Of particular concern to MBDA, given the low levels of minority business participation, are issues involving the formation, growth, and failure of minority-owned enterprises.

Beginning in 1982, MBDA designed and initiated a competitive "Sponsored Research Program." Most of the MBDA-sponsored studies have sought to explain formations, growth, and failures in relation to local market conditions, industry type, timing of the investment and the decision to invest, entrepreneuers' experience and education, urban or locational impact, and individual characteristics, especially the ethnic factor (Ando 1982, 1983; Bates 1982, 1983; Bearse 1982, 1983; Birch 1982; Swinton and Handy 1982, 1983).

GEOGRAPHIC CONSIDERATIONS

Several of these studies also included a geographic variable, and, of those that did, most found this variable to be one of the more important considerations among the research results. This finding is not very surprising in that minority-owned businesses are not uniformly distributed throughout the states but are largely concentrated geographically in the most populated areas. Sixty percent are located in six states, and 83 percent are in Standard Metropolitan Statistical Areas (SMSAs). Although most minority businesses can be correctly classified as having an SMSA location, there are significant numbers of nonfarm MBEs in rural areas. These tend to be black firms in the Southeast and Hispanic and Indian firms in the Southwest. An additional complication is the fact that geographic patterns of minority-owned business activity are not static but change through time.

U.S. CENSUS GEOGRAPHY

Despite these geographic considerations, most reseachers who include a geographic factor utilize U.S. Census geography which divides the country into relatively uniform regions and divisions (see Figure 13.1). The concept of census regions was adopted with the 1940 U.S. Census and was expanded from three to four regions in 1950. These same four regions (Northeast, North Central, South, and West) remain in use today. The current set of nine census divisions (New England, Middle Atlantic, East North Central, West North Central, South Atlantic, East South Central, West South Central, Mountain, and Pacific) reflect modifications initiated in the 1910 U.S. Census.

Although both of these geographic units have a long-standing tradition of use within the U.S. Census Bureau, their basic reason for being is one of providing a convenient structural basis around which to organize, record, and summarize census data. The original formulation of these concepts, and ultimately their configuration, is based more on the logic of geographic proximity than on an effort to identify functional economic or social-cultural units. Even if such were originally the case, social and economic ties have altered substantially in the seventy plus years since 1910 when the current designation of census divisions was established.

For research purposes, a region (or division) within a regional framework should contain identifiable or distinguishing characterisitics that differentiate it from other parts of geographical space with respect to the research topic. Regions may be based on similarities in ethnicity, race, occupation, or whatever criteria might be appropriate to delimit distinct geographical entities for specific research purposes.

RESEARCH PROBLEM

Black business geography is the principal focus of this research endeavor, for most of the previous minority research studies have dealt almost exclusively with black businesses. More specifically, this research asks the question: What geographic structure of regions and divisions might provide a more useful framework for future research efforts involving the formation, growth, and failure of black enterprises? It is hypothesized here that a geographic structure based on descriptive, distributional, and business participation characteristics for blacks would provide a meaningful format for capturing distinctive geographic differences in black business participation rates.

BLACK PATTERNS

In this chapter we will not pursue the somewhat mystical interpretation of the terms *regions* and *divisions.* The more prosaic view adopted here is

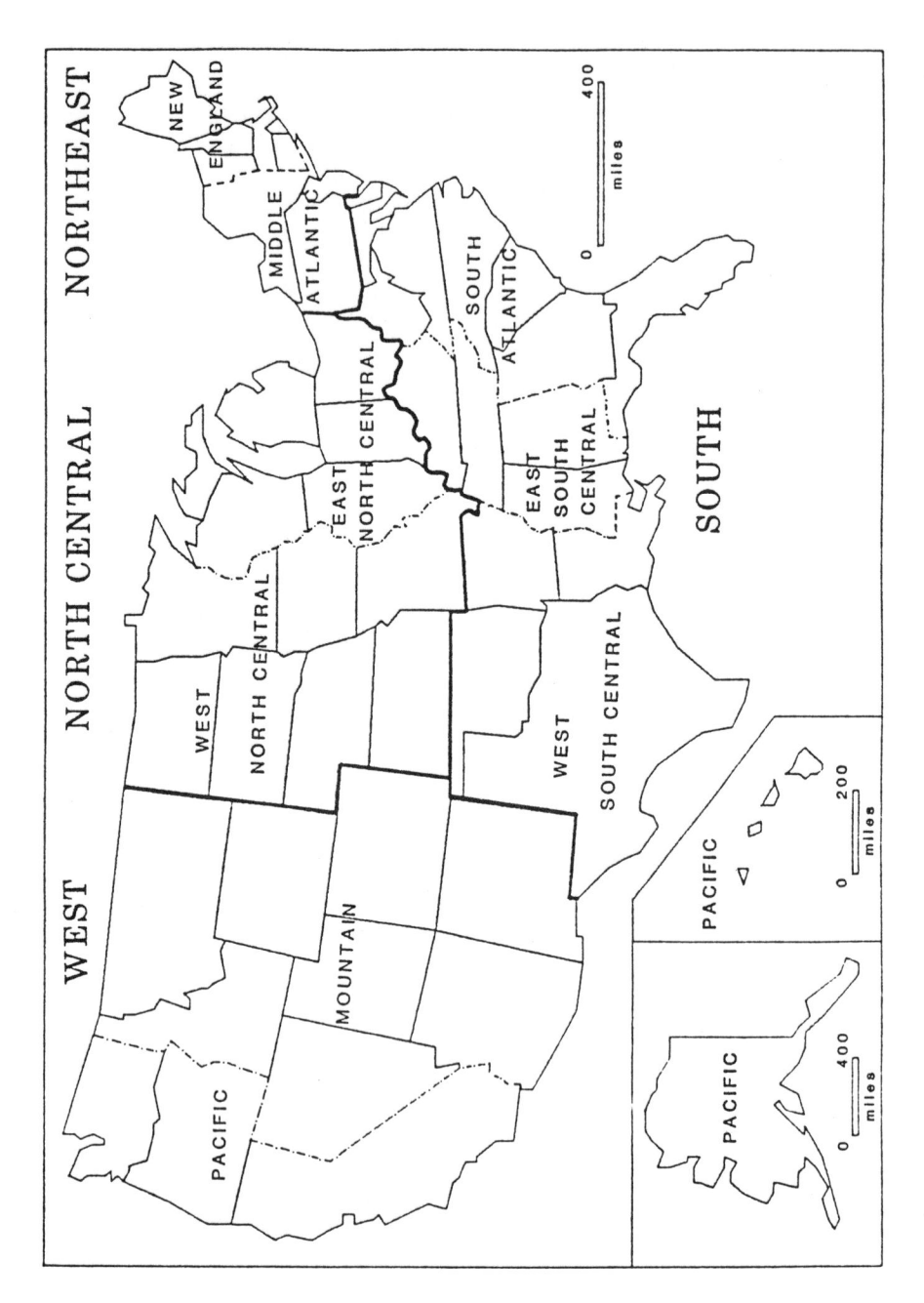

Figure 13.1
U.S. Census Geography: Regions and Divisions

that regions perform much the same role as classification in any science and that regionalization constitutes a special form of classification (Bunge 1966). Classification is a fundamental activity of science and can be viewed as either the beginning or the culmination of scientific investigation (Harvey 1969).

It should not be assumed that regions and divisions can be partitioned or grouped in an unambiguous fashion. In reality, the contrary is much more likely. For example, there is a remarkable range of definitions as to which states constitute an area that has variously been designated as the Midwest, Great Lakes, and (U.S. Census) North Central region (Shortridge 1985:48-57). The primary task is assumed to be one of describing how, and then why, areas (states) differ in characteristics related to black business participation. Although it is essential to identify the regional/ divisional breakdown that serves the particular research purpose, as argued earlier, it is also necessary to be aware of the relative efficiency (loss of detail) of the most representative regional framework. Ultimately, a valid classification is one that reveals meaningful patterns in a data set; all meaningful classifications are, in this sense, purposive and relative rather than absolute (Harvey 1969:326).

Two considerations come into play in the selection of the regional framework: taxonomic space and geographic space. The taxonomic consideration argues that classification methods are not specifically geographic, but merely classify geographic data. For example, California might be classified with New Jersey according to some criteria, despite their geographic separation. In the same way, it can be argued that the implicit inclusion of the concept of location makes for a regional, as opposed to a purely classificatory, scheme (Bunge 1966). It is, of course, possible to modify grouping procedures so that both nearness in taxonomic space and spatial contiguity are taken into account. That is the strategy followed in this analysis.

The first step is to select the characteristics that will be used in building contiguous regions and divisions at the state level. The twenty-five variables selected for analysis (Table 13.1) were identified in a two-step process. The first core set of variables was based on those variables that the literature and previous research have established as having strong relationships with black business participation. Incorporated are such theoretical concepts as market demand; capital availability; human resources, including knowledge and role models; and the opportunity environment, including ethnic group characteristics and social prejudices (Bates and Bradford 1979:202-9; Markwalder 1981:303-12; Scott et al. 1981; Nelson 1979; McClelland and Winters 1969; Doctors 1974; Petroff 1980: 13-17; Vesper 1980). Several additional variables were subsequently identified through exploratory correlation analysis.

Table 13.1
Black Regions and Divisions: Selected Variables

Acronym	Description
PEPOP:	Percent ethnic group population
MDFI:	Median ethnic family income
PCI:	Per capita ethnic income
PUEMP:	Percent of ethnic minority unemployed
MDED:	Median years of education completed by ethnics
PPW:	Percent of employed ethnics working for private wages
PCE:	Percent ethnic construction employees
PME:	Percent ethnic manufacturing employees
PTE:	Percent ethnic transportation, communication employees
PWE:	Percent ethnic wholesale employees
PRE:	Percent ethnic retail employees
PFE:	Percent ethnic finance, insurance, real estate employees
PBSE:	Percent ethnic business, repair, etc.
PPSE:	Percent ethnic professional service employees
PPAE:	Percent ethnic public administration employees
PSEW:	Percent ethnic self-employed workers
FS12:	Average ethnic family size
MDAGE:	Median age of ethnics
PPU18:	Percent ethnic persons under 18
PFEML:	Percent ethnic females in labor force
PMDFI:	Percent ethnic median family income of non-minority
PPCI:	Percent ethnic per capita income of non-minority
PEG78:	Percent ethnic population growth between 1970-80
PEU:	Percent ethnic population living in urban areas
PSH:	Percent ethnic residence in same house 1975-80

SPATIAL DIMENSIONS

The current situation represents a fairly simple type of grouping problem which begins with a series of spatial units (states), for each of which there is a set of descriptive characteristics (twenty-five variables). Analysis starts with a data matrix comprised of locations along the rows and characteristics down the columns. Clearly, the region-building problem is one of assigning locations with similar characteristics into geographic divisions that can subsequently be aggregated into higher level regions.

After transformation into standard normal form and computation of product moment correlation coefficients, a procedure sometimes referred to as R-mode principal components analysis was applied. Then, following the traditional argument that no component with variance less than unity (the variance of an original variable) can possibly be meaningful, only those components with eigenvalues greater than 1 were rotated, using the Kaiser normal varimax criterion, to a position approximating simple structure. Rotation was utilized to insure that, to the degree possible, each variable correlated highly with only one component.

Resulting component loadings (correlations of characteristics with components) can be used to allocate the characteristics into subsets, each representing a particular type of spatial variation among states for blacks. Components scores (values for the states with respect to the components) give quantitative meaning to the new dimensions (components) of spatial variation. Component loadings and component scores are the basic ingredients for interpreting the new dimensions of spatial variation that emerge from the analysis. Ultimately, the component scores are used in what is commonly referred to as Q-mode principal components analysis to group similar states based on their characteristic profiles reflected in the new composite dimensions of spatial variation.

As indicated in Table 13.2, seven dimensions of spatial variation emerged from the state level analysis. Component loadings of less than ± 448 (20 percent of a variable's total variation) have been omitted to make the table easier to read. (One exception is self-employment, which does not have a strong relationship with any of the major patterns of spatial variation.) Although the components are listed in order of the amount of total variance they account for, there is no particular interpretive significance to this ordering. In other words, the greater the number of variables of a particular kind (e.g., economic-related variables loading on the second component) included in the analysis, the greater the likelihood of deriving a dimension of spatial variation accounting for a substantial portion of the problem's total variation. Of equal interest, in most cases, are spatial patterns that are identified by components with fewer variables (characteristics) loading on them. In a region-building problem of this type, who is to say which spatial pattern is more important than another in describing the differing spatial patterns that characterize a set of geographic areas (regions)?

Each of the components reflecting general patterns of spatial variation can be broadly interpreted as follows:

Public/Private Wage-Earners. Represented here is a bipolar pattern with private sector wage employees being found in spatial association with manufacturing employment activities, a very youthful population with larger family sizes, and a tendency to less residential movement by households. Forming the other inversely associated aspect of this pattern (a set of characteristics found in dissimilar locations and/or absent from locations characterized by the preceding variables) are areas characterized by a large number of public administration-related employees. These areas also appear to be characterized by the presence of retail and transportation employment opportunities.

Economic Status. This pattern gives some indication of the general economic health of blacks. High family and per capita incomes, along

Table 13.2
Black State-Level Spatial Dimensions: Component[1] Loadings[2]

Variable Acronym	I Public/Private Wage Earners	II Economic Status	III Black Population Size	IV Financial Employment	V Business/Professional Employment	VI Urban	VII Unemployment
PPW[3]	-.884						
PME	-.835						
PPAE	.794						
PRE	.791						
PPU18	-.714	.480					
PTE	.612						
FS12	-.549						
PMDFI		-.872					
PPCI		-.868					
MDFI		-.828					
MDED		-.762					
PCI		-.685		-.524			
PWE		.460					
MDAGE			.934				
PEPOP			.687				
PSH	-.523		.595				
PSEW		.492	-.423				
PFE				-.805			
PFEML				-.577			
PBSE					.862		
PPSE					-.681		
PEG78					.589		
PEU							
PUEMP						.890	.867
PCE		.498					-.500
Eigenvalues	4.91	4.82	2.49	2.40	2.17	1.90	1.42

[1]The seven components account for 80.4 percent of the original variation.
[2]Loadings less than 0.448 (20% of a variable's variation) have been excluded from this table to make it easier to read.
[3]Variable descriptions appear in Table 13.1.

with low-income differentials compared to whites, have similar spatial patterns and, as might be expected, tend to be associated with higher levels of education. At the same time, these economic-related characteristics tend to be inversely associated, to a lesser degree, with higher proportions of young blacks, stable (nonmover) households, and employment in construction trades. This component would appear to reflect a theoretically sound and rather distinctive pattern of spatial variation within the black population.

Black Population Size. Expressed here in the first of three essentially single-theme patterns are some of the characteristics associated with the larger concentrations of black population. It is a more general pattern than the narrowly defined companion urban dimension to follow. The focus involves some demographic considerations in that larger black populations tend to have an older age character (especially those living in urban areas) and have greater household stability in that there is less residential shifting or movement. Self-employment is negatively associated with these indicators of larger population concentration which, in turn, provides evidence in support of an opportunity costs argument.

Financial Employment. This spatial dimension identifies several interrelated characteristics associated with employment in financial activities. Specific relationships include higher per capita incomes in these areas, which are, in turn, a reflection of greater female participation in the labor force and correspondingly small family sizes.

Business/Professional Employment. This second of two bipolar patterns indicates the separation and/or distinctiveness of areas characterized by business and professional orientations. It would appear that business service employment is more typical of areas experiencing rapid black population growth, whereas black professional employment is associated with regional wholesaling centers that exhibit slower growth.

Urban. The second of three single-theme patterns—percentage of black population residing in urban areas—has only lesser secondary associations with transportation employment and an inverse relationship with percent self-employment. This latter relationship, in conjunction with the self-employment tie to dimension V, suggests that both higher degrees of urban setting and large concentrations of black population are characterized by lower levels of business participation.

Unemployment. The last of the single-theme dimensions is unemployment, which has only one other secondary inverse relationship with construction employment. This suggests that black unemployment is lowest in areas characterized by a relatively high level of construction activities.

PATTERN ANALYSIS

States are now classified in terms of their profiles across the seven basic discriminating spatial patterns from R-mode analysis. This strategy, known as Q-mode analysis, is used to reveal the geographic structure in the data set.

A fundamental problem with such procedures it the degree to which the category-structure revealed is actually inherent in the data versus the degree to which it has been imposed on the data by the procedure itself and is thus an artifact of the procedure (Anderberg 1973). This problem is difficult to resolve. Actually, it is insoluble, but because any geographic structure revealed is useful and valid to the extent that it highlights patterns that might otherwise go unnoticed, and thus promotes new insights and meaningful interpretations, this problem is of little real import (Walker 1985).

This step entails building geographic divisions based on the resultant structural groupings. Unassigned peripheral states are allocated to core groups largely according to their R-mode profiles, and while geographic proximity is considered in resolving potential problems of multiple group membership. However, as a part of this decision-making process, the spatial characteristics of three other variable patterns were examined in arriving at the final set of geographic regions and divisions.

First among these additional variable patterns were the spatial distributions for each of the seven principal types of business enterprises—construction; manufacturing; transporation; wholesale; retail; financial; and selected services firms. A second set of additional variable patterns considered related to several different aspects of firm size includes: the spatial distribution of gross receipts; number of firms with paid employees; and number of paid employees. A final variable was the actual distribution of black population.

BLACK BUSINESS GEOGRAPHY

A synthesis of the taxonomic and spatial analyses yields thirteen geographic divisions for black business enterprises (Figure 13.2). Although each of these geographic groupings is distinctly different from the others, states within each division have characteristics that make the groups internally homogeneous.

The same analyses used to identify the thirteen black geographic divisions in turn facilitate the aggregation of these divisions into geographic regions and provide for their description and interpretation. In all, six regions were derived which accommodate the division pattern (see Figure 13.2).

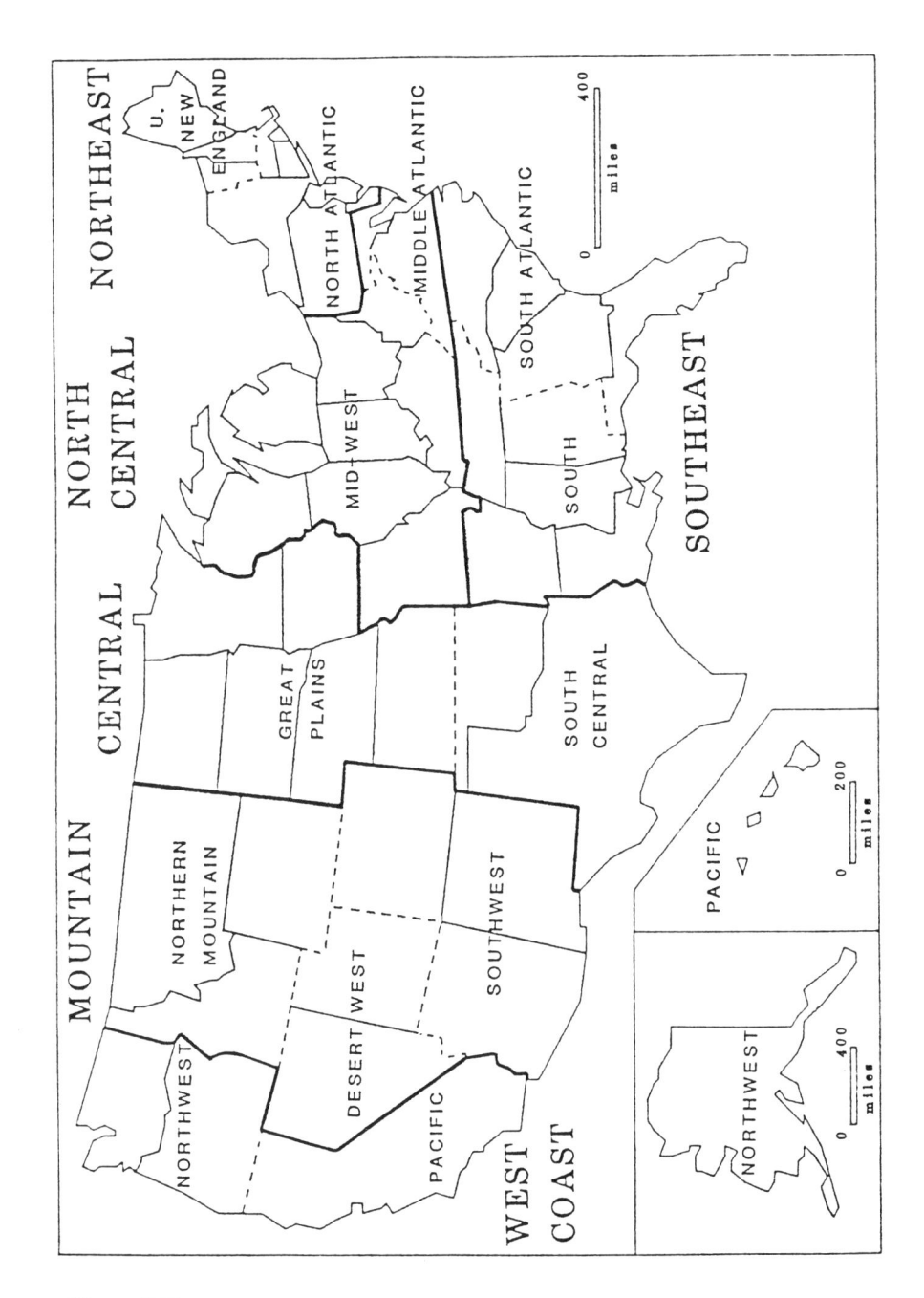

Figure 13.2
Black Business Geography: Regions and Divisions

Divisions

Of the seven original *R*-mode patterns, three assume roles of particular importance in differentiating between divisions. Both ends of the urban continuum (III), measuring the degree of urban concentration from highly urban to an increased rural presence, provide a basis for significant differences. Lack of involvement in financially related enterprises (IV) is another important feature. Still another discriminating pattern is the public versus private sector dichotomy (I), with involvement in public administration being a particularly important source of employment for blacks in a number of areas.

Table 13.3 shows black business participation rates for both the nine U.S. Census divisions and the thirteen-division configurations identified in this study. Participation figures are based on firm counts for 1977 and

Table 13.3
Black Business Participation Rates[1]

Census		Study	
Regions:			
United States	8.73	United States	8.73
Northeast	7.68	Northeast	7.68
North Central	8.65	North Central	9.29
South	8.25	Central	10.62
West	12.78	Southeast	7.05
		Mountain	11.51
		West Coast	14.50
Divisions:			
New England	9.27	Upper New England	21.20
Middle Atlantic	7.51	North Atlantic	7.66
East North Central	8.28	Midwest	8.51
West North Central	10.80	Great Plains	12.04
South Atlantic	8.61	Middle Atlantic	11.02
East South Central	6.33	South Atlantic	7.47
West South Central	9.02	South	6.54
Mountain	11.51	South Central	10.42
Pacific	14.50	Northern Mountain	19.07
		Southwest	12.22
		Desert West	8.17
		Northwest	13.25
		Pacific	14.60

[1] Business Participation Rates are expressed as the number of black firms per 1,000 black population based on 1977 Survey of Minority-Owned Business Enterprises firm counts (MB77-1) and 1980 U.S. Census of Population.

are expressed as numbers of firms per 1,000 black population according to the 1980 U.S. Census.

Overall indications seem to suggest some relationship between size of black population and black business participation rates. The four study divisions with the largest concentrations of black population have the lowest participation rates (the only exception being the Desert West). Statistically, this relationship between black population size and business participation rates has a correlation (Pearson r) value of -0.479, which is significant at the 0.01 level. This persistent inverse relationship would appear to contradict theory which suggests that as black population increases, so does market potential and, as a consequence, greater opportunities for black entrepreneurs.

Other factors may be in operation here, one of which could be a critical threshold effect. Another possibility may be that blacks choosing to live in less populated areas may by nature have a higher degree of risk propensity (an important characteristic for potential entrepreneurs). These individuals may also have greater capital resources at their disposal, better enabling them to enter into and be accepted by the business community in which they have chosen to reside. In any case, this spatial pattern and associated relationship is a very interesting one and warrants further investigation.

Regions

At this higher level of generalization (aggregation), some of the more distinctive detail of the smaller geographic divisions is obscured, and a smaller number of characteristics serve to distinguish between the larger regions. However, these distinguishing features are no less important, and again, it is these R-mode patterns that provide for the greatest differentiation between regions. The public versus private sector dichotomy (I) plays a similar but even stronger role here compared with the divisional analysis. A new entrant discriminating between entities at the regional scale is Economic Status (II), and the Urban continuum (III) is of less importance than was the case in the divisional analysis.

Table 13.3 also lists black business participation rates for both the four census regions and the six proposed study regions. A comparison of the two sets of regions reveals that the two Northeast regions are almost identical (the only difference being the addition of the state of Delaware to the study region). After this, the differences are considerable beginning with the North Central region and including a new Central region. By far the biggest difference, however, is in the composition of the Southeast region. The study region is much smaller and has a lower business participation rate which is probably more representative of the southern setting.

Overall, with the exclusion of the Southeast, there is a very marked zonal trend in black business participation rates from East to West. The smaller number of census regions (and their configuration) does not capture this trend. In fact, there is very little differentiation at all in business participation rates between three of the four census regions.

SUMMARY

Analysis of black population characteristics and black business patterns shows that a six-region structure is the most appropriate format for viewing and/or conducting research on black businesses that may wish to incorporate a spatial dimension. Many economic analyses that include a geographic variable have found that a regional perspective is one of the more important considerations. Therefore, the proposed six-region structure, based on descriptive and distributional business characteristics for blacks, may be even more revealing when used in economic studies of the formation and function of black-owned businesses.

For the researcher who needs to work with a smaller number of regions, it might be feasible to combine the Mountain and West Coast regions which would conform to the original Western census region. However, any further consolidation beyond this point (five regions) would obscure beyond recognition what appear to be some potentially meaningful distinctions between geographic areas with respect to an understanding of black business participation patterns.

REFERENCES

Anderberg, M. G. 1973. *Cluster analysis for application.* New York: Academic Press.

Ando, F. 1982. Analysis of business activity and failure rates of minority-owned businesses. Report prepared for the Minority Business Development Agency, U.S. Department of Commerce under research contract.

_____. 1983. The determination of successful business formation. Report prepared for the Minority Business Development Agency, U.S. Department of Commerce under research contract.

Bates, T. 1982. The nature of the growth dynamic in emerging lines of minority enterprise: Human capital and financial capital considerations. Report prepared for the Minority Business Development Agency, U.S. Department of Commerce under research contract.

_____. 1983. An analysis of the minority entrepreneur: Traits and trends. Report prepared for the Minority Business Development Agency, U.S. Department of Commerce under research contract.

Bates, T., and W. Bradford. 1978. Lending activities of Black-owned and controlled savings and loan associations. *Review of Black Political Economy* 8:202–209.

Bearse, P. J. 1982. An economic analysis of entrepreneurial choice and location with emphasis on factors affecting minority entrepreneurship. Report prepared for the Minority Business Development Agency, U.S. Department of Commerce under research contract.

———. 1983. A dynamic simulation model of the economic development process in minority communities. Report prepared for the Minority Business Development Agency, U.S. Department of Commerce under research contract.

Birch, D. L. 1979. *The job generation process.* Washington, D.C.: Economic Development Administration.

———. 1982. Research on minority business formation, growth, and failure rates. Report prepared for the Minority Business Development Agency, U.S. Department of Commerce under research contract.

Bunge, W. 1966. *Theoretical geography.* Lund, Sweden: C.W.K. Gleerups.

Doctors, S. I. 1974. *Whatever happened to minority economic development?* New York: Dryden Press.

Harvey, D. 1969. *Explanation in geography.* London: Edward Arnold.

McClelland, D. C., and D. G. Winters. 1969. *Motivating economic achievement.* New York: Free Press.

Markwalder, D. 1981. The potential for Black business. *Review of Black Political Economy* 11:303–312.

Minority Business Development Agency, Research Division. 1982. Minority business enterprise today: Problems and their causes. Washington, D.C.: U.S. Department of Commerce.

Nelson, R. E. 1979. Education and entrepreneurial initiatives. In *Small enterprise development: Policies and programmes,* ed, P. A. Neck. Geneva: International Labor Office.

Petrof, J. V. 1980. Entrepreneurial profile: A discriminant analysis. *Journal of Small Business Management* 18:13–17.

Scott, W. C., A. Furino, and E. Rodriguez. 1981 *Key business ratios of minority-owned businesses: Analysis and policy implications.* San Antonio: Center for Studies in Business, University of Texas at San Antonio.

Shortridge, J. R. 1985. The vernacular Middle West. *Annals of the Association of American Geographers* 75:48–57.

Swinton, D., and J. Handy. 1982. Analysis of the determinants of the rate of growth of Black-owned businesses. Report prepared for the Minority Business Development Agency, U.S. Department of Commerce under research contract.

———. 1983. Development of a conceptual framework of minority business enterprise. Report prepared for the Minority Business Development Agency, U.S. Department of Commerce under research contract.

Vesper, K. H. 1980. *New venture strategies.* Englewood Cliffs, N.J.: Prentice-Hall.

Walker, G. T. 1985 High plains depression in Eastern Colorado: Distribution, classification, and genesis. Ph.D. Dissertation. Department of Geology, University of Denver.

White House Commission on Small Business. 1980. *America's small business economy.* Washington, D.C.: U.S. Government Printing Office.

SUMMARY: IMPLICATIONS FOR SMALL BUSINESS AND PUBLIC POLICY

14 A Model for Contemporary Small Business Policy Issues

ROBERT E. BERNEY and ED OWENS

A number of questions are central to the regulation of small business policy. For example, if gaps in the market, financing problems, or significant resource shortages or surpluses occur, should the government intervene in the market through development of new assistance programs? Is it a valid policy goal for government agencies, such as the U.S. Small Business Administration (SBA), to provide loan guarantees or direct loans, or to subsidize in other ways the role and activities of small business? Or is it valid for the Internal Revenue Service to provide tax credits, deductions, or different tax rates to reach similar goals? Or should the government be indifferent to the interactions associated with the operation of large and small businesses in the American "free market" economy?

Over the last several years, a growing body of preliminary information has indicated that the very small businesses within the U.S. economy are being crowded out by the largest of businesses because of the economy's competitive nature. This same body of information further suggests that government policy is not neutral in its impact, rather, it discriminates against the smaller firm.

A strong case could be made in support of the position that special programs should be provided to support small businesses in their competition with larger businesses. However, if we had truly competitive markets or ease of entry into existing markets, the more reasonable government policy would be one of neutrality.

Development and further extension of these concepts was partially funded by SBA 4884-0A-80. The conclusions presented here are solely those of the authors, not those of the Small Business Administration or the current administration.

THE BASIC PROBLEM

T. Scitovisky (1980:2-3,8) has recently provided an excellent statement of the problems which modern capitalistic economies face in striving to maintain efficiency:

Private firms, once so flexible and quick to exploit new opportunities and adapt to price fluctuations, have also become less responsive to changes in market conditions. One reason, probably, is the increasing complexity and size of the most efficient producing unit, due to ever more mechanized and automated productive processes; another perhaps is the increasingly bureaucratic way in which those ever larger units are administered; and both of those factors make it harder, dearer, and slower to innovate, revise production methods, and change input coefficients. A third reason is the great importance of government contracts which encourage the firms that receive those contracts to become just as inflexible as their main customer. Yet another reason is the ever more pervasive regulatory powers of government, promoted by concerns over health, environment, job safety, equity, and similar considerations. The last is generally considered the main impediment to the firm's flexibility . . . the joints of that once wondrously flexible structure are becoming more and more calcified and rigid; the process seems hard to reverse.

One explanation of this deterioration is that the United States capitalistic economy is losing its competitiveness. Currently, the U.S. domestic economy is best described not as the perfectly competitive model of the textbooks, but rather as a two-sector model: a competitive sector and a relatively less competitive sector. Obviously, the more competitive sector is the world of small business with its many buyers and sellers. Of the two operational size groups (large and small businesses), small business more closely resembles the perfect competition model of microeconomic theory but does *not* fit the theories of perfect capital markets. The less competitive sector is the world of big government, big business, labor unions, and other groups that can significantly affect market operations through political or economic power. In short, for the small firm the severity of competition is quite different from that of the large firm (except where there is strong international competition). This level of competition in a capitalistic society provides Scitovisky's flexibility, or the economic efficiency described in our textbooks. The more competition in the economy, the greater will be the drive toward least-cost effciency. Conversely, other things being equal, the larger the organization, the more bureaucratic it becomes; the drive toward cost minimization tends to be blunted; and the more levels of management, the less flexibility the firm has in meeting change.[1]

ARE THERE ECONOMIES OF SCALE?

An argument is often made that economies of scale make the larger firm more productive than the smaller one. However, the available data indicate that economies of scale in production do not vary significantly according to size of firms. Although empirical tests of this hypothesis have been inconclusive (cf. Scherer 1980:81-100), we do not know that a wide range of different-sized establishments survive from year to year, or between economic census periods (Stigler 1958). In the long run, establishment size would tend to be uniform if there were significant economies or diseconomies of scale. The continued existence of establishments of many sizes argues that economies of scale in production are not significant.[2]

As with the argument that economies of scale in production make the larger firm more efficient, some (Scherer 1980:104-108; Scherer et al. n.d.:287; Archer and Faerber 1966) have argued that economies of scale are associated with various types of financial arrangements. However, this economy appears to be related more to institutional change in the financial markets, that is, the concentration of more and more transactions in the national markets (as opposed to local and regional markets) and the growing size of financial institutions. Large financial institutions minimize transaction costs by concentrating their lending activities with large economic units.

In addition to large lenders minimizing transaction costs by lending to the large creditors, a stock or bond issue, to be actively traded, must be large enough to be marketed nationally. Therefore, small and medium-sized local or regional firms find it almost impossible to raise money through the national exchanges unless pooling arrangements are available (e.g., the pooling of SBA loans). Franchising and mergers also enable small firms to tap otherwise inaccessible pools of capital. Because small firms appear to raise more of their capital from small banks, the growing levels of concentration among the financial intermediaries may make it even more difficult for small firms to generate funds for startups and expansion.

As with production and access to capital, some researchers have argued that the growth of large-scale production and distribution units can in part be attributed to economics of scale in distribution, particularly advertising (Scherer 1980: 108-16). Again, it would appear that these economies reflect *structural changes* in the advertising industry rather than any real economies of scale production and distribution. The development of large-circulation national newspapers and magazines, as well as national TV and radio networks with discounts on block time, has encouraged the development of national brands and national distibution chains. The trend toward a regional edition of national publications and the requirement for more local programming (and therefore more local advertising) on radio and television may reduce any existing economies of scale in national advertising.

As more and better data on different-sized firms are collected and analyzed, the hypotheses outlined here can eventually be empirically tested, resulting in a more accurate understanding of how small and large firms interact. In addition, we may learn why one group is more inherently efficient in production, distribution, or obtaining financing. For the present, there is little reason to believe that significant private sector economies of scale act to limit vigorous competition between firms of different size.

In summary, we can state, using the economists' jargon, that the externalities that small business provides to our economy in efficiency and flexibility do not appear to be offset by the diseconomies of their small size.

SMALL BUSINESS EXTERNALITIES

Additional externalities for small business, besides those of efficiency and flexibility, are receiving more attention. There is general agreement that significant benefits accrue from competition. With increased price competition, more products become available. Reservations occur only when there are significant economies of scale in production, innovation, and technological change. As noted earlier, no research consensus exists with regard to production. Small businesses, however, seem to be more efficient in utilizing government R & D dollars to generate innovations. The following extended excerpt from an SBA report (1979:2-3) presents the case for small business:

A recent study by the National Science Foundation concluded that in the post World War II period, firms with less than one thousand employees were responsible for half of the "most significant new industrial products and processes." Firms with one-hundred or fewer employees produced 24 percent of such innovations. In addition, the cost per innovation in a small firm was found to be less than in a large firm since small firms produced twenty-four times more major innovations per research and development dollar expended as did large firms. Yet small firms conduct only three percent of United States research and development. While there is much innovation that can only occur in large resourceful companies, small firms are often more adventuresome and have a greater propensity for risk taking and, accordingly, are able to move faster and use resources more efficiently than large companies. We believe that there is something *fundamental about the unusual ability of small firms to innovate that must be preserved for the sake of healthy economic and social growth in the United States.*

The role of small innovative business in stimulating economic growth can be seen from two recent studies. The first, by the Massachusetts Institute of Technology Development Foundation, shows compounded average annual growth from 1969 to 1974 for the following three groups of companies:

	Sales	Jobs
Mature Companies	11.4%	0.6%
Innovative Companies	13.2%	4.3%
Young High-technology Companies	42.5%	40.7%

The M.I.T. report states:
> It is worth noting that during the five-year period, the six mature companies with combined sales of $36 billion in 1974 experienced a net gain of only 25,000 jobs, whereas the five young, high-technology companies with combined sales of only $857 million had a net increase in employment of almost 35,000 jobs. The five innovative companies with combined sales of $21 billion during the same period created 106,000 jobs.

This study also observed that the *Innovative Companies* produced three times the level of tax revenues as a percentage of sales as did the mature firms. Conclusions similar to those mentioned above emerged from a study of 269 firms by the America Electronic Association. In February 1978, Dr. Edwin V. Zschau of the AEA presented the results of that study to the Senate Select Committee on Small Business. The report showed the following growth employment for newly established firms as contrasted to more mature companies:

Years Since Founding	Stage of Development	Employment Growth Rates in 1976
20+	Mature	0.5%
10–20	Teenage	17.4%
5–10	Developing	27.4%
1–5	Startup	57.5%

Dr. Zschau also reported that annual benefits to the economy realized in 1976 for each $100 of equity capital that had been invested in *Start-up* companies founded between 1971 and 1975 were:

- foreign sales $70 per year
- personal income taxes $15 per year
- federal corporate taxes $15 per year
- state and local taxes $ 5 per year
- total taxes $35 per year

This [sic] data shows that the benefits of investment in small innovative ventures are large (e.g., jobs are created and these jobs are kept at home—exports are created instead of imports—a new $35 per year flow in tax revenues is realized for each $100 initial investment). The large and powerful flow of benefits starts soon after the investment is made and the benefits are substantially greater than those of large corporations.

The tendency for small business to develop a larger number of important advances in technology is often attributed to the separation of ownership and management. In large firms, managers tend to have shorter time horizons than owners. Consequently, managers tend to push projects with short-term payoffs, even when other projects have higher present value to the stockholder. However, both small and large businesses innovate to secure monopolistic profit from innovation. It is unfortunate that many of our "problem" large businesses have apparently attempted to "maintain and enjoy a present business of monopoly" because they have had too much market or political power (Marris and Mueller 1980:34).

D. L. Birch (1979:30, 32), using a data base developed from Dun and Bradstreet records, found that small establishments were more important than medium and large establishments in generating new jobs between 1969 and 1976 (see Table 14.1). Furthermore, Birch found that 58 percent of the new jobs were created by small, independent businesses (as opposed to headquarters and branches or parents and subsidiaries). Almost 8 percent of the new jobs were created by establishments less than five years old. Therefore, if we are concerned about employment opportunity, the obvious conclusion is that we must have a dynamic small business sector.

Similar data from the Brookings Institution's U.S. Enterprise and Establishment Microdata File (USEEM) tabulations for June 1982 show the same basic results for 1978-80; that is, employment growth was concentrated in small establishments, as shown in Table 14.2. The two studies also underscore similar employment growth in independent single establishment firms, as illustrated in Table 14.3.

The major difference between the two studies appears when multiestablishment firms are included, classified by the aggregate employment of the firm. Now the Brookings study shows that only 38 percent of the 1978-80 employment growth is in small firms, whereas Birch shows nearly double that figure. The differences between the two sets of statistics are due to assumptions made in creating the two data bases.[3]

Table 14.1
Percentage of New Jobs Created by Businesses of Varying Size

Size Class	Percent of New Jobs
0-20	66.0
21-50	11.2
51-100	4.3
101-500	5.2
Total: small establishments	86.7
Total: medium and large establishments (500+)	13.3

SOURCE: D. L. Birch. 1979. The Job Generation Process. MIT Program in Neighboring and Regional Change: Cambridge, Mass.

Table 14.2
Comparison of Brookings and Birch Data on Employment Growth

Brookings		Birch	
Size Class	Percent of Employment Growth	Size Class	Percent of Employment Growth
0-19	54.9	0-20	66.0
20-49	14.0	21-50	11.2
50-99	9.5	51-100	4.3
100-499	17.0	101-500	5.2
500+	4.8	500+	13.3
	100.2		100.0

SOURCE: Unpublished data, Brookings Institution, 1982.

Table 14.3
Employment Growth in Single-Establishment Firms, by Size Class

Brookings		Birch	
Size Class	Percent of Employment Growth	Size Class	Percent of Employment Growth
0-19	101.3	0-20	89.6
20-99	4.5	21-50	7.6
		51-100	0.0
100+	-5.8	101-500	-2.6
		500+	5.4
Total	100.0		100.0

SOURCE: Unpublished data, Brookings Institution, 1982.

A MODEL OF GOVERNMENT POLICY

What should the government's policy be toward a sector of our economy that provides significant externalities? Developing an answer to this question requires a number of steps.

First, if we assumed that the perfectly competitive model were in operation, the answer to the question of whether the government should subsidize one group of firms relative to all other firms would be no. In short, the invisible hand of Adam Smith would be operating at its most efficient point, and the economy would maximize welfare as well as minimize the cost of production and the prices of every product. Specifically:

1. Firms would operate on the low point of their long-run average cost curve.
2. Prices would just equal the cost of producing the last unit of output, and there would be no excess profits.

3. There would be many buyers and sellers.
4. Perfect knowledge would exist about supply and demand schedules, products, and processes.
5. Freedom of entry would prevent the development of excessive profits, except for those brief periods of time when new innovations were introduced to the market.
6. Information and transaction costs would be equal to zero.

The realities in our economy are quite different from the assumptions necessary for perfect competition. For example, lack of perfect knowledge about competitors and the most optimum production processes is an obvious basic exception to this perfectly competitive model. Therefore, the greater the number of competitors, the greater the risk and the higher the information costs.

Given the higher information and transaction costs involved when dealing with the many small firms that want relatively small loans, commercial banks prefer to deal with the larger business. Thus, the larger firm tends to face more competitive capital markets, whereas the small firm faces a restricted set of options. Obviously, very few small firms can tap the equity, bond, Eurodollar markets, or pension and trust fund sources to meet their individual capital needs.

The small firm not only is faced with basically the same nonprice competition as the large firm (union contracts, government regulation, etc.), but also tends to compete with many other small firms to sell to fewer buyers because the scope of the smaller business is limited to local or regional markets. Furthermore, the small firm lacks the political and market power of the larger firm. Therefore, even though the two kinds of firms operate in basically similar environments, the competitive fight for firm survival is significantly different for the small firm relative to a large competitor.

More details could be provided, but it is clear that the U.S. economy is not perfectly competitive. The costs of small firms appear to be higher in areas such as banking.[4]

Second, one of the major tenets of public finance theory is that good tax policy should be "neutral" with regard to business decisions and operations. As one example, tax policy would not affect the decision to invest in firms of varying size or affect the cash flow of firms of varying size differently. Nor would it determine to whom the liquidating business owner would sell. The extension of this theory to all government policy suggests that procurement policy, regulatory policy, paperwork policy, monetary and fiscal policy, and so on, should be neutral as to firm size so that small firms have an equal opportunity in the economy.

A small but growing body of evidence suggests that government policy is *not* neutral in its impact. Instead, the burdens of government policy appear to be "regressive" or heavier on smaller firms, and benefits, if any, go to larger firms. Thus, it appears that significant government-induced, *artificial* economies of scale are being created.

Figure 14.1 diagrams this hypothesis. Curve AA reflects the long-run, private sector average cost curve for firms of varying size. Some private economies of scale do exist, making it difficult for the very small business to get started and survive, and some private sector diseconomies of scale exist for the very large firms. Curve BB is the cost curve after both private costs and the net costs of public policy are accounted for. (Net costs are the costs of the policy minus the value of benefits of subsidies.)

Significant diseconomies of scale have been generated by government policy, which make it difficult for new, small firms to enter the market and for existing small firms to stay in the market and effectively compete. Government policies have taken the basic constant cost relationship between firms of varying size and have created a decreasing cost curve. As with other areas, we do not yet have the data by which we can empirically test these hypothesized cost relationships, but most small business owners appear to be convinced that these changes have taken place.

As an antidote to the problem of the very large firm monopolizing an industry, antitrust policy was develped.[5] The effectiveness of antitrust policy has always been open to question, and it may not counteract the advantages derived from other, nonneutral government policies which appear either to benefit firms or to burden them to a lesser extent.

This hypothesis about regressive government costs is considered in

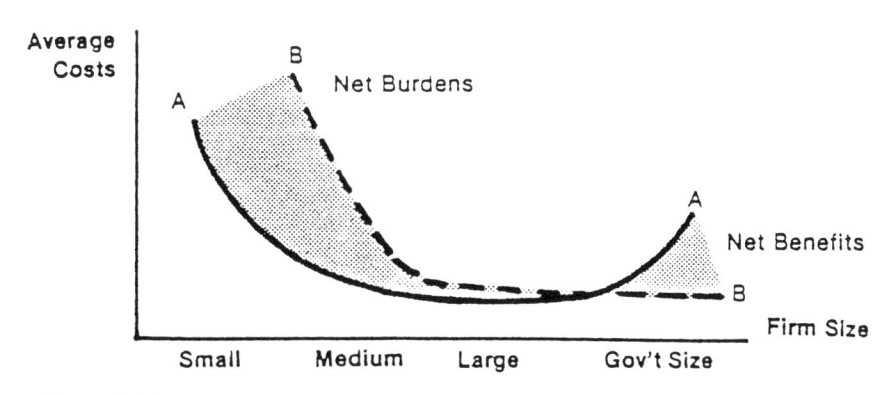

Figure 14.1
The Net Impact of Government Policy on Firms of Varying Size

214 / Summary

some detail in a series of papers by one of the authors (Berney 1979; Berney 1981; Berney and Swanson 1982). Basically, the fixed cost nature of most regulations means that the cost per unit of output or per dollar of sales for a small firm is much higher than for a large firm.

R. J. Cole and P. Sommers (1980; 1985) have developed more fully the theory of how the cost of regulation varies by firm size. Their hypothetical cost function is shown in Figure 14.2, and their empirical results are illustrated in Figure 14.3. Cole and Sommers (1980:24) conclude that the theoretical predictions (that the cost of government regulations are regressive) are strongly confirmed:

Small businesses do face higher compliance costs, in terms of dollars, hours and number of physical and work routine changes than moderate sized businesses. The mean cost level for small businesses is on the average seven to ten times as high as for large businesses. Small businesses also exhibit greater variability in current cost than moderate sized businesses. The standard deviations within the small business class are about five to twenty times as large as the standard deviations within the moderate sized class. These results reflect the greater tensions between compliance cost and enforcement risk faced by small firms.

Kenneth Chilton and Murray Weidenbaum (1980) reviewed the costs on a number of specific regulations for small business and found similar evidence:

There seems to be a naive belief on the part of some government policymakers and much of the public that the regulatory system is neutral with respect to the size of

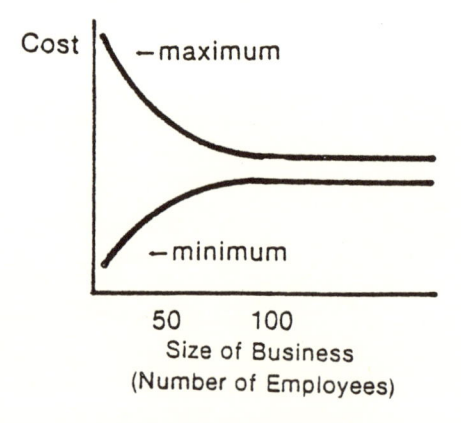

Figure 14.2
Maximum and Minimum Reasonable Compliance Costs
SOURCE: *Cost of Compliance in Small and Moderate-sized Businesses.* 1980. Battelle Human Affairs Research Center, Seattle, p. 13.

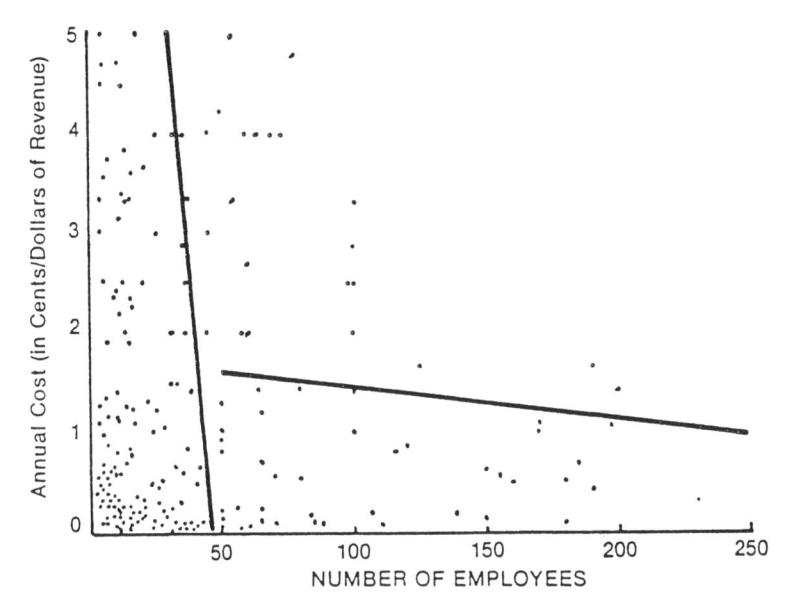

Figure 14.3
Annual Costs of Compliance by Business Size
SOURCE: *Cost of Compliance in Small and Moderate-sized Businessess.* 1980. Battelle Human Affairs Research Center, Seattle, p. 14.

the business firm. In reality, a great deal of government regulation has disproportionately adverse effects on smaller businesses.

One of the most serious threats to the continued existence of the small firm is the requirement for major capital expenditures to meet environmental or workplace safety standards. Less frequent, but no less serious, are regulations that reduce that market for a firm's product, such as a ban on a product, or a performance standard that precludes the use of the product for its normal application.

Typically, the small firm must rely on relatively short-term debt in order to finance its operations, and this reliance tends to make the firm a poor candidate for increased debt to meet regulatory requirements.

As a first approximation, a policy of government neutrality as it would affect firms of varying size is needed. But because of already existing discriminations which favor large firms over small firms, special small business programs may be necessary to provide an equitable policy base.

Unfortunately, programs designed to benefit all business, like the investment tax credit, tend primarily to benefit larger firms.[6] This is the case for two reasons. First, there is a basic difference in production relationships: large firms tend to be more capital intensive and small firms more labor intensive. Second, the more complex a rule or regulation, the more costly it is for small business to use it. Consequently, they do not even use the employment tax credit, which should benefit the small firm. Instead, it tends to benefit the larger firm more.

Neutrality as a governmental policy would appear to demand different treatment for firms of varying size. As an example, the "regulatory flexibility" concept applies different standards to different-sized firms, so that the burden of regulation is more equitably distributed. The concept of encouraging or requiring financial institutions and other lenders to establish "dual prime rates" is a further example. Because small firms appear to have much higher debt-to-equity ratios and rely more heavily on shorter term bank credit, they are more heavily burdened by a tight money policy that forces increased interest rates. Thus, dual prime rates help to spread the burden of rising interest costs more equally.

As many people prefer to work for themselves, equalizing the burden of government policy could only serve to increase the basic growth rate for small business, thus providing an easier start for entrepreneurs, and would encourage a more rapid rate of economic growth.

None of these points, however, argues that small business should be protected from failure. The more efficient firms will succeed and prosper, and the least efficient will not. Many currently successful entrepreneurs learn how to improve their production processes or managerial skills on the basis of their failures.

As a first step government should concentrate on equalizing burdens and benefits in order to achieve true neutrality. If private economies of scale do indeed exist, new firms must grow to survive, but the government should not create artificial economies of scale with public policy.

A strong argument for further action can also be made: it appears that an economic system with a dynamic small business sector produces significant external benefits. Because these benefits go to society as a whole, rather than entrepreneurs alone, in the form of increased profits, a freely operating market without government assistance does not generate as many new small businesses as would be optimal for our society. To internalize the benefits that come from small business, the government needs to devise programs that will increase the rate of return on new, innovative small businesses. Should this happen, we could then anticipate increased rapid rates of innovation and technological change, more rapid rates of employment growth, expanded price competition in all sectors of the economy, and improved export capabilities. In short, the true flexibility in our capitalistic system which Scitovisky and many others feel we have lost will be reintroduced.

CHANGES WITHIN THE U.S. ECONOMY

Is there empirical evidence for the hypothesis that the government has a discriminatory policy against small business? The number of firms within the U.S. economy obviously continues to grow, and most of these firms are small. However, data on birth and death rates, survival rates, and the average age of firms by size are so crude that it is virtually impossible to tell what is actually happening to small business in general, let alone explain the causes for what is happening.[7]

Nevertheless, Table 14.4 presents some preliminary evidence showing that the share of GNP produced by small firms (defined as firms with fewer than 500 employees) has been declining since 1963. From 1963 to 1972 the less competitive sectors (government and large business with 5,000 or more employees) were growing. From 1972 to 1977 the government's share in the production of GNP declined. However, the total large business share continued to grow, and the small business share continued to decline. A more detailed breakdown by firm size suggests that the output of the very small firm (0-19 employees) is being replaced by the output of the very large firm or "government-sized" business (5,000 plus employees).[8]

Other sources tend to substantiate these findings. For instance, Census of Manufactures data through 1977 show that the relative share of the value added by the top 200 companies in the United States has grown continuously since 1947 (Table 14.5). In the same vein, Enterprise Statistics from the Bureau of the Census show how the distribution of output and

Table 14.4
Percentage Share of GNP by Firm Size: 1958, 1963, 1972, and 1977

	1958	1963	1972	1977	(1958-63)	(1963-72)	(1972-77)
Small Business							
0-19 Employees	21.6	21.0	18.2	17.0	- 0.6	- 2.7	- 1.2
20-499 Employees	21.0	22.1	21.7	21.6	+ 1.1	- 0.4	- 0.1
TOTAL	42.6	43.1	39.9	38.6	+ 0.5	- 3.1	- 1.3
Large Business							
500-4,999 Employees	13.7	13.0	12.8	13.2	- 0.7	- 0.2	+ 0.4
5,000 + Employees	26.6	27.2	29.8	31.3	+ 0.6	+ 2.6	+ 1.5
TOTAL	40.3	40.2	42.6	44.5	- 0.1	+ 2.4	+ 1.9
Government	10.5	11.1	13.2	12.4	+ 0.6	+ 2.1	- 0.8
Other†	6.6	5.5	4.2	4.5	- 1.1	- 1.4	+ 0.3
TOTAL	100.0	99.9	99.9	100.0			

SOURCE: Calculations from Joel Popkin, "Gross Product Originating in Small Business: 1977 Benchmark and Revisions of Intervening Years."
*The 5,000 + employees firm is a proxy for government-sized business—a firm with an average of $2 billion in sales and assets. The Office of Advocacy lists 237 government-size; 221 firms had + 5,000 employees, while only 16 had fewer than 5,000 employees.
†Agriculture, Household, Rest of World, Unidentified.

the most important input–labor have changed over time. It appears that, in general, the very large firms are replacing the very small firms in the production processes, underscoring the observation that there is a long-run growing concentration of manufacturing assets in very large firms.[9]

Table 14.5
Share of Total Value Added* in Manufacturing by the Top 200 Companies

1947	1957	1958	1963	1967	1972	1977
30%	37%	38%	41%	42%	43%	43.7%

SOURCE: 1977 Census of Manufactures.
*The concept of value added is similar to GNP produced in manufacturing.

SUMMARY

A number of ideas discussed in this chapter provide a model for contemporary small business issues. The most important are:

- Government policy tends to create artificial economies of scale, giving an unwarranted advantage to the very large firm.
- Government policy should at least be neutral to firms of different size.
- Small firms tend to provide significant externalities to our economic system in the form of price competition, the development of new products and processes, and the generation of new innovations and new employment opportunities.
- Because of the significant externalities that small business provides for our economy, a strong case can be made for government programs that appear to subsidize small business, but in reality are just purchasing the small business' externalities for our economy. Without government programs equal to the value of the externalities, the small business sector of our economy will be too small relative to what would be optimal for the economy.
- Small business would not need special consideration if our economy were basically a competitive one and there were no externalities.
- A large and growing segment of our economy has sufficient market and political power to make our economy basically noncompetitive.

NOTES

1. For an excellent discussion of the research on the benefits of competition versus the benefits of large corporations, see R. Marris and D.C. Mueller (1980).

2. Alternatively, R. Gibrat and others above argued that market structure with varying amounts of concentration is determined by a stochastic process. See F.M. Scherer (1980:145-150).

3. This argument is presented in *The state of small business* (1983:83-87).
4. See *The State of Small Business* (March 1986:51).
5. For a detailed review of antitrust policy, see: F.M. Scherer (1980).
6. Refer to Berney's testimony in *Federal monetary policy and its effect on small business, Part I: Increase in interest rates*, Hearing before the Subcommitee on Access to Equity Capital and Business Opportunities, of the Committee on Small Business, House of Representatives, 96th Congress, 1st Session (October 1979:53-61). See also *Federal monetary policy and its effect on small business*, Report of the Committee on Small Business, House of Representatives, 96th Congress, 2nd Session (September 1980), and Durwood Alkire, "Small business tax problems," unpublished paper for the Office of Advocacy, SBA.
7. The lack of small business data is slowly being corrected. See *The state of small business: A report of the President* (1982; 1983; and 1984). For a discussion on the number of small businesses, see the March 1983 edition:27-37.
8. The best discussion of the percentage share of gross domestic product going to small business is found in *The state of small business* (1983:49-55).
9.

Since around the turn of the century, the 200 largest U.S. manufacturing enterprises (of course, a changing group) have increased their share of total manufacturing assets on average by about one-half of a percentage point per annum, now holding from 58 to 63 percent, depending on the data source. The most official series, provided by the Federal Trade Commission, unfortunately underwent a major break in the period 1971-73, which had the effect of causing an apparent drop in concentration. After the 1973 break the top-200 share, as newly defined, has resumed its upward climb, averaging +0.4 of one percentage point per annum for 1973-78. In the old series, from 1950-70, the trend increase was +0.6 of a percent. From 1910 to 1950, using the best available and appropriately adjusted series, the figure was about .45. Thus the trend for the 1970s, while less than for the 1950s and 1960s, is not significantly lower than for the whole half century. In more recent years, concentration has greatly increased in the financial sector and, during the postwar period, has moderately increased in the distributive sector. [Marris and Mueller (1980:31)]

REFERENCES

Archer, S. H., and L. G. Faerber, 1966. Firm size and the cost of equity capital. *Journal of Finance* 21 (March): 69-83.

Berney, R. E. 1979. *The cost of government regulation on small business.* Washington, D.C.: U.S. Small Business Administration.

———. 1981. *The cost of regulation on small business: An update.* Washington, D.C.: U.S. Small Business Administration.

Berney, R. E., and J. A. Swanson. 1982. The regressive impact of 24 governmental regulations: Some theoretical and empirical evidence. *American Journal of Small Business* 663 (January-March): 16-27.

Birch, D. L. 1979. The job generation process. Cambridge, Mass.: MIT Program in Neighborhood and Regional Change.

Chilton, D., and M. Weidenbaum. 1980. Small business performances in the regulated economy. Working Paper #52. St. Louis, MO.: Center for the Study of American Business, Washington University.

Cole, R. J., and P. Sommers. 1980. *Cost of compliance in small and moderate-sized business.* Seattle, Wash.: Battelle Human Affairs Research Center, SBA-79-2668.

Marris, R., and D. C. Mueller. 1980. The corporation, competition and the invisible hand. *Journal of Economic Literature* 18(March): 32-63.

Scherer, F. M. 1980. *Industrial market structure and economic performance.* 2nd ed. Chicago: Rand McNally.

Scherer, F. M., et al. n.d. *The economics of multi-plant operations.* n.a.

Scitovisky, T. 1980. Can capitalism survive? An old question in a new setting. *American Economic Review* (May): 2-8.

Sommers, P., and R. J. Cole. 1985. Finance costs for small and large businesses. *Policy Studies Journal* 13 (June): 701-708.

Stigler, G. J. 1958. The economies of scale. *Journal of Law and Economics* 1(October): 54-71.

U.S. Small Business Administration (SBA). 1979. *Small business and innovation.* Office of the Chief Counsel for Advocacy.

———. *The state of small business: A report of the President.* 1983. Washington, D.C.: U.S. Government Printing Office.

15 Regulation, Small Business, and Economic Development: A Historical Perspective on Regulation of Business

RICHARD J. JUDD and BARBRA K. SANDERS

The general intent of government policy is to protect citizens from inequity and inefficiency, fraud, or abuse, and to control monopolies, thereby helping to make the marketplace "truly free." The United States, one of the most purely capitalist countries of the Industrial West by the way its economic activity is organized, still relies on market forces (Cochran et al. 1986). The majority of economic enterprise is privately owned and operated; few activities are totally owned and operated within the public interest. Nonetheless, the United States does regulate economic activity to a great extent.

Much of the regulation today is rooted in the nineteenth century. As the country was industrializing, attempts by firms at coordination—whether through collusion or consolidation—were insufficient to assure stable growth. Industry increasingly turned to government to accomplish what industry itself could not—provide a stable environment for planning and coordinating investment decisions among industry participants (Acs et al. 1987). In fact, Gabriel Kolko suggests that the entire Progressive Era was a movement to stablize industry through government intervention (Kolko, 1963). Government policy helped create a stable environment that enabled industrial organizations to undertake long-term investment plans on a predictable or calculable basis. A network of government agencies, regulatory boards, industry advisory boards, and trade associations developed which have permitted companies and industries to coordinate investment, output, and, in some cases, pricing decisions on formal or informal bases. Thus, government policy has been a useful and essential catalyst in the oligopolizing of American energy, extraction, and manufacturing industries.

The regulatory structure, which was meant to support mass production, unintentionally resulted in economic rigidity. As size of firms increased, the bureaucratic mechanisms designed to manage the growth became more rigid, with two economic consequences: (1) price flexibility became reduced and in some sectors was legislated away, and (2) barriers to entry into most established industries created a condition whereby existing firms became comfortable, seeing little need to innovate. However, the long-term consequence of absence of innovation is economic stagnation.

As the American economy slowed down in the 1970s, some large corporations responded by moving some production capacity overseas. They could expand output—using semi- and unskilled labor—in developing countries where primary demand for tangible goods was strong. In today's global economy, the factors historically used by American industries to secure competitive advantage through mass production are of lesser importance. If American industry wants to produce domestically, competing on the same terms it did historically, then it must accept prevailing world wage rates for semi- and unskilled labor. If it so chooses, America should prepare for a massive decline in its standard of living (Carnegie Forum 1986). On the other hand, if the United States chooses to diminish its position in the world economy as a mass production supplier of goods, and not compete with low-wage countries, then it should prepare to abandon the mass production model as the centerpiece of national economic output and with it the largest of its industrial corporations.

Walter Adams and James Brock argue that the return to economic health is through ending government bailouts, maintaining strong antitrust enforcement, supporting strong foreign competition, and continued deregulation of the economy (Adams and Brock 1987). The Reagan administration appears to be fostering these same concepts, except for strong antitrust enforcement. The free trade policy of the Reagan administration has kept pressure on the domestic economy to compete with the rest of the world. The policy reducing the foreign exchange rate has been an important tool in helping American-produced products compete on price in a world market. However, improved price comparatives with other producing countries is only half of the equation. Quality is the other. Many imports into the United States are of higher price and higher quality than the domestically produced goods they have replaced.

The vertically integrated, large-scale mass production organization is gradually being replaced by smaller scale, horizontally integrated "flexible" specialization manuacturers (Piore and Sable 1984). This development has been made possible by technological advances that have led to the development of new products, new firms, and new markets (Rostow 1983) in fields such as microelectronics, telecommunications, and biotechnology. The ability of industry to competitively produce quality specialized products depends on access to advanced technology, availability of skilled labor, flexible supplier networks, a high level of entrepreneurial talent, and continued deregulation of the domestic economy (AmeriTrust Corporation 1986).

SMALL BUSINESS AND ECONOMIC GROWTH

It is becoming more evident that small business is successfully addressing a policy issue with high national priority—economic growth. Unfortunately, we do not have an adequate theory base linking significant economic public policies such as tax regulations, banking regulations, industry-by-industry deregulation, or monetary policy with the small business sector or with entrepreneurial behavior attributes. Since small business does not have the political influence of unions and big business, policymakers have found it easier to address the issues in terms of the interests that are relatively known (e.g., big business, government, and unions) in contrast to that which is unknown or diffuse (e.g., small business). However, empirical evidence suggests the following:

- More new jobs are being created by small businesses than by large business.
- Newer technologies can be utilized by small as well as large businesses, and perhaps better utilized by smaller firms because such firms require much less capital with shorter payback periods, are less dedicated to single-purpose processing, and can produce a wider range of products than can firms with the older, more traditionally known technologies.
- Taxes and "red tape" are considered critical problems confronting small businesses that are unable to get working capital loans considered most crucial.
- The cost of complying with government requirements is much higher per dollar of sales for the small firm than for the large firm, although the compliance burden varies significantly among industries.
- Employment legislation in general works adversely for the smaller firm, in particular in the employee selection process.
- Taxation has had a greater impact on the smaller than on the larger firm, whereas empirical information is not yet available concerning the impact of the 1986-87 tax law changes.
- The most important means of capital formation for small business is believed to be through tax relief.
- Small firms tend to receive proportionately less than large firms in loan monies available from commercial banks.
- Although small firms represent the greatest potential for economic growth, this sector is not receiving its "share" of the funds available for financing economic growth.
- Industry innovation rates fall as the level of firm concentration rises, and the percentage of an industry that is unionized is negatively related to innovative activity (Acs and Audretsch 1986).

- Small firms tend to have higher innovation rates in relation to increases in skill level of labor and R & D intensity than do large firms (Acs and Audretsch 1986).

THE IMPACT OF REGULATION ON SMALLER BUSINESS

Several examples can serve to highlight regulatory impacts on small business. As federal regulatory agencies expanded during the 1960s, smaller firms often experienced adverse effects, disproportionate to their size, from the expanding regulatory powers of government. Capital expenditure to meet environmental and workplace standards has had serious consequences for smaller firms, particularly manufacturers. As the costs of compliance increased, an artificial, government-induced "economy of scale" was placed on such firms by virtue of the higher unit costs associated with meeting regulatory compliance requirements. For example, Kenneth Chilton and Murray Weidenbaum's survey of small firms in the forging industry and chemical specialty industry showed that environmental and workplace safety rules were burdensome, creating new economies of scale in these industries (Chilton and Weidenbaum 1980).

The smaller firm is sensitive not only to increases in capital costs, but also to changes in labor costs. Many smaller businesses are labor intensive. According to U.S. Small Business Administration data (1983), approximately 30 percent of Occupational Safety and Health Administration (OSHA) inspections in 1979 were in firms with ten or fewer employees. Such firms represented only 17 percent of the workforce. Highly specific rules and the issuance of fines for noncompliance tend to increase labor costs. Moreover, an increase in the minimum wage law has a greater adverse effect on the smaller than on the larger firm. Over 20 percent of the nation's small businesses hire full-time teenage help, whereas more than a third employ teenagers on a part-time basis (House Committee on Small Business, 1978). Thus, as regulatory compliance rules are made and disproportionately applied to smaller firms, wage minimums are increased, and the costs to small firms rise significantly. As noted by Bruce A. Kirchhoff (Kirchhoff, 1985), access to capital is a continual problem for small business which is much more dependent on short-term debt than is large business. Therefore, the small firm is sensitive not only to the price charged for short-term debt, but also to the regulations that affect their need for increased debt.

From a macroeconomic perspective, the biggest factor influencing investment decisions in business is the tax code. Regulatory considerations can directly affect venture capital and equity markets for small business. Typically, existing financial institutions such as venture capitalists, commercial banks, and investment bankers assure sufficient capital availability to large, established corporations. However, there is increasing evidence that these same institutions fail to provide appropriate and sufficient amounts of capital to new and small business (Corporation for Enterprise Development 1987).

There are many reasons why capital is unavailable: unwillingness or inability to diversify risk, difficulty and cost of acquiring adequate information on new, young, or small firms, cost of putting deals together, political/geographic/racial/sexual biases, as well as regulatory and taxation policies such as barriers to risk pooling or usury ceilings. Such practices may prohibit existing financial institutions from making substantial capital available to new, young, and small firms, regardless of their soundness and future growth potential (Corporation for Enterprise Development 1987).

THE CHANGING POLICY ENVIRONMENT

Fortunately, economic development has become a central issue at not only the federal but also the state and local levels of government. Entrepreneurship and small business have been rediscovered, and attending virtues have been publicized much as a result of the economic contribution made by entrepreneurial and small-sized firms. President Reagan, the SBA, and trade associations point to the employment, innovation, and economic contributions made by new/small business. However, the role of small business in economic development is often considered the most important argument to be made. The small firm's role as a job generator has important public policy and economic development implications. Public officials faced with declining productivity, plant closings, and rising unemployment within their districts cannot ignore the data, with the result that policy changes have been taking place.

Improvements have been made in a number of critical regulatory areas such as the Regulatory Flexibility Act, Paperwork Reduction Act, and the Equal Access to Justice Act, SEC, OSHA and other labor regulation reforms and Interstate Commerce Commission deregulation at the federal level. Similarly, many states have been undertaking regulatory reform studies as a central ingredient in their economic development programs. Some states have established guaranteed review and decision timetables for authorizing business permits, developed "one-stop" permit offices that also provide guidance and assistance in completing the request forms, created ombudsman offices to handle questions and complaints, and sought ways to improve cooperation between businesspersons and government officials.

Several states have established new agencies or cabinets to plan, market, and respond to the economic development challenges. States have been reexamining their tax codes as well, because stable, attractive conditions for enterprise development can be influenced by the administration and perceived equitability of tax policies.

Financial institutions, licensed and regulated by government, control approximately 80 percent of the $5 trillion in the U.S. economy. Any effort to enhance a state's attractiveness for business development without consideration of the financial regulations in the state will have limited results. At the same time, any change in the investment practices of the primary financial institutions operating within a state will have dramatic impact on the availability, and possibly the cost, of capital available to businesses within the state. Three regulatory initiatives that impact on capital availability are: (1) regulation which allows for statewide branch banking, thereby stimulating aggressive lending practices, (2) local or state reinvestment policies which seek to ensure that banks meet the credit needs of businesses within the community or state, and (3) elimination or loosening of restrictions on pension funds which permit investing of fund assets in qualifying in-state businesses. Other efforts have developed to help channel capital to businesses or to communities seeking to enhance business development. Publicly capitalized venture capital corporations, local or state business, and industrial developmental corporations, as well as the merger of government and private lending programs, illustrate how states are trying to ensure that capital will be available to ensure the successful growth of its businesses.

Another major initiative is being undertaken by various states to address the conditions through which business growth can take place. The attempts undertaken can be divided into one of four categories: creating research and development centers; initiating technology transfer centers; establishing small business development centers; and developing small business incubator facilities. Such efforts seek to provide a climate that will nurture technological innovation, encourage entrepreneurship, and strengthen business management practices.

Other initiatives are being pursued that have direct or tangential relationships to enhancing business or economic development. Increasing high school graduation standards, teacher certification testing, computer literacy, high school graduation testing, and career ladder plans for teachers illustrate developments in public education which are designed to enhance the ability of the next generation of entrepreneurs, workers, and managers to successfully compete in a world economy. Local initiatives include expansion of employee ownership programs, and community-based rapid-response committees to address plant closing or major layoffs and to deal with the related social and economic dislocations; establishment of minority enterprise and job training programs; and promotion of federal transfer payments such as unemployment compensation, welfare, or social security payments for support of individuals to receive training, education, or aid in entering the self-employment/small business arena.

CONCLUSION

The small firm creates most of the jobs that have to be replaced when large firms move out. The past decade has witnessed a dramatic increase in the number and type of programs designed to foster the growth of new/small business. However, the connection between strong economic development and job creation is not well understood.

The issue is how to create the environment that will spark the "spontaneous combustion" from which economic development will flow. In other words, how can a locale, region, or state grow its own small firms? In industry, the ingredients for such growth are being recognized as based on science and related to information technology. Such firms tend to have high wages, produce goods with high value-added, and have a high multiplier effect within the economy.

Conventional thinking may still hold out for programs and policies that seek substantial employment growth in the manufacturing industries based on traditional technology, around which much of our regulatory policies have revolved. It is not the American economy, which is historically considered to be founded on manufacturing, that is being deindustrialized. Rather, the American labor force is being deindustrialized. In the United States, employment grew faster between 1973 and 1985 than during any peacetime period in the nation's history. However, this growth has been primarily in nonmanufacturing areas, especially in white-collar jobs. Thus, an economic development policy designed to enhance manufacturing employment, either high or low tech, is likely to fail. There are three reasons for such failure. First, an accelerating trend is taking place in the substitution of information and capital for semi- and unskilled labor. Second, the economy of scale notion in manufacturing is undergoing a reversal, with smaller firms and new business creations accounting for much of the employment increase when such increases are occurring. Third, industries that are knowledge intensive, such as semiconductors, computers, aerospace, pharmaceuticals, synthetic materials, and other similar sectors, are growing rapidly.

America's mass production, industrial economy was built on the unique national advantages of a large internal market, abundant natural resources, a large and trainable labor force, and effective utilization of the bureaucratic model of organization. The combination of these ingredients produced reliable tangible products through employment of large numbers of semi- and unskilled workers. Today, mass production organizations are gradually being replaced through flexible production technologies that utilize high-skilled workers within smaller sized firms. In today's global economy, if America wants to compete on the same or similar terms as it did in the past, then it may be confronted with prevailing world wage rates for low and semiskilled labor. As a consequence, it may have to prepare for a massive decline in its standard of living. America has historically been an entrepreneurial nation within the industrialized world. Innovation and entrepreneurial success may be the key ingredients to maintaining America's output and political/economic position in the world economy. Sufficient venture capital can fertilize the seeds for growth. But the regulatory environment shapes the conditions (or soil) within which economic growth will take place.

As we move through the late 1980s into the 1990s, there is little question that America is experiencing a revolution in economic development policymaking. Policy and programmatic efforts appear to be developing along two corollary lines: first, attempting to "get out of the way" of business development, and second, creating programs and policies that encourage business formation and job creation, which may contribute to economic vitality and growth.

REFERENCES

Acs, Zoltan J., and David B. Audretsch. 1986. *The determinants of innovation in large and small firms.* Berlin: International Institute of Management.

Acs, Zoltan J., David B. Audretsch, and Richard J. Judd. 1987. *Economic development and public policy: The growth of new/small business.* Springfield, Ill.: Center for Policy Studies and Program Evaluation, Sangamon State University.

Adams, Walter, and James Brock. 1987. *The bigness complex.* New York: Pantheon.

AmeriTrust Corporation. 1986. *Investing in the future: A prospectus for Mid-America.*

Chilton, Kenneth, and Murray Weidenbaum. 1980. *Small business performance in the regulated economy.* St. Louis: Center for the Study of American Business, Washington University.

Cochran, Clarke E., Lawrence C. Mayer, T. R. Carr, and Joseph N. Cayer. 1986. *American public policy: An introduction.* 2nd ed. New York: St. Martin's Press.

Kirchhoff, Bruce A. 1985. Analyzing the cost of debt for small business. *Policy Studies Journal* 13:4.

Kolko, Gabriel, 1963. *The triumph of conservatism.* New York: Macmillan.

Making the grade: The development report card for the states. 1987. Washington, D.C.: Corporation for Enterprise Development.

A nation prepared: Teachers for the 21st century. 1986. Carnegie Forum on Education and the Economy.

Piore, Michael, and Charles Sabel. 1984. *The second industrial divide.* New York: Basic Books.

Rostow, W. W. 1983. Technology and unemployment in the western world. *Challenge* 26:6-17.

U.S. Congress, House Committee on Small Business, 1978. *Hearings.*

U.S. Small Business Administration (SBA). 1983. *The state of small business: A report of the President.* Washington, D.C.: U.S. Government Printing Office.

Selected Bibliography

Abernathy, W. J., K. B. Clark, and A. M. Katrow. 1983. *Industrial renaissance.* New York: Basic Books.
Acs, Z. J. 1984. *The changing structure of the U.S. economy.* New York: Praeger.
Acs, Z. J., and D. B. Audretsch. 1986. *The determinants of innovation in large and small firms.* Berlin: International Institute of Management.
Adams, W., and J. Brock. 1987. *The bigness complex.* New York: Pantheon.
Anderson, J., M. Dubnick, and A. Gitelson (eds.). Forthcoming. *Public policy and economic institutions.* Greenwich, Conn.: JAI Press.
Armington, C., and M. Odle. 1983. *U.S. establishment longitudinal microdata: The weighted integrated USEEM 1976-1982 sample.* Washington, D.C.: Brookings Institution.
Balderston, K. M. 1986. *Plant closings, layoffs, and worker readjustment: The states' response to economic change.* National Governors Association.
Barnett, D. F., and L. Schorsch. 1983. *Steel: Upheaval in a basic industry.* Cambridge, Mass.: Ballinger Book Co.
Berger, S., and M. Piore. 1980. *Dualism and discontinuity in industrial societies.* Cambridge: Cambridge University Press.
Birch, D. L. 1979. *The job generation process.* Washington, D.C.: Economic Development Administration.
Bryce, H. J. (ed.). 1980. *Cities and firms.* Lexington, Mass.: Lexington Books.
Butler, S. 1981. *Enterprise zones: Greenlining the inner city.* New York: Universe Books.
Cole, R. J., and P. D. Tegeler. 1980. *Government requirements of small business.* Lexington, Mass.: Lexington Books.
Donaldson, G., and J. Lorsch. 1983. *Decision making at the top.* New York: Basic Books.
Drucker, P. 1985. *Innovation and entrepreneurship.* New York: Harper and Row.

Hansen, D. 1981. *Banking and small business.* Washington, D.C.: Council of State Planning Agencies.

Hogan, W. 1983. *World steel in the 1980s.* Boston: Lexington Books.

Horvitz, P. M., and R. R. Pettit (eds.). 1984. *Small business finance, part 1: Problems in financing small business.* Greenwich, Conn.: JAI Press.

Hoy, J. C., and M. H. Bernstein. 1981. *Business and academia: Partners in New England's economic survival.* Hanover, N.H.: University Press of New England.

Kent, C., et al. (eds.). 1982. *Encyclopedia of entrepreneurship.* Englewood Cliffs, N.J.: Prentice-Hall.

Kienschnick, M., L. Litvak, and B. H. Daniels. 1980. *Financing new business development.* Washington, D.C.: Council of State Planning Agencies.

Neck, P. A. (ed.). 1979. *Small enterprise development: Policies and programmes.* Geneva: International Labor Office.

Piore, M., and C. F. Sabel. 1984. *The second industrial divide.* New York: Basic Books.

Reich, R. 1983. *The next American frontier.* New York: Time Books.

Scherer, F. M. 1980. *Industrial market structure and economic performance.* 2nd ed. Chicago: Rand McNally.

Solomon, A. P. (ed.). 1980. *The prospective city.* Cambridge, Mass.: MIT Press.

Tornatzky, L. G., J. D. Everland, G. B. Myles, W. A. Hetzner, C. Johnson, D. Roitman, and J. Schneider. 1983. *The process of technological innovation: Reviewing the literature.* Washington, D.C.: National Science Foundation.

U.S. Small Business Administration. 1983. *The status of small business: Programs and activities.* Washington, D.C.: U.S. Government Printing Office.

———. 1984. *The state of small business: A report of the President.* Washington, D.C.: U.S. Government Printing Office.

Vaughan, R., R. Pollard, and B. Dyer. 1984. *The wealth of states: Policies for a dynamic economy.* Washington, D.C.: Council of State Planning Agencies.

Vesper, K. H. 1980. *New venture strategies.* Englewood Cliffs, N.J.: Prentice-Hall.

Weidenbaum, M. L. 1986. *Business, government and the public.* Englewood Cliffs, N.J.: Prentice-Hall.

Wheaton, W. C. (ed.). 1980. *Interregional movements and regional growth.* Washington, D.C.: Urban Institute.

Index

Accelerated Cost Recovery System (ACRS), 83-84, 92
Adams, Walter, 222
Advanced technology firms, 170
Advanced Technology Foundation Act, 177
Age Discrimination in Employment Act (ADEA), 69, 72-73
Ambitious firms, 26-28
American capitalistic values, 22
Antitrust policy, 213
Arthur Anderson and Company, 53-54

Birch, David L., 21, 43, 210
Birth rates, evidence of, 159-63
Black business geography, 189, 196-99
Black enterprises, formation, growth, and failure of, 189
Black participation rates, 198-99
Black population residing in urban areas, 195
Black population size, 195
Black public/private wage-earners, 193
Black unemployment, 195
Blomstrom, R., 183
Boston's Route 128, 169

Bretton Woods Agreement of 1971, 42
Brock, James, 222
Burstiner, I., 114
Bygrave, William D., 28, 30, 32

California's Silicon Valley, 169
Casey, William J., 34
Certified Development Corporations (CDCs), 130
Chilton, Kenneth, 131, 214, 224
Classification schemes, U.S. Small Business Administration, 64
Classifying small firms, basis for, 22
Coalitions, to influence public policy, 8, 12, 134-35
Cole, Roland J., 54
Competitive markets, 205
Compliance costs: by business size, 215; effects of size and industry on, 60; reasonable, maximum and minimum, 214
Comprehensive Income Tax (CIT), 89-90, 92
Constrained growth firms, 28-31
Consumption Tax (CT), 90-91
Conway Data, Inc., 115
Cooper, A. C., 96

Coopers and Lybrand, 116
Corporate social activism, 184-85
Corporate social responsibility: historical evolution of, 182; survival through profit, 182-84

Davies, John O., 53
Davis, K., 183
Davis-Bacon Act, 74
Decline of traditional industries, 171
Deficit Reduction Act of 1984 (DEFRA), 79, 81, 86-87, 92
Depreciation, accounting for, 83, 88-89
Development of new assistance programs, 205
Different-sized firms, 207
Diseconomies of scale, 213
Dun and Bradstreet data, 37

Economic core firms, 23-26
Economic crisis of the 1970s, 42
Economic development movement, 111
Economic development, postwar model of, 41
Economic engine, 18, 20-21
Economic growth, 17-23; impacts and issues of, 9
Economic Recovery Tax Act (ERTA), 33-36, 79-81, 84-87, 91-92
Economic status of blacks, 193-94
Economic suicide of undifferentiated competition, 25
Economies of scale, 20, 206-7, 213
Edwards, Keith L., 43-44
Employment growth, single-establishment firms, 211
Employment Retirement Income Security Act (ERISA), 68-70
Enterprise zones, 115-16
Entrepreneurial behavior, 17-18
Entrepreneurial decisions, government control of, 127
Entrepreneurial development policy, 155
Entrepreneurial economics, 128
Entrepreneurial model, 164-65

Entrepreneurial policies, 155-57, 164
Entrepreneurship and small business as synonymous terms, 17
Environment of price flexibility, 47
Equal Access to Justice Act, 133, 255
Equal Employment Opportunity Commission (EEOC), 68-70, 76-77
Estate tax burden, 86-87
Export finance, 102, 106
Exporting problems, 97
Export management, 102, 106
Export marketing, 102, 106
Export operations, 102, 106
Externalities of small business, 208
Externally constrained firms, 29-30

Fast, Norman D., 28, 30, 32
Federal tax policy, recent developments, 80-87
FIFO (first-in first-out), 82
Financial employment of blacks, 195
Financial institutions, 226
Financial services and venture capital, impacts of, 7
Firm characteristics, 174-75
Firm size, impact on productivity, 141
Flexible specialization technologies, 42, 46-48
Frederick, W. C., 183

Galbraith, John Kenneth, 19-20
Gellman Research Associates, Inc., 31-32
Geographic space, 191
Glamorous firms, 31-32
Godfather's Pizza, 26-27, 32
Government incentives or disincentives, 5
Government policy: a model of, 211; net impact on firms, 213; neutrality of, 206, 215; See Regulation
Government requirements: business impacts of, 59; cost burdens of, 53, 55; policy implications of, 65; See Regulation
Growth of industry output and input, 143-46

Hayes, D. A., 183
Health Maintenance Act, 73
Health Maintenance Organization (HMO), 73
High technology industries, 162
Human capital, development of, 116

Incentives, types offered by state and local governments, 116
Incubators, small business, 155, 226
Industry dummy variables, 62
Industry output, measure of, 143
Industry Sector Advisory Committee on Small and Minority Business for Trade Policy Matters, 95
Inflation, 130
Information-gathering and dissemination capacities, 116
Innovation: copy of, 29; cost of, 29–30; declining rates of, 30; innovation and technology 3, 23–36 passim, 42–44, 228
Integration into the new economic structure, 26
Internally constrained firms, 28–29
Inventories, accounting for, 82, 88
Investment risk, reduction of, 84–87
IRB (Industrial Revenue Bonds), 157

Job training programs, 75
Jobs, creation of, 2, 18, 112, 210–11
Joint Economic Committee of Congress, 117

Large firms, tendency to monopolize industries, 153
Large-scale mass production organization, 222
Large-scale production, 207
Last-in first-out (LIFO), 82
Legal penalties for noncompliance, 131
Life cycle of a company, 97
Local government policy, 164
Longitudinal Establishment Data File, 37
Loss offsets, restrictions on, 85
Low-structure destruction, 23

Management training and assistance, facilitation of, 116
Mass production organizations, 228
Mass production sector, 42
Mature manufacturing, 164
Medium-sized firms, 119, 123
Mini-mills, 44, 45; flexible specialization technologies of, 48; innovation by, 46; productivity of, 46
Minimum wage, 69, 73
Minority business development, 10
Minority Business Development Agency, 187–88
Minority business enterprises (MBEs), 187
Minority enterprise and job training programs, 226–27
Modernization, 45
"Mom and pop" stores, 20

National Chamber of Commerce, 127
National Federation of Independent Business, 38
National Labor Relations Act (NLRA), 68–69, 71, 77
National Science Board, 21
New Industrial State, 19
New steel industry, 44–46
Next American Frontier, 37
Noncompliance choices of small firms, 58
Nonprice competition, 212
North Carolina's Research Triangle, 169

Occupational Safety and Health Administration (OSHA), 68–70, 77, 224
Office of Federal Contract Compliance (OFCCP), 68–69
Oligopolistic legacy of price maker, 47
Organization of Petroleum Exporting Countries (OPEC), 42

Paperwork Reduction Act, 225
Perfect competition, 19; keeper of, 20
Physical capital, improvement of, 116
Policy commitment, 158
Policy innovativeness, 158

Production and access to capital, 207
Productivity growth, rates by firm size class, 149
Productivity, long-term rate of growth, 141
Productivity, measuring growth, 142, 147-48
Productivity, total factor growth, 141
Prompt Payments Act, 133
Public finance theory, major tenets of, 212

Quality of life factors, 115, 118, 123

R&D Scoreboard, 117-18
Reagan, Ronald, 33, 128, 225
Reducing the labor force, difficulties in, 71-72
Regulation, 53, 131; access to information of, 68; employment legislation, 69; employment-related issues of concern, 68; impact of, 4; impact on smaller firms, 58-60, 70-73, 131, 224-225. *See* Compliance costs
Regulatory environment, 65, 131-32, 228
Regulatory flexibility, 216
Regulatory Flexibility Act, 133, 225
Regulatory initiatives, 226
Regulatory structure, 222
Reich, Robert, 37
Research and development centers, 226
Revolving Loan Funds (RLFs), 157
Robinson-Patman Act, 17
Rogers, E. U., 100

Safe harbor leasing of tax benefits, 86
Schumpeter, Joseph A., 21, 31
Schumpeter's theory of creative destruction, 21-22, 36
Securities and Exchange Commission (SEC), 74
Set asides, 75-76
Standard Industrial Classification Codes (SIC), 142, 159-60

Site selection decisions and the small firm, 111, 114-16, 120; by high tech firms, 115
Size, 118
Skitovisky, T., 206
"Small," defined, 18, 55
Small business: categories of, 23, 67; economic growth, 1; government assistance to, 10; impacts on public policy issues, 1; incubators, 155; literature, typology to classify, 96; new view of, 21; policy impact on, 4; policy implications for, 8, 22; problems of, 96-97, 130; regulation of, 205; sector, 42; targeting, 158; virtuous image of, 20
Small Business Development Center (SBDC), 130
Small Business Investment Corporations (SBIC), 130
Small firms: advanced technology, 170; attractiveness of, 112-13; new efforts to attract, 113; responsiveness to regulatory reforms, 113. *See* Small business
Smokestack chasing, 155
Social irresponsibility, 184-85
Social responsibility, 10
Social security taxes, 72
Sommers, Paul, 54
Southland Corporation and Seven/Eleven Stores, 25-26
Spatial dimensions, 192
Stages of the exporting process, 99-100
Standard metropolitan statistical area (SMSA), 188
Startup rates under different policy climates, 156
State and local government, impacts of, 7
"State of Small Business: A Report of the President," 33, 35
State surveys of small businesses: in Connecticut, 53; in Georgia and Massachusetts, 55-57; in New York,

157-63 passim; in Pennsylvania, 175; in Washington, 54-55
Subchapter S, 36
Success continuum, 97; characteristics of each stage, 98-99
Summers, Lawrence, 82

Taft-Hartley Act. *See* NLRA
Taxation, 130; impacts of, 6; relative burdens of, 83
Tax credits, 74
Tax Equity and Fiscal Responsibility Act (TEFRA), 79, 81, 84-86, 92
Taxonomic space, 191
Tax provisions. *See* ERTA
Tax rates, reduction of, 81-82, 87-88
Tax reform: Reagan Administration's proposals, 87; unified gift and estate tax, 86-87; CIT, 89-90; CT, 90-91
Technical progress, measure of, 141
Technology and innovation, 3
Technology transfer centers, 226
Tegele, Philip D., 54
Timmons, Jeffry A., 28, 30, 32

Universities: linkages with small business, 119, 169; measures of importance, 172-73; preference for location near, 121; transfer of scientific knowledge from, 121
University-firm interaction, 172-75
U.S. Bureau of the Census, 37

U.S. Department of Housing and Urban Development, 115
U.S. Department of Labor, 75
U.S. Enterprise and Establishment Microdata File, 21
U.S. Environmental Protection Agency, 132
U.S. Federal Trade Commission, 132
U.S. General Accounting Office, 116
U.S. Internal Revenue Service, 205
U.S. Securities and Exchange Commission, 132
U.S. Small Business Administration 17, 30, 37, 43, 67, 127-28, 169, 205, 224

Venture and Equity Capital for Small Business, 33-34
Venture and expansion capital, generation of, 116
Venture capital and financial services, impacts of, 7
Venture capital corporations, 226
Venture capital pools, 155

Weidenbaum, Murray, 131, 214, 224
Weiss, Randall, 80
Wendy's Restaurants, 27
White House Conference on Small Business of 1980, 91-92
Whyte, William H., 20
World trade, impacts of, 6

About the Editors and Contributors

ZOLTAN J. ACS is Associate Professor of Economics, Sangamon State University in Illinois.

DAVID N. ALLEN is Assistant Professor of Business Administration, Pennsylvania State University.

FRED W. BECKER is Associate Professor of Public Administration, Sangamon State University in Illinois.

ROBERT E. BERNEY is Professor of Economics, Washington State University.

ROLAND J. COLE is an attorney with the firm of Jardine, Foreman, and Appel, Seattle, Washington.

EVELYN M. ERB is Research Assistant at the Wharton School, University of Pennsylvania.

WILLIAM T. GREENWOOD is a private consultant and former Professor of Management, Sangamon State University in Illinois.

R. DUANE IRELAND is Mays Professor at the Hankamer School of Business, Baylor University in Texas.

RICHARD J. JUDD is Professor of Business Administration, Sangamon State University in Illinois.

BRUCE A. KIRCHHOFF is Professor of Entrepreneurship, Babson College in Massachusetts.

DONALD F. KURATKO is Associate Professor and Coordinator of the Small Business/Entrepreneurship Program, Ball State University in Indiana.

VICTOR LEVINE is Visiting Professor at the University of Zimbabwe, Harare, Zimbabwe.

DAVID B. LONGBRAKE is Associate Professor, Department of Geography and Geology, University of Denver.

STEVEN A. LUSTGARTEN is Research Associate at the Center for the Study of Business and Government, Baruch College in New York.

THOMAS S. McCALEB is Associate Professor of Economics and Assistant Vice-President for Academic Affairs, Florida State University.

TIMOTHY S. MESCON is Dean of the Franklin Perdue School of Business, Salisbury State College in Maryland.

BENJAMIN W. MOKRY is Assistant Professor of Political Science, University of Mississippi.

WOODROW W. NICHOLS, JR., is Professor of Geography, North Carolina Central University.

HERBERT R. NORTHRUP is Professor of Industry and Director of the Industrial Research Unit of the Wharton School, University of Pennsylvania.

ED OWENS is Director of the Washington State Small Business Development Center.

BARBRA K. SANDERS is Managing Partner of the Certified Public Accounting firm of Nosari & Sanders, Springfield, Illinois.

PAUL SOMMERS is Research Associate at the Graduate School of Business Administration, University of Washington.

PHILIP M. VAN AUKEN is Chairman of the Department of Management, Baylor University School of Business in Texas.

GEORGE S. VOZIKIS is Professor of Management, Memphis State University.

DEBORAH McCORKLE WAUGH is a doctoral candidate in accounting, Georgia State University.

WILLIAM L. WAUGH, JR., is Associate Professor of Public Administration and Political Science, Georgia State University.

POLICY STUDIES ORGANIZATION PUBLICATIONS ISSUED WITH GREENWOOD PRESS/QUORUM BOOKS

Intergovernmental Relations and Public Policy
J. Edwin Benton and David R. Morgan, editors

Policy Controversies in Higher Education
Samuel K. Gove and Thomas M. Stauffer, editors

Citizen Participation in Public Decision Making
Jack DeSario and Stuart Langton, editors

Energy Resources Development: Politics and Policies
Richard L. Ender and John Choon Kim, editors

Federal Lands Policy
Phillip O. Foss, editor

Policy Evaluation for Local Government
Terry Busson and Philip Coulter, editors

Comparable Worth, Pay Equity, and Public Policy
Rita Mae Kelly and Jane Bayes, editors

Dimensions of Hazardous Waste Politics and Policy
Charles E. Davis and James P. Lester, editors